Hair

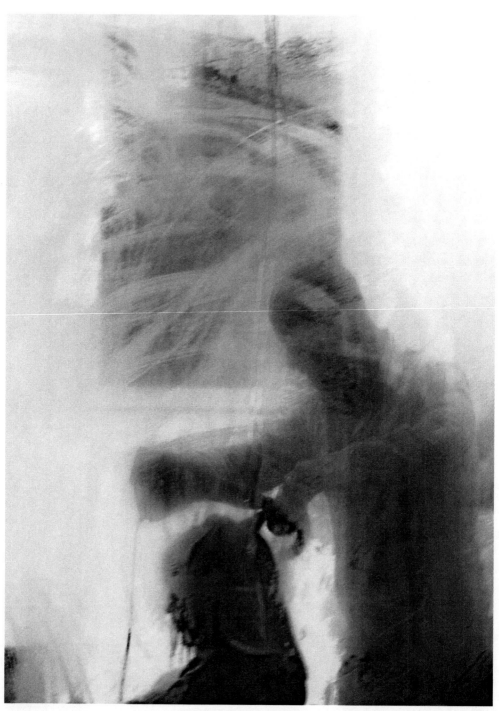

Hairdressing.
Photo by Colin Miller. © Colin Miller.

Hair

Styling, Culture and Fashion

Geraldine Biddle-Perry and Sarah Cheang

Oxford • UK

English edition
First published in 2008 by
Berg
Editorial offices:
First Floor, Angel Court, 81 St Clements Street, Oxford OX4 1AW, UK
175 Fifth Avenue, New York, NY 10010, USA

Berg is the imprint of Oxford International Publishers Ltd.

Library of Congress Cataloging-in-Publication Data

Hair : styling, culture and fashion / [edited by] Geraldine Biddle-Perry and
Sarah Cheang.—English ed.
p. cm.
Includes bibliographical references and index.
ISBN-13: 978-1-84520-791-5 (cloth)
ISBN-10: 1-84520-791-2 (cloth)
ISBN-13: 978-1-84520-792-2 (pbk.)
ISBN-10: 1-84520-792-0 (pbk.)
1. Hair—Social aspects.   2. Hairstyles—Social aspects.   3. Hairdressing—
Social aspects.   I. Biddle-Perry, Geraldine.   II. Cheang, Sarah.
GT2290.H25 2008
391.5—dc22
2008036533

British Library Cataloguing-in-Publication Data

A catalogue record for this book is available from the British Library.

ISBN 978-1-84520-791-5 (cloth)
978-1-84520-792-2 (paper)

Typeset by Apex CoVantage, Madison, WI, USA
Printed in the United Kingdom by Biddles Ltd, King's Lynn

www.bergpublishers.com

CONTENTS

ACKNOWLEDGEMENTS

We are grateful to Angela Drisdale-Gordon, Joanne Entwistle, Sandra Gittens, Paul Jobling, Sarah Norris, Lucy O'Brien, Susanna Peretz, Denise Redd, Mellany Robinson, Jimo Salako, Hannah Shakespeare and Andrea Stuart for their valuable input during the development of this volume. We would also like to thank Barbara Burman, Reina Lewis, Louise Purbrick, Lou Taylor, Helen Thomas and Lesley Whitworth for their advice and encouragement along the way. Last but not least, this book could never have been produced without the unstinting support of our two wonderful husbands Graham and John and our five patient sons—thank you to Ben, Simon, Misha, Lucian and Marius.

This project was supported by the Research Project Fund, London College of Fashion.

FOREWORD

CAROLINE COX

Editors' Note: This volume presents a range of ideas, reflections and theoretical perspectives on hair, in response to hair's exciting and diverse potential as an academic topic, and the needs and aspirations of students across disciplines. Hair, and its management, is part of everyone's everyday experience, so critical analysis of its practice and experience provides a fascinating and engaging entry point to contemporary debates around the body and its fashioning. This positioning of theory in relation to the creative, the experiential and the practical is a key part of this edited collection. It is a serious approach to a subject area richly deserving of new research.

My life has always been bound up with hair in one way or another—my great-grandfather Peter Karel Sartory, chairman and founder of Superma Ltd, born in Amsterdam in 1881, was one of the pioneers of the chemical perm and had a hairdressing salon in Leinster Terrace, Paddington, called Sartory et Cie. I was a hair model for Keith Hall, Derby, in the 1970s and spent most of my early adult life experimenting with post-punk DIY dye jobs. I have written about hair, talked about hair and thought about hair for the past twenty-five years, first at the London College of Fashion and now at Vidal Sassoon's Advanced Academy alongside International Creative Director Mark Hayes and his sublime team of creative directors. So what is it about hair that preoccupies me? I think it's because haircuts are magical configurations, pieces of performance art that are never the same from one moment to the next—they are the most intangible and fleeting form of fashion there is. They are also the most ubiquitous because everyone does something with their hair—and even when the choice is to do nothing, a definite sartorial statement is being made. Haircuts are talismanic, too, embodying such symbolic capital that they can be responsible for determining 'good' as opposed to 'bad' hair days. The processes used to manipulate hair are seemingly endless; it can be shaved, braided, waxed and woven or permed, extended and layered, and today there are more techniques available than ever before, although hair's Holy Grail, a cure for male-pattern baldness, is yet to be found. A nimble-fingered hairdresser is an alchemist with the ability to transform the way we think about ourselves and how we are perceived by others. So why then do we think so little of the profession? Perhaps because of hairdressing's long associations with women and the concomitant 'trivialities' of femininity, an association which has hindered its serious study until the last decade. Fashion has successfully gained recognition as a legitimate area of cultural analysis, and as hair and fashion are so inextricably linked, the meanings of hair are beginning to be teased out, particularly in arena of African diasporic style. The history of hairdressers is yet to be written and the careers of Antoine de Paris, Freddie French, Raymond Bessone, Rose Evansky, Irma Kusley and Rene remain pretty much undiscovered even within the hairdressing industry. Yet their time will come and this book, wholly pertinent and much welcomed, goes a long way towards untangling the relationship between hair, its relationship with culture and with our identities, revealing hair as a rich and rewarding source of study.

AUTHOR BIOGRAPHIES

Alice Beard is Senior Lecturer in Design History at Kingston University. Her teaching and research is focused on the intersections between fashion, graphic design and photography, and she is particularly interested in fashion media and magazine cultures. Her publications include articles in *Fashion Theory: The Journal of Dress, Body and Culture;* on fashion editorial in *Nova* magazine for the 'Fashion & Photography' special edition (2002), and on the innovative and influential Web project showstudio in a special edition on 'Fashion Curation' (2008). She curated 'Beauty Queens: Smiles, Swimsuits and Sabotage' (2004) and 'Remembering *Nova* Magazine 1965–1975' (2006) at The Women's Library, London. She is currently completing doctoral research on *Nova* magazine at Goldsmiths, University of London.

Geraldine Biddle-Perry is Associate Lecturer at London College of Fashion/University of the Arts, London where she is currently completing her doctoral research in the development of recreational leisurewear in Britain in the postwar period. Her research interests include fashion and class, and the use of oral historical approaches to fashion historical study and its pedagogy. Her publications include 'Bury Me in Purple Lurex: Promoting a New Dynamic between Fashion and Oral Historical Research' in *Oral History*, 33: 1 (2005) and she co-organized the conference *What About Us? Oral Historical Approaches to Fashion, Dress and Textiles* held at London College of Fashion in 2007.

Sarah Cheang is Senior Lecturer in Cultural and Historical Studies at the London College of Fashion. Her publications include 'Selling China: Class, Gender and Orientalism at the Department Store', *Journal of Design History*, 20: 1 (2007), 'Women, Pets and Imperialism: The British Pekingese Dog and Nostalgia for Old China', *Journal of British Studies*, 45: 2 (April 2006), and 'The Dogs of Fo: Gender, Identity and Collecting', in A. Shelton, ed, *Collectors: Expressions of Self and Other*, London/Coimbra: Horniman Museum/Museu Antropologicao da Universidade de Coimbra (2001).

Pamela Church Gibson is Reader in Cultural and Historical Studies at London College of Fashion/University of the Arts, London. She has published extensively on film, fashion, fandom, history and heritage and has co-edited three anthologies, including *The Oxford Guide to Film Studies* (OUP 1998) and *Fashion Cultures: Theories, Explorations, Analysis* (Routledge 1998). She edited *Dirty Looks: Gender Power Pornography* for the British Film Institute in 2004; she is now writing a monograph on fashion and celebrity culture.

Shaun Cole is Research Fellow in the Centre for Fashion, the Body and Material Cultures, University of the Arts, London. He was formerly Head of Contemporary Programmes at the Victoria and Albert Museum in London, where his exhibitions included 'Dressing the Male' (1999) and 'Black British Style' (2004–2005). Shaun's research focuses on men's fashion, particularly underwear, and subcultural and gay style. His publications include *'Don We Now Our Gay Apparel': Gay Men's Dress in the Twentieth Century* (2000) and *Dialogue: Relationships in Graphic Design* (2005).

Caroline Cox is an international authority on fashion history and works as a cultural trends advisor for Vidal Sassoon's Advanced Academy as well as lecturing throughout the world. Her books on fashion history and theory have been published internationally and include *Stiletto* (Mitchell-Beazley, 2004), *Hair and Fashion* (V and A, 2005), *Seduction* (Harper Design, 2006), *Bags* (Aurum, 2007), and *Vintage Shoes* (2008). She also broadcasts regularly on fashion and beauty culture for the BBC. In 2005 she was awarded a Visiting Professorship at the University of Arts, London, for her contribution to cultural history.

Louisa Cross works as an Administrator in the University of Dundee where she is studying towards a PhD in the School of Humanities researching the display of fashionable dress in urban Scotland in the late eighteenth and early nineteenth centuries. She has delivered conference papers at the Universities of Dundee and Stirling, to Women's History Scotland and at the Costume Society Annual Conference. Louisa's MPhil study looked at the theatrical display of extreme hairstyles in England in late 1700s.

Eiluned Edwards is Researcher in Design History and Material Culture, specializing in textiles, dress and the construction of identity with a regional focus on South Asia. Recent publications include 'Cloth and Community: The Local Trade in Resist-dyed and Block-printed Textiles in Kachchh District, Gujarat', *Textile History*, 38: 2 (2007) and 'Marriage and Dowry Customs of the Rabari of Kachchh', in H. B. Foster and D. C. Johnson, eds., *Wedding Dress Across Cultures*, Oxford and New York: Berg (2003).

Thom Hecht is a dance scholar and expert in applied emotional intelligence in the performing arts. He is Associate Lecturer at London College of Fashion, University of the Arts, London. Thom is the author of numerous scholarly publications on cultural studies and dance education, including a research monograph, *Emotionally Intelligent Ballet Training—Facilitating Emotional Intelligence in Vocational Dance Training* (Saarbruecken: VDM Publishing, 2007).

Royce Mahawatte holds a PhD in English Literature and Language from the University of Oxford and also an MA in Creative Writing from the University of East Anglia. He is an Associate Lecturer in the Department of Cultural and Historical Studies at the London College of Fashion, University of the Arts, London. This year, he has essays appearing in *Gothic Studies, Women's Writing Special Issue on the Silver Fork Novel* and *Queering the Gothic* (MUP). He is currently preparing a monograph on George Eliot and the Gothic novel.

Leila McKellar is Leverhulme Junior Research Fellow at the University of Sussex. Her interests include contemporary women's art, and art and the senses. Publications include 'The Word Made Flesh: Re-embodying the Madonna and Child in Helen Chadwick's *One Flesh*', in Griselda Pollock and Victoria Turvey Sauron, eds., *The Sacred and the*

Feminine: Imagination and Sexual Difference (2007). She is working on a monograph on the work of Helen Chadwick.

Janice Miller is Lecturer in Cultural and Historical Studies at the London College of Fashion. She has published essays and conference papers around music and fashion, make-up and performance and dress in literature. She is currently working on a book on fashion and music to be published in 2009.

Dene October is Senior Lecturer in the School of Graphic Design at London College of Communication/University of the Arts, London. His major research interest is fashion and performativity.

Jack Sargeant is the author of numerous books, including *Deathtripping: The Extreme Underground* (1995, rev. 2008) and *Naked Lens: Beat Cinema* (1997, rev. 2009). He has written essays on various aspects of sexuality, subcultures and cinema for numerous collections and journals.

Faegheh Shirazi is a native of Iran. She is Associate Professor in the Department of Middle Eastern Studies and Center for Middle Eastern Studies—Islamic Studies programme at the University of Texas at Austin. Shirazi specializes in studying textiles, rituals and material cultures as they relate to the social and cultural practices of Muslim women and men in contemporary Islamic societies. She is the author of numerous scholarly publications and two books: *The Veil Unveiled: Hijab in Modern Culture,* Gainesville: University of Florida Press (2001, 2003), and *Velvet Jihad: Muslim Women's Quiet Resistance to Islamic Fundamentalism,* Gainesville: University of Florida Press (forthcoming).

Kim Smith graduated from the Royal College of Art in 2001 and is presently Senior Lecturer of Fashion and Design History and Theory at University of East London where she is also pursuing a PhD in London West End hair salons in the 1960s. She has presented a paper for the Design History Society in 2007 entitled *Dial F for Fear*—a cross-disciplinary study of design in film; a forthcoming paper for the DHS 2008 conference examines the transmission of design modernity in Fritz Lang's 1922 *Dr. Mabuse, Der Spieler.*

Carol Tulloch is the TrAIN/V&A Senior Research Fellow in Black Visual Culture. Her interest in dress, the African diaspora, and style narratives has been discussed through exhibitions and a number of articles. These include the shows *Black British Style, Tools of the Trade: Memories of Black British Hairdressing,* and the publications *Black Style* (ed), 'Out of Many, One People?: The Relativity of Dress, Race and Ethnicity to Jamaica, 1880–1907', '"My Man, Let Me Pull Your Coat to Something": Malcolm X', and 'Altered States: Susan Stockwell and the Politics of Paper'.

Rachel Velody is Senior Lecturer in Fashion Studies at the London College of Fashion. Her major area of interest concerns the representation of the female detective in British and American television detective series.

LIST OF ILLUSTRATIONS

INTRODUCTION

I INTRODUCTION
THINKING ABOUT HAIR

GERALDINE BIDDLE-PERRY AND SARAH CHEANG

THEORIZING THE MEANING OF HAIR

Just as the human body is dressed and adorned in order to participate in society, so human hair is combed, cut, coloured, curled, straightened, plaited, swept up, tied back, decorated, plucked and shaved (Synnott 1993; Cox 1999; Corson 1965; McCracken 1996). Like fashion and dress, hair can be situated as a fundamental part of 'the means by which bodies are made and given meaning and identity' (Entwistle 2000: 7). Humans are, of course, born naked; the flesh is totally unmarked by culture and at its most natural. But we are almost simultaneously assigned a visually communicated identity, not just through dress (such as the gendering of babies through the colour of their clothing) but also through the cultural coding of our skin, our eyes and our hair colour (Figure 1.1). Hair's physiological properties and symbolic representations, regulations and rituals are, therefore, a fundamental part of any culture and its ordered relations of class, gender, race and sexuality (Weitz 2001; Hiltebeitel and Miller 1998; Peterkin 2001; Banks 2000; Lesnik-Oberstein 2006).

A combination of psychoanalytical and anthropological approaches to hair have produced a number of influential concepts around the role of hair in human society. Hair's function as an extension of the body and as social object has led to the theorizing of hair as a phallic symbol, and the cutting of hair as symbolic castration (Berg 1936, 1951; Leach 1958; Hershman 1974). Because of its constant growth, removal and manipulation, hair cannot be easily ignored. Hair can be freely touched and played with in full view of one's fellow humans in a way that other parts of the body cannot, and is therefore seized upon by the human unconscious for its ability to represent and manifest repressed latent thoughts (Berg 1936: 73–88). For Charles Berg, that such phallic symbols are considered sacred is evidence of their origin in sexual taboo. Edmund Leach (1958: 157) contends that it's the other way round. 'Sacred objects are taboo because they are sacred ... because they are full of dangerous potency, including sexual potency'. The magical power of 'body dirt', including hair, works like verbal expletives; potency is gained through their association with sexual and excretory functions or with a deity, to make explicit powerful and dangerous thoughts that are *liable* to become repressed (Leach 1958: 159).

The growing and cutting of hair has also been related to control in society, where long hair stands for social freedom or defiance, and short or covered hair is a sign of social regulation, obedience and disciplined religious or cultural conformity (Hallpike 1969). Such

Figure 1.1   Newborn baby boy with a full head of hair.
Photo by Anthea Sieveking. Wellcome Images.

theories may be challenged by the specific local meanings of hair practices; the balance between personal, individual and public symbolism has also to be considered (Obeyesekere
1981). A sociological understanding of hair and its manipulation as a part of everyday life
also focuses on the ways in which the body and its functions must be negotiated according
to the social situation. The work of Anthony Synnott (1993: 104) uses such an understanding to argue for a system of oppositional meanings in hair; women cultivate their head and
body hair in opposition to men and vice versa; head hair is treated as conceptually opposite

to body hair, and opposing social ideologies choose opposing hair strategies. Accordingly, hair is theorized as pivotal to the mechanisms of social and cultural differentiation. Its practices and representations are shaped by both social exterior and psychic interior regulatory forces, worked and reworked as markers of individual and collective identity, and frequently invested with gendered and racialized assumptions (Lesnik-Oberstein 2006; Hiltebeitel and Miller 1998; Mercer 1994).

HAIR: STYLING, CULTURE AND FASHION

This edited collection builds on these debates, and several themes emerge as central to thinking about the special significance of human hair. Hair functions at both a symbolic and an operational level to maintain social boundaries, and an understanding of hair as polluting and pollutant is common to many societies. The psychoanalytical and the social are brought together in the imaginative and material experience of hair. Across cultures, the practices of hair's cutting, shaving, colouring, styling, dressing and collecting provide a presentational and representational dynamic for a diverse range of subjectivities.

The essays in this volume employ a variety of approaches and are part of a significant shift of academic focus on to the body as an object of study in the humanities and social sciences, and a corresponding emphasis on interdisciplinarity. The collection as a whole draws on key theorists in the study of cultural identity and the body (Foucault 1977, 1979; Butler 1990; Kristeva 1982) to present a study of hair and self-fashioning, representation, manipulation and material culture. The book is arranged in three sections to critically engage with the cultural meanings of hair from a range of different perspectives: firstly, histories of hair on the head, face and body; secondly, the powerful associations and symbolic value of hair in the production of social identity and the maintenance of its rituals; and, finally, the role of hair in literature, art, performance and the media.

HISTORIES OF HEAD, FACE AND BODY HAIR

Throughout human history, the presentation and manipulation of hair, wherever it grows, has been fundamental to embodied social and symbolic practices that inscribe it with meaning. Hair's self-conscious cutting and growth, and then display and concealment, therefore provides a continuum of human hair experience. This section examines how historical discourses surrounding human hair and its removal have operated as ideological mechanisms that regulate class, gender, race and sexuality. Louisa Cross (Chapter 2) explores how excessive hair display served as a form of conspicuous consumption in eighteenth-century Britain, when elaborately ornamented and extremely high hairstyles and wigs were worn by both men and women as very obvious symbols of gender and class. Cross argues that hair's spectacle played a vital part in the ever-more theatrical performance of everyday life in the emerging arenas of commercial leisure and entertainment.

The significance of human hair rests not just in the materiality of maintaining a range of hairy cultural differentials, but also in how this functions to visibly define what it is to be human according to an imperialist racial hierarchy. Sarah Cheang (Chapter 3) examines the ways in which museums and anthropological collections of hair were amassed through processes of colonial control. The classification of people through the possession and study of their hair was used to maintain a racial pecking order and was closely allied to assertions of white Western authority. In the struggle for self-determination under racial discrimination and/or colonialism, the symbolic and biological connections between hair and notions of race and breeding accorded a heavily loaded significance to the nineteenth-century scientific hair sample.

Various transformations of human hair also affect gender power relations through hair's potential to both mirror and mould cultural meanings. Women with short or shaven head hair and inversely hairy bodies and faces are consistently historically stigmatized as masculine, sick or even monstrous according to regimes of idealized gendered identity (Lesnik-Oberstein 2006). Hair's abundance and/or lack, and its visible absence or presence, operates as a form of social and somatic 'border control'. It is the continued proscription of cultural invisibility surrounding female hirsuteness that, Lesnik-Oberstein (2006) argues, makes visible the power inherent in the politics of the gendered body. Jack Sargeant (Chapter 4) explores the representation of female pubic hair since the mid-nineteenth century as intrinsically sexual. Through a range of sources he examines pubic hair and its removal, trimming and shaping as a source of fascination and eroticism, using Freudian understandings of fetishism as the source of a sexually inquisitive gaze and the desire to both conceal and reveal the sight of the female genitals.

The locations in which hair can be displayed are allied to gendered sites of cultural proscription and permission. Whilst the barber's shop was for centuries a socially fluid masculine space and a forum for male social intercourse (Lewis 1995: 436), women's hair was styled and dressed at home by women themselves, more frequently by household servants, but also by attendant professional hairdressers. The development of the commercial ladies' hair salon in the twentieth century was therefore a distinctly modern phenomenon that paralleled the emergence and expansion of new spaces of feminine consumption in the metropolis. Kim Smith (Chapter 5) examines how the growth of these dedicated locations altered not only the social dynamics between hairdresser and client, but also the spatial environment within which women's hairstyles were produced and consumed.

Conversely, the invention of the safety razor at the turn of the twentieth century effectively shifted the cutting of men's facial hair from the exterior, public spaces of the barber's shop to the interior private spaces of the domestic. Stylistic variations in the appearance (and dis-appearance) of men's whiskers, beards and moustaches can similarly be located in relation to a centuries-old diverse rhetoric of masculinity and patriarchal control (Peterkin 2001). Dene October (Chapter 6) looks at the promotion of shaving in the twentieth century and the rituals of normative Western masculinity promoted by advertisers of male shaving and grooming products. Many such advertisements dwell on contemporary anxieties around hygiene and social performance through the representation of a contradictory range of masculinities, implying a sense of agency whilst at the same time reinforcing the wider structures of patriarchal control.

HAIR AND IDENTITY

The ambiguities of masculine power and social control are also particularly pertinent to our second section, Hair and Identity. Considering issues around the negotiation of sexuality, Shaun Cole (Chapter 7) argues that within Western gay male culture, the care, control and management of hair 'on top' and 'down below' is dominated by strategies of both conformity to, and subversion of, 'straight' masculinity. Again, these can be situated as part of a historical continuum of shifting contra-distinctions of shaving and growth, here in relation to the gay male body, from the bushy moustached, hairy-bodied 'clone' of the 1970s to the smoothly cropped head and shaved or waxed body of the muscle man in the 1990s.

The rituals of hair, dressing and artifice can be understood as markers of a 'natural' performative identity whose achievement is fundamental to the practices and processes of 'selfhood'. Geraldine Biddle-Perry (Chapter 8) explores the way that the sight of both head and body hair, or its visible absence, operates as a spectacular dynamic in the creation of Western ideals of masculinity and femininity, from its earliest representation in Greek classicism through to contemporary advertising. Human hair is a powerful thing, she argues, because the sight of it exerts social and cultural power. Foucault's theories of the disciplined body (1977, 1979) provide a critical springboard for Biddle-Perry's chapter to argue that hair is central to the articulation of gendered looking, and analyse the presentational and representational symbolic potential for gendered identity.

In some cultures and religions, women's hair is seen as a source of temptation and pride, and is therefore too dangerous to be seen at all. In Islam, covering the head and hair can signal a woman's virtue and respectability, the historical and cultural roots of which also resonate with hair's relationships with religious proscription, and also the concept of concealment and privacy (El Guindi 1999; Shirazi 2001; Pfluger-Schindlbeck 2006). In this volume, however, Faegheh Shirazi (Chapter 9) examines historical and contemporary influences on the management and grooming of men's facial hair in the context of Islamic religious practice and societal rules. Men's individual choices of facial hair are bound up in wider collective cultural understandings of patriarchy, extremism, secularism, tradition and modernity.

Shirazi's study of the beard in Islam raises important issues about the potential of hair to reinforce, reinvent and reappropriate cultural traditions. Such strategies are also pertinent to the history of the Afro hairstyle, where the curly texture of black African hair was exploited to unite and unify black consciousness and proclaim 'black is beautiful'. The Afro was created by encouraging hair to grow upwards and outwards into a characteristically large rounded shape, using a pick, or Afro comb (Mercer 1994: 104–9). Carol Tulloch (Chapter 10) provides a detailed analysis of the Afro comb as a 'hero' of the Black Power movement through its pivotal role in the hairstyling practices of the African diaspora, and its complex position within African-American culture. Tracing the comb's history in America, Tulloch considers how a seemingly simple tool can unpack a variety of historically and culturally significant moments and meanings.

Hair's malleability gives it great power but its growth and re-growth forces us to constantly deal with our biological roots on a regular basis. This gives rise to a diversity of ambiguous readings and ambivalent ideologies rooted in both culturally constituted ideals of normative 'natural' beauty and the culture and the technologies of self-fashioning. Pamela Church Gibson (Chapter 11) explores such ambiguity in the potential for men and women to dress, style and colour their hair in ways that challenge—at least superficially—the proscriptive boundaries of gender, race and ethnicity. Mikhail Bakhtin's (1981) notion of the carnivalesque, Church Gibson argues, is one way to explain the phenomenon. From the *ganguro* girls of contemporary Japan, to David Beckham and the blond-black footballers of the English football league, blondeness functions as a form of playful inversion.

Cultural constructions of race and gendered identity are constantly 'naturalized' through the idea of the body as a transformational project, where hair is integral to synthetic processes of social and self-management. According to Mary Douglas (1970), societies symbolize the body and its functions through rituals as a way of articulating fears and anxieties around pollution and purity. Hair, or the meaning of hair, and the ceremonies and rituals that surround its dressing, cutting and collection act as a safeguard against transgression and as a marker of the maintenance of the social order. Eiluned Edwards (Chapter 12) examines this in the context of hair care and grooming customs in the rural areas of western India. Ethnographic material is allied to an analysis of the symbolism of hair on the subcontinent and to the changing influences on traditional hair grooming practices.

HAIR IN REPRESENTATION: FILM, ART, FASHION, LITERATURE AND PERFORMANCE

In the final section of this volume, we consider how hair is used in a variety of creative media to convey social meaning. Leila McKellar (Chapter 13) explores the complex and compelling work of artist Mona Hatoum. Through detailed analysis of various works such as the installation *Recollection* (1995), McKellar reveals how Hartoum exploits the potential for hair to introduce both the pleasurable and repulsive. Much of this artist's work, she argues, examines the compulsive rituals hair invites. Hair can be situated as part of the social customs of cleanness that are central to all societies; rejected 'bits and pieces' or 'dirt' such as hair, or certain kinds of food and waste body products, are first seen as 'out of place' (Douglas 1966: 197), and then as taboo (a spontaneous code of prohibition). Between these two stages such substances have a 'half-identity' and are at their most powerful because they demonstrate the 'danger which is risked by boundary transgression' (Douglas 1966: 198). Hair's meanings depend on whether it is 'in place' or 'out of place' creating a network of sensory responses and memories and revealing the emotive power of hair to evoke the absent body.

Relics of the body such as hair or nail clippings perform a vital role in remembrance, but also act as eerie reminders of death itself. Janice Miller (Chapter 14) uses Freudian notions of the 'uncanny' to examine how human hair carries not only these connotations, but operates as an ambiguous mechanism of familiarity and alienation. With reference to both literary and cinematic narratives, Miller explores how hair that is separated from the body is loaded with cultural meaning. Many cultures believe in the special powers possessed of human hair, even after the physical connection is severed (Frazer 2003: 193; Hallpike 1969: 258). However, cut locks of hair are also part of the more prosaic realm of economic exchange. Royce Mahawatte (Chapter 15) interrogates the styling and dressing of women's hair, as well as its cutting, selling and buying, as a literary device in two nineteenth-century novels, George Eliot's *The Mill on the Floss* (1860) and Thomas Hardy's *The Woodlanders* (1887). In these narratives, hair is used to characterize the conflict that arises between conventional and errant femininity, and as a metaphor for the human and social cost of modernity.

In fictional representation, the narratives to be found in women's hair are frequently exploited to evoke the kinds of meanings different types of hair and hairstyles might have for women in specific social and moral contexts. Since antiquity, women's hair has served as a vehicle for all kinds of cultural meanings aligned with a host of moral attributes or their lack, and connotations of both innocent natural beauty and vainglorious, implicit deceit (Synnott 1993: 103–27). For example, the 'looseness' of women's hair can symbolize a moral 'looseness' but also a 'natural' sensuality. Loose hair's reverse—'disciplined' female head hair, tightly scraped back into buns, chignons and topknots and secured with pins—operates in opposition but can be equally ambiguous. Thom Hecht (Chapter 16) argues that disciplined hair is a significant aesthetic determinant and a complex cultural signifier of both controlled, and controlling, feminine sexuality. In a range of cultural forms he looks at how the typical figures of the schoolmistress, the dominatrix, the spinster and the classical ballerina characterize a feminine typology of frigidity and fetishistic sexual potency through the discursive power of female head hair. This ambiguity is part of a long tradition in Christian ideology that separated female sexuality from sociality, encoded in a dualistic 'game of modesty and sexual explicitness, denial and celebration of pleasure' (Tseelon 1997: 14).

An exploration of a contemporary manifestation of these themes is provided by Rachel Velody (Chapter 17), in a discussion of the popular American TV series *Desperate Housewives* (ABC Inc.). Velody considers the differential functions of hair's styling, colouring and dressing in relation to the implicit economic and ideological exchange involved in the production and consumption of the show's female stars and their on-screen characterization. The presentation of different and conflicting feminine identities in popular culture exploits the meanings attached to variations in hair's physical qualities. These operate to visibly mark out the parameters of idealized femininity and their potential transgression.

Hair's fashioning and display are pivotal to the presentation and representation of social identity, so that its shifting practices, styles and processes frequently come to embody the wider historical political and social changes of which they were a part. The inter-connection between a hairstyle and a fashionable 'look' has always been an organic one. Men and women's hair and their changing hairstyles can be seen as a discreet and distinctive part of key historical moments in fashion and fashion photography. Alice Beard (Chapter 18) examines this concept in the particular context of the young female consumer in the late 1960s and early 1970s and the influential and innovative style magazine *Nova* (published in Britain from 1965–1975). *Nova* aimed to be a new kind of magazine and to offer a different way of writing about and representing style and fashion. Beard considers how haircutting and styling was more than just an accessory to this pivotal shift in fashionable dress and the iconography of style, but functioned as an essential element in the narrative drive of fashion itself and in the fashion spread.

CONCLUSION

As Marina Warner very aptly argues: '[T]he language of the self would be stripped of one of its richest resources without hair: and like language, or the faculty of laughter, or the use of tools, the dressing of hair in itself constitutes a mark of the human' (1995: 371). Hair is loaded with cultural meaning because it signifies a very human capacity for self-conscious manipulation, management and display. In our final chapter (Chapter 19), we explore how hair is used to delineate supposedly innate human identities. However, concepts of hair as either natural and biological, or cultural and synthetic, are equally manufactured through ideologies of race, sexuality and gender. Hair and hairstyling mark out identity, and function as a key signifier of social status through a whole repertoire of culturally and historically specific meanings.

Hair's manipulation and care has discursively operated throughout history as a powerful vector of human identification. The relationship between cutting and growth, exhibition and concealment, provides an oppositional paradigm through shifting culturally coded sequences of emphasis and de-emphasis that at any one time mark out differences between and within different individuals and social groupings. Technological innovation, commercial development and social change constantly intersect in the history of human hair, effecting corresponding shifts in its spatial and social interface (Cox 1999; Cooper 1971) (Figure 1.2). The cultural and commercial forces of hairstyling's production and consumption combine to reinforce old, and negotiate new, social hierarchies.

The daily practices of hair are part of a complex network of normalizing standards and discursive mechanisms, to perform and police social boundaries. However, 'The boundary between the "everyday" and the special uses of hair is a hard one to draw' (Sleeman 1981: 325). On and off the body, hair functions as a form of social and corporeal border control invested with power through its liminal status betwixt and between the body and the self. Hair as fetish or fashion serves as a powerful vehicle for all kinds of anxieties and their social proscription. It presents a narrative of human experience and a significant and historically consistent vocabulary of subjective identification and performative expression. Thinking

Figure 1.2   Identity hair salon, High Street, Whitstable (2008).
Photo by Geraldine Biddle-Perry.

critically about human hair involves engaging in its stories, histories, performances and rituals to understand the significance of hair's styling, culture and fashion.

BIBLIOGRAPHY

Bakhtin, M. (1981), *The Dialogical Imagination*, trans. C. Emerson and M. Holquist, ed M. Holquist, Austin: University of Texas Press.

Banks, I. (2000), *Hair Matters: Beauty, Power and Black Women's Consciousness*, New York: New York University Press.

Berg, C. (1936), 'The Unconscious Significance of Hair', *International Journal of Psycho-Analysis*, 17: 73–88.

Berg, C. (1951), *The Unconscious Significance of Hair*, London: George Allen and Unwin.

Butler, J. (1990), *Gender Trouble: Feminism and the Subversion of Identity*, London: Routledge.

Cooper, W. (1971), *Hair: Sex, Society, Symbolism*, London: Aldus Books.

Corson, R. (1965), *Fashions in Hair: The First 5000 Years*, London: Peter Owen.

Cox, C. (1999), *Good Hair Days: A History of British Hairstyling*, London: Quartet.

Douglas, M. (1966), *Purity and Danger,* London: Routledge.

Douglas, M. (1970), *Natural Symbols: Explorations in Cosmology,* London: Barrie and Rockliff/The Cresset Press.

El Guindi, F. (1999), *Veil: Modesty, Privacy and Resistance,* Oxford: Berg.

Entwistle, J. (2000), *The Fashioned Body: Fashion, Dress and Modern Social Theory,* Cambridge: Polity Press.

Foucault, M. (1977), *Discipline and Punish,* Harmondsworth: Penguin Books.

Foucault, M. (1979), *The History of Sexuality,* vol. 1; *Introduction,* Harmondsworth: Penguin Books.

Frazer, J. (2003), *The Golden Bough,* London and New York: Routledge Curzon.

Hallpike, C. R. (1969), 'Social Hair', *Man,* New Series, 4 (2): 256–64.

Hershman, P. (1974), 'Hair, Sex and Dirt', *Man,* New Series, 9 (2): 274–98.

Hiltebeitel, A. and Miller, B. D. (1998), *Hair: Its Power and Meaning in Asian Cultures,* Albany: State University of New York Press.

Kristeva, J. (1982), *Powers of Horror: An Essay on Abjection,* New York: Columbia University Press.

Leach, E. (1958), 'Magical Hair', *Journal of the Royal Anthropological Institute,* 88: 147–64.

Lesnik-Oberstein, K. (2006), 'The Last Taboo: Women, Body Hair and Feminism', in K. Lesnik-Oberstein, ed, *The Last Taboo: Women and Body Hair,* Manchester and New York: Manchester University Press: 1–18.

Lewis, S. (1995), 'Barbers' Shops and Perfume Shops: "Symposia without Wine" ', in A. Powell, ed, *The Greek World,* London: Routledge: 436–42.

McCracken, G. (1996), *Big Hair: A Journey into the Transformation of Self,* Woodstock, NY.: The Overlook Press.

Mercer, K. (1994), *Welcome to the Jungle,* New York: Routledge.

Obeyesekere, G. (1981), *Medusa's Hair: An Essay on Personal Symbols and Religious Experience,* Chicago: University of Chicago Press.

Peterkin, A. (2001), *One Thousand Beards: A Cultural History of Facial Hair.* Vancouver: Arsenal Pulp Press.

Pfluger-Schindlbeck, I. (2006), 'On the Symbolism of Hair in Islamic Societies: An Analysis of Approaches', *Anthropology of the Middle East,* 1 (2): 72–88.

Shirazi, F. (2001), *The Veil Unveiled: The Hijab in Modern Culture,* Gainesville: University of Florida Press.

Sleeman, M. (1981), 'Medieval Hair Tokens', *Forum for Modern Language Studies,* XVII (4): 322–36.

Synnott, A. (1993), *The Body Social: Symbolism, Self and Society,* London and New York: Routledge.

Tseelon, E. (1997), *The Masque of Femininity,* London: Sage Publications.

Warner, M. (1995), *From the Beast to the Blonde: On Fairy Tales and Their Tellers,* New York: Farrar, Straus & Giroux.

Weitz, R. (2001), 'Women and Their Hair: Seeking Power through Resistance and Accommodation', *Gender and Society,* 15.5 (Oct.): 667–86.

PART I
HISTORIES OF HAIR ON THE HEAD,
FACE AND BODY

2 FASHIONABLE HAIR IN THE EIGHTEENTH CENTURY
THEATRICALITY AND DISPLAY

LOUISA CROSS

Fashionable display was a key feature of eighteenth-century British society, particularly in the urban environment. Public buildings, their furniture and ornamentation all acted as signifiers of fashionable display, whilst for individuals, fashionability was portrayed by dress, manners and hairstyles. Hair and wig styles were a significant element of this fashionable display, and highly visible and theatrical symbols of gender and class. A great variety of hairstyles was displayed during this period, with hair becoming a focal part of the overall 'look', as well as the focus of social comment. Styled and dressed hair was integral to eighteenth-century fashionability in what Powell and Roach have called 'the social performance of everyday life' (2004: 81). New 'arenas of display' for entertainment, socializing and commerce, particularly in cities such as Bath (Corfield 1990: 33), all provided a vital 'social theatre' that afforded both the production and consumption of more stylized and various hairdressing practices for both men and women.

WOMEN'S HAIR: FASHION AND EXTREME HAIRSTYLES

In the eighteenth century, it was not enough just to be seen to be conspicuously in fashion, it was important to be seen to be fashionable in spectacular style. Changing or accessorizing hairstyles was a more economical way of keeping in the fashion than buying material to make up new items of clothing. For women, this brought about great fluctuation in the heights and variety of hair dressing and its display. There were some high styles at the beginning of the century such as the 'fontange' where the front of the hair was supported by wire and decorated with lace; and the 'commode', where hair was set high on a wire silk-covered frame (Stevens Cox 1984: 45, 66). Hairstyles fell in height towards the middle of the eighteenth century, but began to rise and increase in size again gradually through the 1760s, reaching their greatest heights in the 1770s and 1780s, when the most spectacular excesses of these styles became prominent for women (Corson 1965: 327). A letter from the Hon Mrs Osborn in 1767 notes: 'Lady Strathmore's dress is the wonder of the town, her head a yard high and filled, or rather covered with features to an enormous size' (cited in Laver 1996: 140); a commentary on the styles of 1768 reported that after composure over a structure of wool and gauze, and dressing with ribbons and other ornaments, these added some 24 to 36 inches to the actual height of the wearer (Corson 1965: 327). Hairstyles became increasingly elaborate with the addition of feathers and combs, and sometimes featuring flowers or other items, including model ships. Such styles were held together by wires and a glue-like paste called 'pomatum' which was usually made from the fat of pigs, calves or bears, and finished off with a final covering of powder to set the style and make it look clean (Barrell 2006: 149). A contemporary account in the *Lady's Magazine* of March 1776 described fashionable ladies with 'features quite distorted, by the horrid drag of their hair to a height absolutely half as tall as themselves.' (Cunnington and Cunnington 1957: 377). Such styles also took a great deal of time and a hairdresser could take more than two hours to prepare, style and dress the hair of a fashionable figure such as the popular wit and novelist Fanny Burney in the 1780s (Rosenthal 2004: 10).

The creation of these female high 'heads' for public display involved almost obsessive attention to detail and was achieved often at great personal discomfort. Hair was enlarged by being set on top of a cushion and by being 'frizzed and piled up', further augmented with various ornaments as well as powder and pomatum. This resulted in a potential breeding ground for insects which then required them to be dealt with by items such as head-scratchers and flea-traps (Powell and Roach 2004: 92). The fact that time and money were not always sufficient to enable the elaborate hairstyles to be cleaned and 'dressed' resulted in cases of poor levels of hygiene frequently being associated with 'high heads'. This unhealthiness was observed by a letter writer to the *London Magazine* in August 1768, describing his aunt's 'head' being combed by her hairdresser thus: 'Swarms of animalculas running about in the utmost consternation ... the quantity of powder and pomatum formed a glutinous matter ... And prevented their migration' (Corson 1965: 338). It was not just a case of mere discomfort; the effects of extreme hairstyling could also prove fatal as shown by a contemporary response to the death of a lady in Bath in 1776, following her hair being burned by being caught in a chandelier:

> Yet miss at her rooms
> Must beware of her Plumes
> For if Vulcan her feather embraces
> Like poor Lady Laycock
> She'll burn like a Haycock
> And roast all the Loves and the Graces
>
> (cited in Stroomberg 1999)

That hairstyles were an integral, and prominent, part of overall fashionable display is demonstrated by the use of fashion plates which were included in an increasing number of contemporary magazines subscribed to by milliners, hairdressers, dressmakers as well as individual ladies (Ribeiro 1995: 76). Fashion plates were also inserted into the Ladies' Pocketbooks or almanacs which were popularly given as New Year gifts as a relatively inexpensive means of providing social guidance for young gentlewomen throughout Britain, and which included advice on fashions and hairstyles (Langley Moore 1971: 1, 2; Vickery 1998: 175–82) (Figure 2.1).

Twelve fashionable Head dreſses of 1773

Figure 2.1 '12 most fashionable hairstyles of 1773' in *Ladies Own Memorandum Pocketbook* (1773). Harry Matthews Collection of Fashion Plates and Pocketbooks, Museum of London.

This illustration shows what middle rather than upper-class women would view as fashionable hairstyles, incorporating a number of different styles that could be achieved relatively simply and inexpensively by curling the hair and changing the headwear. The regularity of monthly stylistic change emphasizes how hair and its accessorizing was an essential and accessible means of being fashionable for many women. The examples shown in this plate do not show the most extreme heights of hair display, rather they show styles which could have been managed by household servants and would not have taken the same length of time to prepare. Nonetheless, these styles evidence an aspiration to greater heights of fashionable display for all, and echo the sentiment expressed by the contemporary hairdresser, David Ritchie: 'All young ladies, and those of low stature, should have their hair or cap dres'd high at the top of the head, and terminate in a point, as by that means it adds to their height' (Ritchie 1770: 60).

The greater extremes of fashionable hairstyles were frequently parodied and circulated in prints of the social caricatures which had such a strong impact in the 1770s. Contemporary satirical engravings and prints were a predominant feature of political and social life and were displayed in coffee houses, libraries and print shops—such as that of Matthew and Mary Darly—where the very subjects of the satire themselves gathered. In this way spectacular hair display worked as a dynamic as both the subject and object of parody, and in the production and consumption of cosmopolitan fashionable excess. Matthew Darly's prints often used fashionable female high hairstyles as the theatrical backdrop for biting political commentary, with hair ornaments in a variety of forms acting as satirical props. Darly's *A Speedy and Effectual Preparation for the Next World* (1777) (Figure 2.2) is one such example featuring the republican historian, Catherine Macaulay. In this representation, Macaulay is pictured in front of her mirror, while behind her a skeleton holds an hourglass, running through and spilling out on to the table, lampooning the futility of her actions.

This contemporary theme of the 'Dance of Death' makes a strong attack on the folly of Macaulay's fashionably high hairstyle, further mocked by the funeral procession riding

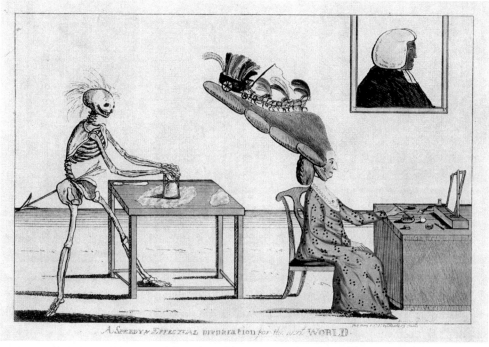

Figure 2.2   M. Darly, *A Speedy and Effectual Preparation for the Next World* (1777).
© The British Museum Register No J,5.109.

down the hair, topped by feathered plumes (Paulson 1970: 544–59). Darly's caricature emphasizes both the amount of time being wasted on fashion, and the artifice of female make-up and extreme hairstyles which, despite all such attempts, fail to ward off the inevitable: old age, physical decline and death. However, equally cutting is the way Darly constantly directs the spectator's gaze from Macaulay's extravagant hairstyle to the adjacent portrait on the wall depicting one of Macaulay's male contemporaries in Bath. His simple and sober clerical wig acts as a foil for Macaulay's ridiculous excess, visibly demonstrating masculine distaste for excessive fashionable display while implicitly contrasting Macaulay's short-sighted preparations to face this world with his implicit preparation for the next. This satirical personal attack on feminine vanity is symptomatic however of a wider prevailing discourse of male perceptions of female obsession with fashion and shopping for fripperies. Female display, particularly its most extreme examples, was seen as distasteful

Figure 2.3   William Hoare, *Christopher Anstey with His Daughter Mary* (1776). National Portrait Gallery, London.

and profligate and contributed to a widespread understanding of the gendered nature of the consumption of fashionable goods seen as wantonly destructive and 'other' to the more ordered male arena (Kowaleski-Wallace 1997: 2–3).

William Hoare's portrait of the poet Christopher Anstey with his daughter Mary (1776) (Figure 2.3) somewhat ambiguously reinforces the point. It again shows a masculine disdain for extremes in dress and hairstyles. However, at the same time, the image demonstrates not only the crucial role hair played in signifying status and fashionability, but also how high hairstyles formed a part of a young girl's training in fashion and femininity. Anstey's daughter brandishes a fashion doll wearing the characteristically high hair of the period, but the doll's function extends beyond that of a mere plaything. In the early- to mid-eighteenth century, fashion dolls formed the main avenue for communicating fashion ideas, and offered an ideal medium through which to disseminate hairstyles. In 1768 an Academy of Hair was set up in Paris by the French hairdresser Jean Legros for ladies' maids and valets who dressed dolls which were sent all over Europe, and featured in publications such as of *L'Art de la Coiffure Des Dames Francoises* (1768) (Ribeiro 2002: 155). In Hoare's portrait, Christopher Anstey, wearing a conservative powdered wig suitable to his rank and social standing, averts his eyes from daughter Mary's fashion doll, demonstrating his disapproval for feminine excess and also once again the cultural superiority of masculine sobriety and good sense (Rosenthal and Myrone 2002: 160).

MEN IN WIGS

For the majority of eighteenth-century men such as Anstey (and Macaulay's clerical admirer), hair in the form of wigs—and from the 1790s hair powdered and cut to resemble a wig—comprised a wide range of styles which related to a man's professional and social status (Pointon 1993: 128). The wearing of a wig beneath a man's 'Quality and Estate' could have marked social consequences and lead to him being given less preferential treatment in fashionable meeting places such as the coffee houses where, a contemporary account noted, a good 'full bottom'd Wig', which could reach down to the waist, could command great respect (cited in Budgell 1711: 92–3). Considerable importance was attributed, and status accorded, to the wearing of wigs and they were clearly central to masculine sartorial display in terms of both fashionable and social status. A wig was one of the most expensive items of clothing in a man's wardrobe, costing anything between 10s 6d and £1 15s (Pointon 1993: 120; McNeil 2000: 376; Picard 2000: 296). The famous social commentator, James Boswell, lost his wig in August 1789 when sharing a room at an inn, and felt impelled to send more than 20 miles (some distance in the eighteenth century) to buy a replacement (Pointon 1993: 120). As with women's wigs, they were equally subject to stylistic shifts in height and length: they also decreased in size in the middle of the century and then rose again towards the end.

The professional hierarchies denoted by wigs were famously satirized by the artist William Hogarth in his *Five Orders of Periwig* of 1761 (Figure 2.4). This image shows the use of wigs worn by different groups of men at the coronation of George III, from 'Episcopal or Parsonic', 'Old Peerian or Aldermanic', 'Lexonic', 'Composite, or Half Natural' and

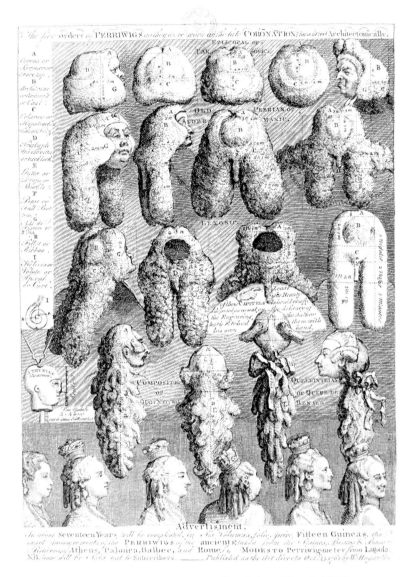

Figure 2.4 William Hogarth engraving, *The Five Orders of Periwig* (1761).
Guildhall Art Gallery, City of London.

'Queerinthian'. This print demonstrates the varieties of parts performed by styles of wig in a theatrical way, using names such as 'Queerinthian', combining a synonym for 'odd or unusual' with the classical architecture term 'Corinthian'. In this way, Hogarth highlights the levels of importance accorded to professional men by virtue of their wigs, whilst he places female wigs, with the profiles of Queen Charlotte and her ladies, at the bottom of the print, marking the feminine styles as subordinate to the masculine styles in the social hierarchy (Powell and Roach 2004: 85–6).

More extreme male wigs were worn as fashionable, rather than professional, statements, particularly by an aristocratic elite such as those popularly known as the 'macaronis'—a relatively small group of wealthy young men who were so named following their travels to Italy and France on the fashionable Grand Tour of Europe. These men were the archetypal effeminate 'fops' of the eighteenth century, creating and responding to passing fads and indulging in extravagant styles beyond 'the ordinary bounds of fashion.' (Rauser 2004: 101). In the 1770s when the fashion for men was to appear tall and thin, for example, the macaroni men's height was emphasized by the front roll of their wigs (Ribeiro 1975: 113) which were powdered and worn ridiculously high (Rauser 2004: 101; McNeil 1999: 425). Macaroni style was in effect an extra high toupee constructed around wire frames or pads of wool or felt (Cooper 1971: 101), and consisting of about 'two pounds of ficticious hair, formed into what is called a club, hanging down their shoulders as white as a baker's.' (Corson 1965: 295).

While this stylistic excess clearly connects fashionable wigs to the wealthier classes, in the eighteenth century fashion was progressively an ideal to which all social groups aspired, including the labouring classes. For example, usually small, less comfortable, 'scratch' wigs were worn by many labouring men in the eighteenth century until after the 1770s (Brewer and Porter 1993: 538). However, towards the end of the century, the prevailing socio-political climate for men of all classes was one of increasing industrialization within a more secular society. There was a growing professional middle class, with a strong work ethic. In terms of dress for men, this led to a more sober and less ostentatious fashion (Kuchta 2002: 165–6) which increasingly served as a contrast to both the excesses and theatricality of female and, of course, male macaroni fashions. By the 1790s there was a move towards wigs being worn only by men of professional status—a trend reinforced, in 1795, by Pitt's one-guinea tax on hair powder to raise money for the war with France, which also further highlighted a concept of indulgence and luxury in the use of hair powder. (Barrell 2006: 155).

'ARENAS OF DISPLAY': HAIR AND CONSPICUOUS CONSUMPTION

Excessive and expensive hair and wig styles for men and women visibly communicated luxurious expenditure of both time and money, and can be situated within the wider context of the expansion of 'conspicuous consumption' and the needs of an emerging middle class in the eighteenth century (McKendrick, Brewer and Plumb 1983: 34–99; Brewer and Porter 1993). Growing numbers of traders responded to this desire for fashionable products, goods and services, and the desire to very visibly show them off. Extreme hairstyles were an obvious example of, and channel for, social aspiration and its expression through such 'conspicuous consumption'. In Britain, the number of hairdressers expanded considerably with one report stating that the profession had grown from 2 in London at the coronation of George II in 1727 to 50,000 in the whole of Britain by 1795 (Corson 1965: 360).

Advertisements and trade cards demonstrate the growth of 'puffing' (advertising) as retailers became more aware of competition and the need to market both their wares and their professional skills. In the *Bath Chronicle* (1782), for example, local businesses advertised scented hair powders and pomades, whilst Lady Molyneux advertised her 'LIQUID, which changes red or grey hair to a beautiful brown or jet black.' Amongst advertisements for perfumeries, silk-makers and mercers, which all related to fashionable personal display of the times, the frequency of specifically hair-related examples demonstrate the prominence of hair and its dressing and display for the middle-class readers of the *Chronicle*.

The mid- to late-eighteenth century saw a widespread growth in the production and consumption of all types of luxury goods that provided opportunities for spectacular fashionable display. The corresponding commercialization of leisure activities such as the races, the theatre, walking in the new pleasure gardens, socializing in assemblies and coffee houses equally created exciting 'arenas of display' that fuelled the mechanisms of conspicuous consumption in urban centres. These new venues emerged alongside the development of fashionable shopping streets that allowed people to view the latest fashions in the shops for themselves but also to visibly parade their own fashions and hairstyles, and to note those of other people's (Clark and Houston 2000: 579; Stobart 1998: 19). The more elaborate the hairstyle, the more wealth and leisure time was shown to be available to the individual. Hair and its styling visibly demonstrated the wearer's ability to consume but more important, to do so in a conspicuously and theatrical manner (Rosenthal 2004: 11; Powell and Roach 2004: 87).

THE THEATRICALITY OF HAIR DISPLAY: PERFORMANCE AND THE 'SOCIAL THEATRE'

The nature of fashionable display in the eighteenth century meant that men and women were constantly trying to outdo each other in order to stand out from the crowd—particularly in the crush of indoor venues. High and highly dressed hairstyles and indeed some of the more extreme fashions, such as wide hoop petticoats and cork rumps, created figures of extraordinary and theatrical proportions. The novelty achieved by the high hairstyles was intended to gain attention in these new public arenas, where their display and 'performance' was an integral part of the 'social theatre' of public life and theatrical behaviour was a major feature in a number of different ways (Hundert 1998: 141–72). The popularity of the theatre as a highly fashionable form of entertainment and as a social venue increased. Theatre audiences had vastly grown in size throughout the eighteenth century, in fact at a greater rate than the increase in the overall population of London, with almost 12,000 people attending the theatre each week by 1760 (Brown, 1995: 267–8). Actors, such as David Garrick and Sarah Siddons, achieved iconic status and became prominent members of fashionable society. Garrick even introduced a style called the 'Garrick cut' which was a small wig 'with five crisp curls on either side' (Corson 1965: 301). Social commentary on hair and its everyday practice was incorporated into theatrical performance itself, demonstrated in this quote from Oliver Goldsmith's very popular comedy of errors, *She Stoops to Conquer* (1773):

> Pray how do you like this head, Mr Hastings?
>
> Extremely elegant and degagee upon my word madam. Your frisseur is a Frenchman,
>   I suppose?
>
> I protest, I dressed it myself from a print in The Ladies Memorandum Book for the last
>   year. (cited in Buck and Matthews 1984: 89).

It was also in the 1770s that the 'masquerade' achieved the height of popularity with the elite classes in England. These events not only provided, but positively encouraged, a focus for fashionable and spectacular extravagance in both clothing and hairstyles (Ribeiro 1977: 385). The masquerade was a formal social assembly or ball, where the participants were disguised by a mask, so allowing them the opportunity to display their fashions literally and metaphorically as actors on a public stage. However, elements of 'social theatre' equally extended into the middle-class home. Here, there was an increasing social and spatial de-marcation between the public 'front stage' area where visitors circulated and were lavishly entertained, and the 'back stage' or more private areas of the home where fashionable display was assembled—in the case of hairstyles, in the time-consuming 'building of the head'.

Wealthy visitors to Bath, for example, a prime venue for fashionable display during the eight months of the season, went to see and be seen, and equally performed their fashion-able status in the constant 'play' of social life: promenading, dancing, shopping and social-izing (Borsay 1989: 150). In cities such as Bath, the built environment itself only further contributed to a sense of theatricality: the façades of the most fashionable addresses such as 'The Circus' were akin to theatre boxes from which a fashionable elite might observe the 'company' parading themselves in the streets below (Borsay 1989: 279). Furthermore, as Peter Borsay has argued, the height of some of the larger hairstyles paralleled architectural ornaments such as the obelisk in Queen's Square which was built to some seventy feet; and the addition of flowers and even vegetables in the larger hairstyles were equally reminiscent in terms of extravagance and spectacular display to the ornamental gardens that were such a feature of Bath's fashionable squares (1989: 78, 279).

THE NEW PUBLIC STAGE

Theatrical display at a number of levels was pivotal to the articulation of social and fash-ionable status in the eighteenth century. Participation in a range of social activities and a new public 'stage' of conspicuous consumption afforded greater opportunities for the display of the rapidly changing fashions by both men and women. Increasing numbers of fashionable individuals behaved in a theatrical way, wearing extreme dress and hair-styles to achieve spectacular effect. The gendered nature of hair and its dressing and styling marked female fashionable display as excessive and extreme. The small group of flamboy-ant, aristocratic macaronis equally highlighted the hedonism of conspicuous consumption in the late-eighteenth century in a very obvious way. Both these forms of hair display contrasted with the increasingly professional and progressively less ostentatious appearance of male wigs.

However, the more sober wigs and powdered hair of middle-class men also provided an element of theatricality. If they functioned to clearly demarcate the boundaries of both female fripperies and aristocratic excess, then they also enacted a social theatre of public and professional life. Women might study dress to add to their beauty; men should dress suitable to their various 'roles' in life:

> [W]hether as a magistrate, statesman, warrior, man of pleasure, &c, for the hair, either natural or artificial, may be dress'd to produce in us different ideas of the qualities of men, which may be seen by actors, who alter their dress according to the different characters they are to perform. (Ritchie 1770: 78 quoted in Adler and Pointon 1993: 175)

It was the extreme nature of the styles of the 1770s in particular that most sharply emphasize the theatrical, and often spectacular, nature of fashionable hair display. However, hairstyles for both men and women in the eighteenth century performed and were performed as a key indicator not only of fashionable status but also of the changing nature of the social and political environment. This idea of the wider 'social theatre' as a circuit of cultural meanings is a useful one: hair and its dressing and styling was just one part of a range of contemporary responses to the growing importance of the performance of the eighteenth-century self, but an extremely significant one.

BIBLIOGRAPHY

Adler, K. and Pointon, M. (eds.) (1993), *The Body Imaged: Representation and the Human Body since the Renaissance,* Cambridge: Cambridge University Press.

Barrell, J. (2006), *The Spirit of Despotism,* Oxford: Oxford University Press.

Bath Chronicle, 11 and 25 April 1782.

Borsay, P. (1989), 'All the Town's a Stage: Urban Ritual and Ceremony 1660–1800', in P. Borsay (ed), *The English Urban Renaissance,* Oxford: Oxford University Press.

Brewer, J. and Porter, R. (eds.) (1993), *Consumption and the World of Goods,* London and New York: Routledge.

Brown, J. R. (1995), *The Oxford Illustrated History of the Theatre,* Oxford: Oxford University Press.

Buck, A. and Matthews, H. (1984), 'Pocket Guides to Fashion: Ladies' Pocketbooks Published in England 1760–1830', *Costume,* 18: 35–48.

Budgell, E. (1711), *The Spectator* No 150, Wednesday 22 August in D. F. Bond (1965), *The Spectator,* Oxford Vol. II.

Clark, P. and Houston, R. A. (2000), 'Culture and Leisure 1700–1840', in P. Clark (ed), *The Cambridge Urban History of Britain II,* Cambridge: Cambridge University Press.

Cooper, W. (1971), *Hair: Sex, Society, Symbolism,* London: Aldus Books.

Corfield, P. (1990), 'Georgian Bath: The Magical Meeting Place', *History Today,* 11 (40): 26–33.

Corson, R. (1965), *Fashions in Hair: The First 5000 Years,* London: Peter Owen.

Cunnington, C. W. and Cunnington, P. (1957), *Handbook of English Costume in the 18th Century,* London: Faber.

Defoe, D. (1979), *A Tour Through the Whole Island of Great Britain*, Harmondsworth: Penguin Books.

Donald, D. (2002), *Followers of Fashion: Graphic Satires from the Georgian Period*, London: Hayward Gallery Publishing.

Hundert, E. (1998), 'Performing the Passions in Commercial Society: Bernard Mandeville and the Theatricality of Eighteenth-Century Thought', in K. Sharpe and S. N. Zwicker (eds.), *Refiguring Revolutions: Aesthetics and Politics from the English Revolution to the Romantic Revolution*, Berkeley: University of California Press.

Kowaleski-Wallace, E. (1997), *Consuming Subjects: Women, Shopping and Business in the 18th Century*, New York: Columbia University Press.

Kuchta, D. (2002), *The Three-Piece Suit and Modern Masculinity: England, 1550–1850*, Berkeley and Los Angeles: University of California Press.

Langley Moore, D. (1971), *Fashion through Fashion Plates 1771–1970*, London: Ward Lock.

Laver, J. (1996), *Costume and Fashion*, London: Thames & Hudson.

McKendrick, N., Brewer, J. and Plumb, J. H. (eds.) (1983), *The Birth of a Consumer Society: The Commercialisation of Eighteenth Century England*, London: Hutchinson & Co.

McNeil, P. (1999), '"That Doubtful Gender": Macaroni Dress and Male Sexualities', *Fashion Theory*, 3 (4): 411–47.

McNeill, P. (2000), 'Macaroni Masculinities', *Fashion Theory*, 4 (4): 373–403.

Paulson, R. (1970), 'Rowlandson and the Dance of Death', *Eighteenth-Century Studies*, 3 (4): 544–59.

Picard, L. (2000), *Dr Johnson's London*, London: Phoenix Press.

Pointon, M. (1993), *Hanging the Head: Portraiture and Social Formation in 18th Century England*, New Haven: Yale University Press.

Powell, M. K. and Roach, J. (2004), 'Big Hair', *Eighteenth-Century Studies*, Fall 2004: 79–99.

Rauser, A. (2004), 'Hair, Authenticity and the Self-Made Macaroni', *Eighteenth-Century Studies*, Fall 2004: 101–17.

Ribeiro, A. (1975), *The Dress Worn at Masquerades in England, 1730–1790 and Its Relation to Fancy Dress in Portraiture*, PhD thesis, Courtauld Institute of Art, University of London.

Ribeiro, A. (1977), 'The King of Denmark's Masquerade', *History Today*, 27: 385–9.

Ribeiro, A. (1995), *The Art of Dress: Fashion in England and France 1750–1820*, New Haven and London: Yale University Press.

Ribeiro, A. (2002), *Dress in Eighteenth Century Europe*, New Haven and London: Yale University Press.

Ritchie, D. (1770), *A Treatise on the Hair*, London.

Rosenthal, A. (2004), 'Raising Hair', *Eighteenth-Century Studies*, Fall 2004: 1–16.

Rosenthal, M. and Myrone, M. (2002), *Gainsborough*, London: Tate.

Stevens Cox, J. (1984), *An Illustrated Dictionary of Hairdressing and Wigmaking*, London: Batsford.

Stobart, J. (1998), 'Shopping Streets as Social Space: Leisure, Consumerism and Improvement in an Eighteenth-century County Town', *Urban History*, 25 (1): 3–21.

Stroomberg, H. (1999), *High Head: Hair Fashions Depicted in Eighteenth-century Satirical Prints Published by Matthew and Mary Darly*, Enschede: Rijksmuseum Twenthe.

Vickery, A. (1998), *The Gentleman's Daughter: Women's Lives in Georgian England*, London and New Haven: Yale University Press.

3 ROOTS
HAIR AND RACE

SARAH CHEANG

The Natural History Museum in London holds more than 5,000 samples of human hair from around the world. These specimens are currently used in the study of human DNA to reveal the genetic affiliation of different ethnic groups, patterns of human migration and genetic change (Kruszynski 2008). However, when many of the samples were collected as the result of scientific expeditions in the nineteenth and early-twentieth century, it was the colour and texture of the hair that appeared to hold the key to human biological identity. The purpose of this chapter is to investigate how hair has been used in the study of human racial difference (ethnography), by looking at hair's role in the categorizing of race, and in the history of anthropological collecting. Like the colour, patterning and texture of animal fur, human hair has been strongly linked to notions of breeding, race and lineage, and has been used as a natural indicator of racial identity. Such readings of hair relied on a particular understanding of nature, culture and 'race', in which the body serves as the touchstone of 'authentic being' for humanity. Thus, hair as a sign of corporeal authenticity has been powerfully utilized in debates around racial identity.

In ethnographic collections, hair samples form part of a wider set of photographs and objects that were used to delineate cultures. For example, the British colonial civil servant and anthropologist Edward Horace Man (1846–1929), an authority on the cultures of the Andamese and Nicobar Islands, made museum donations of seventy-five specimens of Andamese hair, along with vast quantities of other objects such as tools and utensils.[1] However, it could be argued that hair possesses an almost talismanic quality of authenticity that is lacked by other, nonbiological forms of recording and collecting 'race'. Wet film photography and cinematography is indexical (Sontag 1977; Barthes 1984), bearing an 'I was there'/'it was there' authority. Yet, ethnographers, through judicious framing and the use of props, have been accused of recording images that fitted in with their own visions of 'pure' and 'traditional' communities, denying the existence of 'modern', 'external' influences on their subjects (Edwards 1992). The cultural authenticity of the traditional craft object can similarly be questioned on the grounds that it may have been produced for the tourist industry (or to please the visiting anthropologist) and thus seem to have less value as an expression of 'true' ethnicity (Ames 1992: 59–69). Hair, on the other hand, grows involuntarily from the body of the subject, so that its validity as a true token of biological identity cannot be denied. Whatever is done to it, it is gradually and ceaselessly renewed at the roots, enabling researchers to get at what has seemed like the roots of 'natural' 'racial' identity.

HAIR, RACE AND BIOLOGICAL DIFFERENCE

Human beings are a single species who share ninety per cent of their DNA, and rarely live in isolated, 'pure-bred' societies (American Anthropological Association (AAA) 1998; Cole 1965: 27). Physical diversity within 'racial' groups is much wider than the differences between the 'races', and there is no link between variations in anatomy, physiognomy or colouring, and qualities such as 'intelligence' or 'natural aptitude'. For a human group to qualify as a 'race', seventy-five per cent of its individuals must be 'taxonomically' different to another group (Cole 1965: 9), so that the basis of 'race' lies in comparative anatomy. To understand how and why hair is used to communicate ideas of racial difference, it is necessary to look at the history of Western scientific theories of race which divided human beings into separate groups, on the grounds of biological difference.

At the time when Europeans began meeting with non-Europeans in the late-fifteenth century, humans were understood to differ in terms of a combination of cultural and physical markers, such as skin colour, language and customs. The colour and texture of head, facial and body hair, hairdressing and hair removal, were remarked upon as part of these distinctions, but the term *race* was not much used (Banton 1998: 25). It was during the eighteenth and nineteenth centuries that comparative studies of human anatomy were used to separate humans into 'races'. The idea was set in place that cultural differences between human groups had a biological, and hence inescapable, origin in the body (Banton 1998; Gould 1997: 62–175). However, the biological concept of race still involved cultural values and distinctions. As Christine Bolt (1971: 9) writes: 'Cultural characteristics, such as language, and physical features were used to classify the different divisions of man. Ultimately the two became confused, so that something called 'race' came to be seen as the prime determinant of all the important traits of body and soul, character and personality, of human beings and nations'.

The new 'scientific' understanding of race had its conceptual roots in an older medieval system known as the Great Chain of Being, in which all of creation was organized in order of ascending superiority like a chain of command, from the most lowly amoeba at the bottom to God himself at the top; the races of man were arranged with white people above all others (Lovejoy 1964; Jahoda 1999: 32–35). It should also be noted that by the eighteenth century, racial theories were being developed along with white Western imperialism and slavery, so that the racial hierarchy confirmed a worldview in which white socio-economic domination over nonwhites was somehow 'natural'.[2] The influence of climate on human evolution, and the notion that the races constituted separate species with separate origins, were debated as the possible causes of racial difference (Stocking 1991). Biological divergence was placed at the root of difference between human societies, whether this was seen as a direct cause (natural disposition), or through evolutionary changes in the species caused by environmental factors (natural selection). The Great Chain of Being had positioned human beings in strong association with apes, but the discovery that humans were descended from apes prompted the search for a 'missing link' between man and ape and gave a new scientific impetus to the study of bodies in order to ascertain who was closest and who was furthest away from the ape (Jahoda 1999: 36–50, 53–74).

Investigations into race and human anatomy therefore also involved an interest in anthropoid apes. Pruner-Bey's 1864 study of human hair and 'race-character' concluded with a section on the head hair of chimpanzees, gorillas, orangutans and baboons (Pruner-Bey 1864: 22). This linking of men and apes in the study of hair can also be seen in the activities of the twentieth-century British zoologist William Charles Osman Hill (1901–75). His collection of more than 800 samples of primate hair (human and nonhuman), mounted on glass slides for examination under the microscope, is now in the Wellcome Museum of the Royal College of Surgeons of England.[3] Osman Hill was a well-respected primatologist who also collected skeletal and wet-tissue specimens, and he published on the comparative anatomy of apes, and on the relationship of man to apes (Osman Hill 1954, 1957). His human hair collection was overwhelmingly focused on the Malayalam, Tamil, Sinhalese and Veddah people of southern India and Sri Lanka, and his approach was extremely comprehensive. His collection played a significant part in his very full anatomical description of the Veddahs, including diagrams of Veddah hair 'streams' (the direction that the hairs grow on the body) (Osman Hill 1941: 61–72). Osman Hill collected hair from the scalp, eyebrow, beard, moustache, armpit, breast, abdomen, pubis, buttock, leg, and the anal area from both sexes. This was achieved through several years of fieldwork in Sri Lanka, and also through the use of native cadavers, obtained after 'surmounting considerable difficulties' (Osman Hill 1941: 28). His collection even includes the scalp and facial hair of a Sinhalese foetus at six months gestation.[4]

Concepts of race have led to the erroneous, deeply prejudiced and highly damaging notions that, for example, black people or Jewish people were not merely culturally different but also fundamentally inferior to white people by birth, biology and nature, and could therefore be subjected to the horrors of oppression, atrocity, enslavement and even mass extinction (Banton 1998: 1–16). Race, unlike ethnicity (Eriksen 1993), was therefore a category assigned to people according to their physical characteristics, and it placed them in a hierarchy; a racial pecking order which historically positioned 'white' people ('causcasoids') above 'yellow' and 'red' people ('mongoloids'), and 'yellow' and 'red' people above 'black' people ('negroids'). These three main categories were subdivided into ethnic groupings called 'sub-races', according to common ancestry and shared physical (and supposed mental) characteristics.

Hair characteristics, along with eye and skin colour, were treated as a primary indicator of racial identity in the nineteenth and twentieth centuries (Figures 3.1 and 3.2) (Rowland 1853: 19–54; Trotter 1938). Hair's attraction for anthropologists was at least threefold. First, unlike internal skeletal structures, or observations based on behaviour, hair can be examined at a distance, with a minimum of social and physical invasion and without the need

Figure 3.1   Mid-nineteenth-century illustration of female ethnological differences in hair, showing a European, a Patagonian, an 'Esquimaux', a 'Bisharee' woman, a Fijian and a woman of the Warrau tribe, South America. (Rowland 1853: Plate 1).
Wellcome Library, London.

for dissection or specialist training. Second, hair has an immediate visual impact, enabling an almost instant identification of race at the first moment of contact. Last of all, although eye and skin colour can also be quickly ascertained, a more detailed analysis involves careful comparisons with colour charts in the field, whereas hair can be cut, taken away and studied at a later date, and hair keeps its colour and texture whether the donor is living or dead.

Figure 3.2   Mid-nineteenth-century illustration of male ethnological
differences in hair, showing a European, a 'negro', a Papuan, a Bosjesman,
a Kutchin Kutchin warrior and an 'Aboriginal native of Van Diemen's
Land'. (Rowland 1853: Plate III).
Wellcome Library, London.

As outlined in John Crawfurd's mid-nineteenth-century study, 'caucasoid' (cynotrichous)
hair was understood to come in a wide range of colours and positive textures such as 'fine,
soft and silky' (Crawfurd 1868: 146) so that whites were handed the cultural advantage of
differentiated, distinct and aesthetically pleasing identities. In contrast, 'mongoloid' (leiotri-
chous) hair was said to be 'coarse' and uniformly straight and black, implying sameness

and an innate lack of innovative powers; African 'negroid' (heliotrichous) hair was described as black and 'woolly', as in the title of Peter A Browne's *Classification of Mankind by the Hair and Wool of Their Heads* of 1852, in which Browne argued that wool-like hair qualities proved that the black race(s) were a completely separate species to whites (polygenesis) (Riss 2006: 98–106). Hair therefore became an important plank in monogenesis/polygenesis debates around the abolition of slavery that divided the discipline of anthropology (Sillitoe 2005: 1–6). In a robust defence of monogenesis, the nineteenth-century British ethnologist James Cowles Prichard (1843: 104, 546) also examined the hair of men and of sheep and stated 'I am convinced that the Negro has hair properly so termed, and not wool', therefore announcing that 'all human races are of one species and one family'.

Thus, in the mid-nineteenth century, the character of African hair was a 'controversial' subject (Rowland 1853: 31), and it was typically described as 'like the wool of a sheep' (Hunt 1863: 22), stigmatizing such hair as more closely related to animals than humans. In North America, white slaveowners would insist upon the term *wool* instead of *hair*, even, in one documented case, when a slave's hair was straight (White and White 1995: 56–8). Clearly, the possession of straight hair by a black slave was a significant disturbance to the boundaries of race and social identity in eighteenth- and nineteenth-century American society. To adamantly use the word *woolly*, against all common sense, shows how hair as a sign of racial difference also operated as a fetish (McClintock 1995: 185–9) that denied the existence of racial mixing as unthinkable.

In the 1920s, explanations of 'race' still relied heavily upon hair, arguing that whilst head size, facial features, skin colour, height and other body-related data can be used to determine race, 'the most useful character, because the least variable, is the hair' (Hammerton c.1925: 6454). Hair has also served as a means of examining racial mixing. For example, a 1950s study of hair in South Africa found that a man whose mother has the 'peppercorn' hair of the Hottentots (small knots close to the scalp with gaps in between), and whose father has 'woolly' hair of the Bantu, can have hair that is 'tufted, tending towards peppercorn at the margin. But the scalp ... has a covering with an irregular surface, like the waves in a choppy sea.' (Ruggles Gates 1957: 81).

Late-nineteenth and early-twentieth-century anthropological debate in Britain over the significance of hair colour was not confined to race, or to comparisons between the three major racial groups. Anthropologists also tried to demonstrate links between hair colour and insanity, and susceptibility to disease, arguing that dark-haired people were more likely to have cancer, whilst people with red hair were less likely to be lunatics (MacDonald 1911: 14). However, as notions of racial purity and racial fitness became more important, giving rise to eugenics, hair studies were ultimately linked to the delineation of the British people in racial terms. D. MacDonald (1911) observed the colouring of children with scarlet fever, diphtheria, measles and whooping cough in a Glasgow hospital. He concluded that dark and red-haired children were the least susceptible to these diseases, whilst medium-haired children were more susceptible and more likely to suffer permanent disability. However, if they became infected, fair-haired children seemed the most likely to die. MacDonald

(1911: 34–9) then used death and disability statistics to speculate on how the European 'race' was likely to be affected if certain hair colours were being selected by nature for extinction, finding that medium-coloured hair was most likely to die out.

Fifty years earlier in 1862, John Beddoe, a leading member of the Royal Society, the Ethnological Society and the Anthropological Institute of London, had published *Races of Britain,* in which he used hair and eye colour to investigate the origins of the British people. Beddoe, in line with much scientific and popular thought of the time, positioned the Irish and Welsh peoples between man and ape, on the same rung of the racial ladder as black peoples (Curtis 1971). He went on to argue that British hair was generally getting darker, because dark-headed people of Celtic descent from Ireland, Wales and Scotland were moving into towns and cities across England as a result of industrialization (Beddoe 1863). In his view, this situation was exacerbated by the way in which people with dark hair appeared to have greater resistance to the diseases of the city, and also the notion that fair-haired women were statistically more likely to die single, contributing to the demise of fair hair. Beddoe (1866) was also a prominent figure in discussions around hair colour, race and the effects of climate.

The claims made by Beddoe, his colleagues and his successors, in common with much anthropometric work (Gould 1997), do not stand up to close scrutiny. Clearly, they were fundamentally affected by the imperatives of justifying and maintaining a racial hierarchy. The search for links between hair and race, and hair and pathology, established a wider idea about hair as a sign that humans beings existed in fundamentally and naturally different groupings, but also contained implicit concerns over British racial degeneration. The scientific study of hair colour was also fraught with difficulties, the most basic of which was how to objectively and consistently decide what constituted dark brown as opposed to brown hair, or definitions of red, so as to create any meaningful results; hair observed indoors might look several shades darker than hair seen out of doors, hair might be dirty, and a child's hair often changes as the child grows (Tocher and Beddoe 1907; Parsons 1920: 160). The validity of casual observations of hair in the street was questioned, and it was deemed preferable to obtain hair data from situations where the anthropologist's subject could be better controlled, such as the hospital and the barracks (Parsons 1920: 159). Such institutions have been identified as crucial locations for the exertion of power and control over society (Foucault 1977; Tagg 1981). They offered researchers direct access to passive bodies—people placed in a compliant position where it would be difficult to evade scientific enquiry—and enabled the collection of supporting information such as parentage. At schools and hospitals all over the world, docile children, and sick or even dead patients, also afforded an opportunity to cut off specimens of hair and take them away for analysis. These hair samples still exist today as objects of study and as proofs of racial identity, in museums of ethnography, anatomy and natural history.

COLLECTING HAIR: FURTHER INVESTIGATIONS IN RACE

When scientific papers were given at learned institutions on the racial characteristics of hair, they were sometimes illustrated by specimens that could be passed around and examined (Barnard Davis 1873). These were sometimes just a few strands, and sometimes entire locks, and occasionally an entire scalp. An even closer scrutiny of hair involved a structural analysis of the hair shaft under the microscope, and this was used to investigate race from the 1850s onwards (Trotter 1938: 106). In 1863, Dr Franz Pruner-Bey read a paper at the Anthropological Society of Paris, in which he outlined how the transverse section of a single hair viewed under the microscope was of 'incontestable value for the study of characters inherent in the races of man' (Pruner-Bey 1864: 23). Pruner-Bey argued that where hair colour was shared between 'races', the shape of the hair shaft alone would reveal all: broadly speaking, 'negroid' hair was elliptical and flattened in section, 'mongoloid' hair was circular, and 'caucasoid' hair was somewhere in between these two extremes. The various sub-races demonstrated subtle differences that allowed him to use just one hair to distinguish, for example, Japanese from Chinese, Papuan from Melanesian, or German from Italian (for whom he also analysed facial and body hair). Of course, in order to carry out this work, Pruner-Bey needed samples. He obtained these through fellow anthropologists, explorers and collectors, and had access to the Musée National d'Histoire Naturelle in Paris. However, the number of specimens that Pruner-Bey used to confirm his thesis seems surprisingly small—usually only one or two samples for each racial sub-category, with the notable exception of sixteen specimens from East India, obtained through connections with English colonialists, and forty-eight samples of Irish hair from a single collection. He also made use of antique hair from the dead, taken from mummified bodies from South America and Egypt, and from an Irish turf pit.

Some of his specimens carried more cultural weight than others. In addition to a sample of Hottentot hair, Pruner-Bey added a pubic hair from Sara Baartman, a Khosian woman known as the Hottentot Venus. Baartman had been exhibited in England and in France between 1810 and 1815, as a natural and exotic curiosity, becoming a symbol of black racial difference at a time when the movement for the abolition of slavery gave images of black people a political impact (Qureshi 2004). When alive, her body was the subject of great scientific and popular excitement in Europe, and particular attention was paid to the size of her buttocks, and the shape of her genitalia (which she never displayed when alive), as a sensational proof of black women's animalistic sexuality, and of Hottentot racial status as extremely low (Gilman 1985). After her early death in Paris in 1815, Baartman's body was dissected by the anatomist Georges Cuvier, and her skeleton, brain and genitalia were preserved in the museum, as objects of knowledge for future researchers such Pruner-Bey.

The notoriety of Baartman's story finally led to the repatriation of her remains in 2002 (Qureshi 2004: 233). However, this is unlikely to happen to the vast majority of museum hair collections because they are classified as 'replaceable' body parts, in a different category from bone and tissue, even though they are similarly implicated in the unequal and racist histories of Western imperialism (Peers 2003: 75–8; 2007: 141). Many hair samples were collected in the pursuit of knowledge of colonial subjects, the better to control them, along with photographic images of native people (Pinney 1997: 17–71), whilst entire villages of native peoples from the colonies were exhibited in Europe and America as informative and entertaining attractions (Corbey 1995; Coombes 1997: 85–108). The metonymical

Figure 3.3   A shrunken head,
Jivaro Indian, Ecuador.
Wellcome Library, London.

relationship between hair, bodies and identities means that hair makes a good substitute for the whole person. Hair is also easily transported—it can simply be sealed in an envelope and posted—it will not break, and does not deteriorate like other body tissues. Hair samples can be taken from the living or from the dead, and can even be preserved 'in situ' as it were, still attached to a scalp, to mummified remains, or to a shrunken head (Figure 3.3).[5]

Whilst the imperial project was seldom an explicit aim, concerns over 'miscegenation' (inter-racial breeding), racial 'degeneration', and the destruction/disruption of native communities by Western colonialism, very consciously spurred anthropological collecting as a way of recording what might soon cease to exist. This is termed the *salvage paradigm* (Figure 3.4). Osman Hill (1941: 34) saw it as his 'duty' to obtain a record of the 'dwindling race' of the Veddahs, and he claimed to have examined 'probably every existing Veddah worthy of the name' (Osman Hill 1941: 27–8). That he, and not his subjects, decided who should be named 'Veddah' on the strength of a physical inspection is the basis of the difference between 'race' and 'ethnicity', and a fundamental part of the social inequalities that concepts of 'race' maintain. Hair was being used as an index of racial purity that gave power to the anthropologist. Hair specimens also provided scientific proof of racial mixing, and stood for the body of the native in the archive who had, in a sense, been collected.

Figure 3.4   Glass phial containing a sample of hair from an unnamed inhabitant of Tasmania, said to represent a 'now extinct race'. Wellcome Library, London.

PROBLEMS WITH HAIR: RACIAL POLITICS AND NATIVE RESISTANCE

Although hair's physical qualities and symbolic meanings gave it an important role in the material culture of 'race', nineteenth- and early-twentieth-century anthropologists were in fact all too aware of certain problems in studying mankind through hair. In 1868, John Crawfurd, President of the London Ethnological Society, argued that hair, along with skin and eyes, makes 'a very inadequate and ambiguous test of the races of man' (Crawfurd 1868: 144). He reasoned that whilst 'the Hindu, the Hindu-Chinese, the Chinese, the Japanese, the Malays, the Mongols, and the other races of Tartary, with the fairer races of the South Sea Islands, and with the two races of America' have the same kind of hair, the 'negroes' of Africa, Papua, the Pacific Islands and Australia all have markedly different hair (Crawfurd 1868: 146). Crawfurd (1868: 146–7) also observed that differences in male facial hair made no sense in terms of the established racial divisions and attendant hierarchy; the full beard grown by Europeans seemed such a symbol of 'vigour and manliness', and yet some 'inferior' races had abundant beards, while other 'superior' races had very scanty beards.

Anthropometric measurements were designed to give scientific certainty to the messy business of assigning racial identity, but in the information that accompanies many museum hair samples, moments of uncertainty are sometimes captured. At the Pitt Rivers Museum, Oxford, Malaysian hair collected in 1884–5 has the following notes: 'Heavy moustache (yellow) high cheekbones. Skin lighter than usual amongst Malays [,] cheeks tinged with red appearance like a typical peasant. Probably has white blood but could not persuade him to tell me.'[6] Thus, although the hair may be in the researcher's hand, a hint of native resistance can be detected; the Malaysian man's refusal to supply information on parentage ultimately undermines the hair specimen's function as a proof of racial lineage. The need to negotiate the slippery and politically loaded nature of racial identity can also be seen in the collecting of Beatrice Blackwood, who did anthropological fieldwork in North America from 1924 to 1927, researching the relationship between 'intelligence' and 'race'. During three weeks in 1925 she took samples from Ojibwe (Chippewa) communities of Red Lake and Cross Lake, Minnesota, accompanied by notes on the name, age and parentage of her subjects, and also their eye and skin colour; these samples were subsequently deposited at the Pitt Rivers Museum.

Here, the scrutiny of hair and the need to identify who was 'full blood' and who was 'mixed blood' was no academic project, but a political and economic imperative (Peers 2003: 87–8). Full-bloods were not allowed to lease or sell their reservation lands, whereas mixed-bloods could, and hair colour had been used by anthropologists in the employ of the government to decide the classification of Ojibwe individuals. Working in North America also gave Blackwood a heightened sense of the role that physical anthropology had played for African Americans within a racist and segregated society, where the identification of race and lineage had an especial significance (Cornell and Hartmann 1998: 23–5; Young 1995: 180–2).

It appears that Blackwood never looked at most of her samples after they were collected, and this has been interpreted as a crisis in their value and meaning (Peers 2007). Blackwood's research report concluded that there was no direct link between 'intelligence and physical inheritance' (Peers 2003: 80). Nevertheless, her work was always complicit with colonial frameworks, through her use of governmental and missionary agents to access the Ojibwe, and because of the power relations inherent in the taking and keeping of other people's hair. First, in the most direct sense, hair is considered to have magical properties in some cultures, where the possession of a person's hair can give power over that individual through the use of spells and charms (Peers 2003: 87). Second, the cutting of hair often occurs as part of the imposition of authority, in schools, barracks, prisons and workhouses. Native American girls' hair was worn long, loose or in braids, but their hair was put up or cut off in Federal schools in order to eliminate native cultures and overwrite them with white American culture (Peers 2007: 136; Weitz 2005: 7–9).

Collections of hair described as 'cut from the heads of the natives'[7] as a token of their authenticity are thus highly problematic, and connected on multiple levels to the imposition of cultural identities through the manipulation of hair. Museums collections formed around objects acquired by exchange or by force in the course of colonial expansion and maintenance can be seen as imperial knowledge and power made tangible (Richards 1993; Hooper-Greenhill 1992). At a meeting of the Anthropological Institute of Great Britain and Ireland, London, in 1873, a letter was read out from H. Blanc, civil and army surgeon in India and Fellow of the Royal Geographical Society, giving the details of a specimen of hair that he was sending for the Institute's museum (Blanc 1873). The hair had come from the head of a Brahmin turned fakir, who had not cut his hair for sixteen years, and whose appearance as a long-haired, 'religious mendicant' rendered him a fascinating figure, so that the collected hair represents race, custom, caste, gender and religion. The man had died in hospital, effectively delivering his body into Blanc's hands, although Blanc reported that at first, the other fakirs refused to allow the hair to be cut. However, when they understood that the hair was to be sent to England, they let Blanc take his sample. Blanc did not indicate the precise reason for this change of heart, but this very omission in an otherwise detailed account implies that the London Anthropological Institute saw itself as a universally acknowledged power, synonymous with reason, and positioned at the all-seeing and all-knowing heart of the British empire. In such reports, issues of complicity, coercion and ethics are effectively erased; hair's sentimental, magical and personal qualities shrink away at the moment of scientific cutting.

CONCLUSION

Since the mid-twentieth century, the biological determinism of 'race' has been discredited, but the tensions between the biological and the social (nature/nurture) have always to be reconciled or at the very least explored (Wade 2004; Dunbar 2007; Ulijaszek 2007). The usefulness of hair historically as a visual and material part of racial identity means that even attempts to break down the unacceptably racist assumptions of nineteenth-century racial constructions are made with reference to hair. The American Anthropological Association, in a recent statement outlining the immense problems and negative consequences of historical meanings of 'race', has commented that: 'Dark skin may be associated with frizzy or kinky hair or curly and wavy hair or straight hair, all of which are found among different indigenous peoples in tropical regions' (AAA 1998). Thus, hair type is still hard to escape from in discussions of 'race'.

Hair is indexically linked to race, but race is a very reductive concept. It reduces the immense complexities of human life—biological variation at an individual level, environmental factors and social influences—to a single organizing principle. The hair collections discussed in this chapter were all formed before the discovery of DNA and modern genetics, and were understood in terms of inheritance and morphology—the identification and classification of inherited traits. Today, the problematic postcolonial status of these hair collections (Peers 2007: 139–41) reflects the reintroduction of the voices and concerns of people who can claim a genetic, cultural, historical and emotional connection to the hair samples that are, after all, human remains.

ACKNOWLEDGEMENTS

Thank you to Cory Willmott, Lou Taylor and to the staff of the Wellcome Library, London.

NOTES

1. Pitt Rivers Museum (PRM) 1887.11.90.1–3; 1884.106.1–23.
2. The association of social privilege with whiteness has not been confined to European societies. European whiteness is a particular construction of the eighteenth and nineteenth centuries that erased access to white identities for non-Europeans, for example, in China and in the Middle East (Bonnett 2000: 7–27).
3. Wellcome Museum, RCSMS.Osman Hill 3–7, 20, 56, 867–949, 1831–80, 1891–1983.
4. Wellcome Museum, RCSMS.Osman Hill 932, 937.
5. See, for example, the scalp of an Andamese man who died in hospital in 1885, the scalp of a Plains Blackfoot man collected in Canada, and hair from a shrunken head from Ecuador. PRM 1887.1.45; PRM 1887.1.375.1–2; PRM 1884.106.33–34.
6. PRM 1887.1.399.13. This hair is part of a box of twenty-four samples that were collected in the Perak area of Malaysia by Mr A. Hale. Collectors Miscellaneous XI Accession Book: 63, 68, Pitt Rivers Museum.
7. PRM 1887.11.90.1–3.

BIBLIOGRAPHY

American Anthropological Association. (1998), 'American Anthropological Association Statement on "Race"', http://www.aaanet.org/stmts/racepp.htm, accessed 13 March 2008.
Ames, M. M. (1992), *Cannibal Tours and Glass Boxes: The Anthropology of Museums*, Vancouver: University of British Columbia.
Banton, M. (1998), *Racial Theories*, 2nd edn, Cambridge: Cambridge University Press.

Barnard Davis, J. (1873), 'A Few Notes upon the Hair, and Some Other Peculiarities of Oceanic Races', *The Journal of the Anthropological Institute of Great Britain and Ireland*, 2: 95–104.

Barthes, R. (1984), *Camera Lucida*, London: Fontana.

Beddoe, J. (1862), *The Races of Britain: A Contribution to the Anthropology of Western Europe*, Bristol and London, John Beddoe, J. W. Arrowsmith, Bristol & Trübner, London, 1885; republished by Hutchinson, London, 1971.

Beddoe, J. (1863), 'On the Supposed Increasing Prevalence of Dark Hair in England', *Anthropological Review*, 1 (2): 310–12.

Beddoe, J. (1866), '[Comments on:] On the Evidence of Phenomena in the West of England to the Permanence of Anthropological Types', *Journal of the Anthropological Society of London*, 4: xviii–xxvi.

Blanc, H. (1873), 'On the Hair of a Hindustanee', *The Journal of the Anthropological Institute of Great Britain and Ireland*, 2: 102.

Bolt, C. (1971), *Victorian Attitudes to Race*, London: Routledge and Kegan Paul.

Bonnett, A. (2000), *White Identities: Historical and International Perspectives*. Harlow: Prentice Hall.

Cole, S. (1965), *Races of Man*, London: British Museum.

Coombes, A. (1997), *Reinventing Africa: Museums, Material Culture and Popular Imagination*. New Haven: Yale University Press.

Corbey, R. (1995), 'Ethnographic Showcases, 1870–1930', in J. Nederveen Pieterse (ed), *The Decolonization of Imagination: Culture, Knowledge and Power*, London: Zed Books.

Cornell, S. and Hartmann, D. (1998), *Ethnicity and Race: Making Identities in a Changing World*. London: Sage Publications.

Crawfurd, J. (1868), 'On the Skin, the Hair, and the Eyes, as Tests of the Races of Man', *Transactions of the Ethnological Society of London*, 6: 144–9.

Curtis, L. P. (1971), *Apes and Angels: The Irishman in Victorian Caricature*, Newton Abbot: David and Charles.

Dunbar, R. (2007), 'The Biological and the Social: Evolutionary Approaches to Human Behaviour', in D. Parkin and S. J. Ulijaszek (eds.), *Holistic Anthropology: Emergence and Convergence*, New York: Berghan Books.

Edwards, E. (ed) (1992), *Anthropology and Photography 1860*, New Haven: Yale University Press.

Eriksen, T. H. (1993), *Ethnicity and Nationalism: Anthropological Perspectives*. London: Pluto Press.

Foucault, M. (1977), *Discipline and Punish: The Birth of the Prison*, London: Allen Lane.

Gilman, S. (1985), 'Black Bodies, White Bodies: Towards an Iconography of Female Sexuality in Late Nineteenth-Century Art, Medicine and Literature', *Critical Inquiry* 12.1 (Autumn): 204–42.

Gould, S. J. (1997), *The Mismeasure of Man*, London: Penguin Books.

Hammerton, J. A. (ed) (c.1925), 'Race', *Harmsworth's Universal Encyclopedia*, Vol. 10, London: Educational Book Co.

Hooper-Greenhill, E. (1992), *Museums and the Shaping of Knowledge*, London: Routledge.

Hunt, J. (1863), *On the Negro's Place in Nature*, London: Anthropological Society.

Jahoda, G. (1999), *Images of Savages: Ancient Roots of Modern Prejudice in Western Culture*, London: Routledge.

Kruszynski, R. (2008), Personal communication, curator, anthropological collections, Natural History Museum, London, 25 March.

Lovejoy, A. O. (1964), *The Great Chain of Being*, Cambridge, MA: Harvard University Press.

MacDonald, D. (1911), 'Pigmentation of the Hair and Eyes of Children Suffering from the Acute Fevers, Its Effects on Susceptibility, Recuperative Power and Race Selection', *Biometrika*, 8 (1/2): 13–39.

McClintock, A. (1995), *Imperial Leather: Race, Gender and Sexuality in the Colonial Contest*, New York: Routledge.

Osman Hill, W. (1941), 'The Physical Anthropology of the Existing Veddahs of Ceylon', part 1, *Ceylon Journal of Science;* reprinted from Section G, *Anthropology*, 3, part 2, July 10 and part 3, August 4, 1942.

Osman Hill, W. (1954), *Man's Ancestry: A Primer of Human Phylogeny*, London: Heinemann.

Osman Hill, W. (1957), *Man as an Animal*, London: Hutchinson.

Parsons, F. G. (1920), 'The Colour Index of the British Isles', *The Journal of the Royal Anthropological Institute of Great Britain and Ireland*, 50 (Jan–June): 159–82.

Peers, L. (2003), 'Strands Which Refuse to Be Braided: Hair Samples from Beatrice Blackwood's Ojibwe Collection at the Pitt Rivers Museum', *Journal of Material Culture*, 8 (1): 75–96.

Peers, L. (2007), 'On the Social, the Biological and the Political: Revisiting Beatrice Blackwood's Research and Teaching', in D. Parkin and S. J. Ulijaszek (eds.), *Holistic Anthropology: Emergence and Convergence*, New York: Berghan Books.

Pinney, C. (1997), *Camera Indica: The Social Life of Indian Photographs*, London: Reaktion.

Prichard, J. Cowles (1843), *The Natural History of Man: Comprising Inquiries into the Modifying Influences of Physical and Moral Agencies on the Different Tribes of the Human Family*, London: Brailliere.

Pruner-Bey, F. (1864), 'On Human Hair as a Race-Character, Examined by the Aid of the Microscope', *Anthropological Review*, 2 (4): 1–23.

Qureshi, S. (2004), 'Displaying Sara Baartman, the "Hottentot Venus"', *History of Science*, 42: 233–57.

Richards, T. (1993), *The Imperial Archive: Knowledge and the Fantasy of Empire*, London: Verso.

Riss, A. (2006), *Race, Slavery and Liberalism in Nineteenth-Century American Literature*, Cambridge: Cambridge University Press.

Rowland, A. (1853), *The Human Hair, Popularly and Physiologically Considered with Special Reference to Its Preservation, Improvement and Adornment, and the Various Modes of Its Decoration in All Countries*, London: Piper.

Ruggles Gates, R. (1957), 'Forms of Hair in South African Races', *Man*, 57 (June): 81–83.

Sillitoe, P. (2005), 'The Role of Section H at the British Association for the Advancement of Science in the History of Anthropology', *Durham Anthropology Journal*, 13 (2): 1–17.

Sontag, S. (1977), *On Photography*, London: Penguin Books.

Stocking, G. W. Jr. (1991), *Victorian Anthropology*, New York: The Free Press.

Tagg, J. (1988), *The Burden of Representation: Essays on Photographies and Histories*, Basingstoke: Macmillan Press.

Tocher, J. F. and Beddoe, J. (1907), 'Observations on the Scottish Insane', *Man*, 7: 129–33.

Trotter, M. (1938), 'A Review of the Classifications of Hair', *American Journal of Physical Anthropology*, 24 (1): 105–26.

Ulijaszek, S. J. (2007), 'Bioculturalism', in D. Parkin and S. J. Ulijaszek (eds.), *Holistic Anthropology: Emergence and Convergence*, New York: Berghan Books.

Wade, P. (2004), 'Human Nature and Race', *Anthropological Theory* 4 (2): 157–72.

Weitz, R. (2005), *Rapunzel's Daughters: What Women's Hair Tells Us about Women's Lives,* New York: Farrar, Straus and Giroux.

White, S. and White, G. (1995), 'Slave Hair and African-American Culture in the Eighteenth and Nineteenth Centuries', *The Journal of Southern History,* 61 (1): 45–76.

Young, R. (1995), *Colonial Desire: Hybridity in Theory, Culture and Race,* London: Routledge.

4 REVEALING AND CONCEALING
OBSERVATIONS ON EROTICISM AND FEMALE PUBIC HAIR

JACK SARGEANT

[H]e strained until the corners of his eyes began to ache. He tried all the obscenity he knew, but words alone couldn't penetrate that thicket.

—Yukio Mishima, *The Sailor Who Fell from Grace with the Sea*

While male pubic hair has been a physical and philosophical signifier of adulthood and masculinity, female pubic hair, like female sexuality, has occupied more uncertain territory.[1] The cultural traditions of the West demand that female genitals belong to the domain of the hidden; the labial folds and creases that frame the vagina vanish from sight, hidden between the thighs and behind the matted curls of pubic hair (Figure 4.1).[2] As Mishima's youthful protagonist found, as his spied upon his own mother and her lover, he could not see that which he knew was there: the promise of the sex was whispered invisible. In Freudian theory, it is precisely this inability to see the female genitals behind the female fur that plays a central role in the establishment of sexual identity. Yet the hair that conceals is itself subject to elision—shaved away on the body, and disguised or airbrushed out in representation—so that that which effectively hides the female genitals also disappears, until all that remains is vanished and unspoken. The following exploration of eroticism and the representation of female pubic hair in the West shifts between literature, psychoanalysis, art history, pornography and body fashion, and multiple parallel discourses. To simply privilege one narrative strand would be to negate the myriad of ways in which something as commonplace as pubic hair has both affected, and been affected by, culture.

LITERATURE, EROTICISM AND HAIRLESSNESS

The body exists as a zone in which manifestations of power compete. The work of French philosopher Michel Foucault examines the mechanisms and technologies of power that surround the human body, and suggests that these not only emerge from external discourses such as gender and class, but also from within the individual (Foucault 1980). The contested nature of the correct form of pubic hair, and the individual's response to this, can be viewed as one form of this discourse. The manifestations of power that play in, through and across the body can be seen in the rituals that define the sexual practices associated with sadomasochism. If dominant culture did not acknowledge sex, then eroticized subcultures did. 'The Basque and Bijou' stands out amongst the transgressive erotic stories written

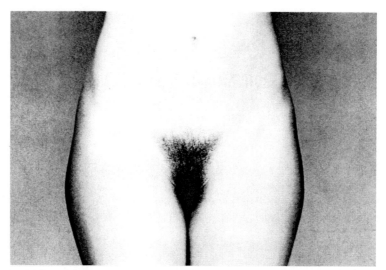

Figure 4.1   A woman's naked abdomen.
Daniel Sambraus/Science Photo Library.

by bohemian authoress Anaïs Nin, its narrative presentation of sadomasochism tracing the limitations associated with consent and abuse. Originally written to satisfy the whims of a private client in the 1940s, her collected short erotic stories were subsequently published under the title *Delta of Venus*.

Focusing on the purity of the unrestrained, raw sadomasochistic relationship between its protagonists, 'The Basque and Bijou' is delirious in its episodic structure which drifts through numerous oneiric scenarios. While contemporary sadomasochistic relationships are often weighed down under rigorous self-policing and notions of consent, in Anaïs Nin's fiction such niceties are rendered obsolete, instead presenting scenes that float and drift between incidents of cold rejection and forced bestiality. In the narrative, the heroine Bijou, is seduced by the Basque, a man who enjoys tormenting her, teasing her to the edge of orgasm with numerous subtle cruelties. One such ordeal is the ritualized humiliation of the shaving of her pubic hair.

In this sequence the Basque uses a straight razor to remove her hair, while a trio of his associates hold her still and look greedily on. As the sequence progresses, so Nin describes the process of shaving in meticulous detail, which climaxes in the men looking at Bijou's vulva, while the Basque uses the bristles on the shaving brush to arouse her, caressing her clitoris, opening her labia, and forcing dampness from her vagina. The scene of the shaving of pubic hair creates an evocative sensuality, and while the resulting unrestricted view of the character's aroused genitals creates the narrative climax, it is the description of the shaving that forms the bulk of the narrative. Each detail—the texture of the hair on her belly, the coldness of the razor, and so on—contributes to the building sensuality of the piece. It is not the result that matters; rather it is the eroticized process of hair removal that forms the *mise-en-scene* of the narrative's eroticism.

Yet here the process of shaving can also be understood as a form of dominance and subjugation, indeed it is this emphasis that makes Nin's story powerful, as Bijou does not choose erotic submission but is held down by her lover's associates. In reality such events may be a form of vicious traumatic abuse, but the power of fantasy is that it knows no limits, existing unrestrained and unpoliced.

FETISHISM AND EROTICISM

The rituals of eroticized violence, fantasy, desire, and gaze that are manifested in Nin's story also find an echo in the psychoanalytical writing of Sigmund Freud, the undoubted master theorist of the phallocentric gaze. However, unlike Nin's quartet of monomaniacal sadists, Freud was never fully able to come to terms with the female genitals. Again and again he turned his attention to them, but despite the rigor of his scoptophilic investigations he finally saw nothing.

Understanding the certainty, both in function and discursively, of the penis, in the vagina Freud saw only 'orifice', castration, and 'cloaca' (a variant of the *down-there* which conflates the anus and genitals in the sexual understanding of children and which also means 'sewer') (Freud 1977: 104, 144). Citing Lou Andreas-Salome, Freud observed that the vagina was merely 'on lease' (Freud 1977: 104) from the anus. The female genitals are thus not merely a lack, but a zone of filth and utter contagion (Freud 1977: 104).[3] The Viennese doctor was blinded *by* and *to* the sight of the vagina, unable to render it as psychoanalytic discursive certainty. Yet, despite and because of his understanding of the vagina as a space needing to be filled, Freud turned his attention elsewhere, finding psychoanalytic truths in the curls of matted hair that framed the 'space' that he could not render within his discourse.

Freud founded the entire psychosexual and moral development of males on the sight of the female genitals and the instant understanding of the vagina as castrated lack. He saw that pubic hair offered an explanation for the fetishes for fur and velvet that his patients spoke of on his early-twentieth-century analyst's couch. In psychoanalysis, seeing woman as castrated becomes evidence for the threat that all male children perceive in the actions of parents, guardians or nursemaids. In this instant of understanding—the instantaneous 'unforgetting' of truth—the boy child must take on his father's morality manifested in the instantaneous formation of the super-ego, and simultaneously he must renounce his incestuous desires for his mother, repress his polymorphic infantile sexuality and understand sexual difference via castration.

The fetishist, Freud argued, repressed knowledge of the sight of the wound of castration, replacing the acceptable target for his penetrating desire with the last exquisite vision before the resplendently horrific evidence of sexual difference. Thus a fur fetishist would find his libidinal obsession (cathexis) reflected in a repressed desire for pubic hair, his last sight before the horror of the vagina, realized in the luxurious, soft warm sensuousness of fur or velvet. 'Spared' (Freud 1977: 354) from the evidence of castration the fetishist was still able to view women as phallic yet also as desirable, the fetish representing 'a substitute for the mother's penis' (Freud 1977: 352).

Such a mechanistic view of development, of sexuality, and of fetishism serves to essentialize sexuality and reduce it to a psychosexual developmental certainty, but this is less interesting than Freud's descriptions of pubic hair in this particular scenario. Freud is unable to fully engage with the female genitals as anything other than horrific, but his positioning of pubic hair in fetishism as that which both hides the genitals and seduces the gaze suggests a sense of subtle eroticism.

DEPILATION IN ART

Pubic hair appears as excess; it fulfills no immediately recognizable function, rather it seems to be a biological trace of our primal animal roots. Moreover, the very location and time of its appearance can be seen as the punctuation of our ferine sexuality; as Freud wrote of the genitals, 'they have remained animal' (Freud, 1977: 259). It is not surprising that the hairy mons veneris was largely unknown in Western art history, the curves of the female body vanishing and the crotch hidden by carefully placed hands or legs, or ending in wispy shadow, or hidden behind carefully positioned foliage (Figure 4.2). If artists depicted the rich smear of hair across the mons pubis of the supine mystic nudes that populate classical

Figure 4.2   Eugène Delacroix (1798–1863), *Odalisque*, c. 1825 (oil on canvas).
Fitzwilliam Museum, University of Cambridge, UK/The Bridgeman Art Library.

Western art, then sexually repressive cultures and societies would have to understand women as sexual, with all of the concomitant drives, urges, desires and fantasies. In classical Western art the denuded pudendum exists in contrast to the swell of the breasts, its smooth hairlessness a symbol of 'sexual innocence' and of virginity. These nude female bodies occupy a contradictory zone, they are infantile yet adult, sexless yet erotic, maternal yet virginal; such are the inconsistencies of these artworks and the cultures that spawned them.

In sharp contrast to the majority of coy nudes that are presented in the mainstream of Western art, and predating the frequent depiction of realistic nudes in modern art, is Gustave Courbet's painting *The Origin of the World* (1866) (Figure 4.3). Depicting a woman's torso, her legs parted, this is one of only a handful of artistic images that depicts the vulva surrounded by pubic hair.[4] This painting was, and still is, scandalous, unashamed in its desire to illuminate that which had previously been rendered unseen, the thin-lipped slit glimpsed through the dark matted brown curls of hair that have sprung from the artist's brush. Moreover in painting the vulva as both an object of desire and as a personal subject it becomes as important as the face; most nudes include the woman's face, but here the portrait is of the vulva.

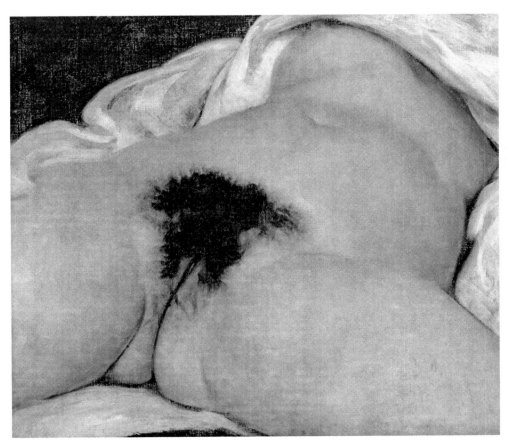

Figure 4.3   Gustave Courbet (1819–77), *The Origin of the World,* 1866 (oil on canvas). Musée d'Orsay, Paris/Giraudon/The Bridgeman Art Library.

Origin was painted for Khalil-Bey, a diplomat and renowned collector of erotic art, in 1866, the year in which a young Sigmund Freud turned ten (presumably having already been traumatized by the sight of the female lack which would forever haunt his writings). It celebrates the artist's gaze upon the female genitals, not as a zone of non-knowledge waiting to be decoded but as an affirmation of unleashed sexual passion. This is an image of veneration and devotion, but free of the staid vestiges of religion, it is an icon of the sacred found within the profane, of mana manifested in the taboo, presenting the viewer with an unrestricted look at the nude female. Where Freud would come to understand this sight merely as a single moment in *psychological time* that re-enforced his own phallocentric worldview, Courbet saw his own lusts in *physical space* simultaneously affirmed and hidden by the hair.

In 1955, *The Origin of the World* was acquired by the psychoanalyst Jacques Lacan and Sylvia Bataille. The ferocious and lascivious power invested within the work was contained by Lacan who commissioned the surrealist Andre Masson to construct a frame for the painting, fitted with doors that could be used to cover the artwork. Among modern art movements few had the desire to explore sexuality more overtly than the surrealists, who repeatedly alluded to genitals and copulation in their works. However, framing these images in dream logic invariably meant that even an explicit work such as Rene Magritte's *The Rape* (1934) could be positioned as phantasmagoric rather than naturalistic. Masson and Hans Bellmer—both dissident surrealists—produced extreme erotic illustrations graphically depicting sexual acts to illustrate the erotic/philosophic novel *Histoire de l'oeil* by Georges Bataille, but the circulation of the images was clandestine.[5]

In 1860, a contemporary of Courbet, the poet Charles Baudelaire, wrote 'Un fantome', which was subsequently published in *Les Fleurs du mal* (1861). Baudelaire (1961), who became notorious for the erotic content of his work, describes the sight and sensuous smell of the vagina, barely hidden by poetic metaphor,

> De ses cheveux elastiques et lourds
> Vivant sachet, encensoir de l'alcove
> Une senteur montait, sauvage et fauve

There are various published translations of this poem—most literally translate *encensoir de l'alcove* as 'censer of the alcove' which certainly evokes images both religious and vaginal, sacred and profane, but the term *incense burner* evokes the notion of scent more readily. The opening line, with the use of 'its' rather than the gender specific 'her' suggests that the hair belongs to the 'living sachet' of the next line, in other words to the vagina. The description of 'heavy and elastic' hair could be translated as 'luxuriant' hair, but the notion of elasticity in hair certainly evokes the coils of pubic hair. Thus Baudelaire's verse can be broadly translated as: 'From its pubic hair / Living sachet, incense burner / a scent rises, savage and musky'. Like Courbet, Baudelaire is seduced and intoxicated by the stimulation offered to the senses. This is desire in the raw. The pubic hair that so intoxicates and fascinates these two artists frames the genitals, but is also seen as a sensual pleasure in itself.

Not just as a source of visual fascination, this is pubic hair as both tactile and aromatic; as seductive hair, which serves the vagina with its warm softness and rich scent. This dance with the erotic takes on a new intensity with the advent of photography and, as the twentieth century progressed, the increasing availability of explicit visual sexual materials.

FROM CONCEALED TO REVEALED

In erotic postcards and magazines of the first half of the twentieth century, images of nudity were carefully shaded or airbrushed in order that the pubic hair vanish behind fleshy tones in a mimesis of classical art (Figure 4.4).[6] Women, like toy dolls, have abdomens delineated by smooth curves that merely lead back upon themselves. The torso is rendered as a curved redundant stump that sprouts legs, there is no hair and no holes, no points of entry and no points of exit, such is the absurdity of censorship.

It was nudist magazines that were first exempt from this censorship, in a landmark 1958 case in America when the representation of pubic hair was allowed in supposedly non-erotic nudist magazines. This led to a growth in the popularity of nudist magazines, and eventually, by 1967, a few clandestine erotic magazines began to depict pubic hair. Even in the nudie cuties—short sexy films that promised unfettered flesh but actually only showed bottoms and breasts—pubic hair remained unseen until 1968, when some pornographic film directors dared to show it (McNeil, Osborne and Pavia 2006: 10). The representation of female pubic hair as a sign of sexual maturity and as a zone for an eroticized gaze emerged fully in the early 1970s with the growth of hardcore pornography. *Penthouse* magazine was the first mainstream magazine to publish explicit photographs that included pubic hair in 1971.

Originally, the sexualized pleasures associated with pubic hair removal existed as a minority interest, catered for in specific pornographic magazines such as *Shaven Ravers*, and often this eroticized hair removal focused—like Nin's story—on the process of shaving as a sexual act with its locus in sexual transgression and making visible, performed as a ritual of dominance and submission. However, female pubic hair has also been regarded as undesirable on both medical and cosmetic grounds, and the sight of the carefully manicured or bald *mons pubis* has moved from minority fantasy to mainstream culture with the appearance of fashions for the removal of pubic hair within the pornography industry and more widely.

Since the nineteenth century the 'correct' appearance of the female body has increasingly been the subject of medical and cultural discourses in the West. In 1877 the American Dermatological Association was founded and it soon began to address the 'issue' of female body hair. As Labre (2002) notes the 'issue' was constructed as a pseudo-medical discourse and it is telling that the removal of what was deemed excessive body hair was described as a treatment. During the second half of the twentieth century, the increasing medicalization of childbirth saw women shaved 'clean' prior to the delivery of the newborn in hospital. Hygiene was commonly cited by medical professionals as the reason for this activity, although the damaged skin left by the razor was actually more of a potential zone of

Figure 4.4   1920s French postcard.
Mary Evans Picture Library.

infection than the presence of pubic hair. This shaving prior to labour can be traced to the nineteenth century, was widespread in the English-speaking world and was still routinely practiced in sixteen per cent of Canadian hospitals in 1993 (Cassidy 2007: 184).

The cosmetic removal of body hair became increasingly popularized in the early-twentieth century, and in the years following the Second World War numerous products became readily available, designed to remove 'unwanted' hair from armpits and legs. This hair was no longer even viewed as an excess, but simply as something that would 'normally' be removed. As fashion increasingly revealed more of women's bodies, more hair was subsequently removed in displays of normalized femininity that posited a hairless female body. Furthermore, the smooth legs and armpits became associated with a degree of affluence, simply: the depilated woman could afford to follow fashion.

The Brazilian Wax was first documented in the 1990s, referring to the removal of hair from the mons pubis, the vulva and between the buttocks, to leave a thin vertical strip of hair on the mons pubis. The Brazilian was commonly associated with women who presented their splayed labia for a public eroticized gaze, either at strip clubs or in pornographic films, but by the end of the decade the procedure had gained in popularity in the wider community and was the source of numerous, often titillating, magazine articles (Valhouli 1999; Ellen 1999; Crisp 2006). Although it reportedly emerged from a New York beauty salon, notions of cultural otherness and exoticism located the procedure's origins in Brazil, seen as a result of the scanty thong-style bikini costumes that are commonly associated with the country's beaches. Invariably, the desire to trim and shape pubic hair suggested by the Brazilian led to the complete removal of all pubic hair in what is colloquially referred to as the Hollywood Wax.

The increasing popularity of bikini waxing, and the complete removal of all female pubic hair, may have its roots in the desire to pay witness to the aroused female genitals as envisioned in *The Basque and Bijou* or in hardcore pornography, but paradoxically the results often appear to resemble the carefully stylized nudes of art or the carefully airbrushed nude photography of softcore pornography. While during sex acts the 'nakedness exposed every nuance' (Nin 1990: 147), at other times hairlessness often merely emphasizes the curve of the belly downwards.

While some celebrate the increased manifestation of sexual awareness felt by baldness, and the breakdown of the clear distinction between the border between inside and outside, such overt pleasures are not mooted as reasons for women to undergo the procedure. Magazine articles that discuss the various manifestations of the Brazilian often quote actress Kirstie Alley who celebrated her Brazilian, saying 'It feels like a baby's butt, only all over' (Valhouli 1999: 1). Such descriptions remove the activity from any sexual or eroticized context, positioning it instead with a *cutesy nausea* discourse of infantilization that owes less to Anaïs Nin and more to Hello Kitty.

The move to the fashionable Brazilian Wax as part of a common beautification regime has recontextualized the process of hair removal to an experience akin to any other beauty treatment rather than as an intimate sexual activity. Part of the pleasure is in the inability to fully see the vulva but in *trying* to, as Nin understood, the process of shaving is the pleasure of the gradual unveiling. As an erotic activity it becomes seduction, foreplay, and, for some, a ritual of submission. The erotic frisson of both seeing and feeling the bare vulva may be a transgressive and exotic experience, and an exploration that reconfigures notions of dominance and sexuality through a consensual engagement with power.

As hairlessness increasingly becomes a commonplace, so the excitement and novelty associated with difference is eradicated. Moreover, while once illicit pleasures could best be found in the eroticized difference of otherness, now there appears to be merely the desire for physical homogeny. In part this is because pubic hair is seen as unclean and its presence to some suggests that the female genitals belong in some intrinsic way to the realm of the animalistic, to the primitive, to the musky bouquet that fascinated Baudelaire. To remove it merely for the vagaries of fashion serves to negate this animalism. But in denying the animalistic, the sexual and the pleasure of difference, what is left has little do with the pleasures of the body and more to do with commodification of appearance regardless of personal preference.

ACKNOWLEDGEMENTS

My thanks to those anonymous individuals who answered my questions regarding their own pubic hair and their experiences with shaving, trimming, waxing and cutting, and to those who helped by providing the illustrations. Thanks also to Alexander Lawrence and Missy P who assisted in my sourcing of Baudelaire poems and Dr Angus Carlyle and Peter Osborne who commented on my translation. Dr Annie Sprinkle, Charles Gatewood, Jack Stevenson, David McGillervery, Monte Cazazza and Fergus Armstrong all provided valuable leads and insights into the history of erotic and pornographic representation of pubic hair. Finally thanks to Donkey Girl for the photograph of her pubic hair.

NOTES

1. The phallocentric nature of knowledge in the West assumes that that which is male, or coded as male, is eternally self-present, while the female is veiled, confused and aleatoric.
2. The vagina has often been viewed as a 'passage' that flows one way: outward, dedicated merely to birth. When the female genitals emerged as a subject of medical and scientific discourse in the nineteenth century, it was as a source of trouble, the clitoris and female masturbation were seen by doctors as sources of psychological disturbance, and medical texts recommended the removal of the clitoris as a treatment for female psychological maladies into the twentieth century.
3. See also the aphorism widely attributed to early evangelical Christian philosopher and repentant pagan St Augustine, noting that we are all born *inter faeces et urinam* (between shit and piss).
4. Among the handful of mainstream erotic images to depict pubic hair prior to Courbet is Goya's *Naked Maya* (1800), which depicts a supine nude with a dash of visible pubic hair. Such images were considered to be pornographic and obscene, and, like Courbet's work, this was painted for a private commission. Other images of nudity that depicted female pubic hair included private drawings and prints designed to be sexually stimulating (Tang 1999).
5. The 1928 Masson illustrated edition was of 134 copies, while the Bellmer edition of 1944 consisted of 199 copies.
6. I am excluding clandestine and illicit hardcore stag movies and pornography.

BIBLIOGRAPHY

Baudelaire, C. (1961), 'Un fantome', in *Les Fleurs du Mal.* Paris: Gallimard.

Cassidy, T. (2007), *Birth: A History,* London: Chatto and Windus.

Crisp, M. (2006), '7 Steps to Looking Good on Holiday', *Daily Mirror,* 18 July.

Ellen, B. (1999), 'The Brazilian Wax ... Have the Americans Gone a Pluck Too Far?', *Observer,* 6 June.

Foucault, M. (1980), *Power/Knowledge,* Hemel Hempstead: Harvester Wheatsheaf.

Freud, S. (1977), *On Sexuality,* Pelican Freud Library, Vol. 7, Harmondsworth: Penguin Books.

Labre, M. P. (2002), 'The Brazilian Wax: New Hairlessness Norm for Women?', *Journal of Communication Inquiry,* 26 (2): 113–32.

McNeil, L. and Osborne, J. with Pavia, P. (2006), *The Other Hollywood: The Uncensored Oral History of the Porn Film Industry,* New York: Regan Books.

Nin, A. (1990), *Delta of Venus,* London: Penguin Books.

Tang, I. (1999), *Pornography: The Secret History of Civilization,* London: Channel 4 Books.

Valhouli, C. (1999), 'Faster Pussycat, Wax! Wax!', *Salon.com,* 3 September, http://dir.salon.com/story/health/feature/1999/09/03/bikini, accessed 12 June 2007.

5   FROM STYLE TO PLACE
THE EMERGENCE OF THE LADIES' HAIR SALON IN THE TWENTIETH CENTURY

KIM SMITH

As a site of production and consumption, the modern ladies' hair salon can be seen as the concrete sign of a craft whose work has no permanence, its exterior and interior design mirroring the changing concerns of both hairdresser and client. The salon may be viewed similarly to the atelier of the fine artist or couturier: as a space in which creative ideas are formulated and consolidated into a fashionable product ready for display and consumption. While fashion is created away from the catwalk, and the artwork usually made at a distance from the gallery, the salon space is simultaneously a site of industry and of exhibition. Within this commercial environment, the act of creation and the practices of consumption become inextricably fused; the hair salon itself not only accommodates the cutting and styling processes, but is also seen as indicative of the hairdresser's skill, creativity and fashionability.

This chapter focuses on the emergence and development of the ladies' hair salon, which has received little academic attention, being only briefly incorporated into larger works on hair culture (Corson 1965; Cooper 1971; McCracken 1995; Cox 1999; Zdatny 1999). Cox's study (1999) demonstrates that the advent of women's salons in the West was determined by socio-political factors, which delayed its appearance in the nineteenth century, and which both retarded and accelerated their growth during the twentieth century. This chapter explores how these new dedicated locations were a feature of the emergent metropolis in the twentieth century and altered the social dynamics between hairdresser and client. Moving the activity of hairdressing from the private and domestic sphere to the commercial and public influenced the design interior and exterior spaces, which were progressively affected by wider developments in science, technology, art and fashion and the emergence of a modern aesthetic.

THE HISTORICAL ORIGINS OF THE HAIR SALON

The dressing of women's hair was only considered acceptable if performed by other women; and the notion of a solitary male ministering in public to what was a very private part of a lady's *toilette* was unthinkable. However, records indicate that a seventeenth-century French peasant named Champagne opened the first ladies' hair salon in Paris (Cooper 1971: 164), although any rapid expansion in the number of Parisian salons was halted as a result of the

Catholic Church's condemnation of them on the grounds of immorality. The Church may have had good reason to be concerned about the vulnerability of young women to the attentions of male advances since as one contemporary critic observed,

> This prig Champagne, by his cleverness in dressing the hair, and by his pushing ways, was run after and caressed by all the ladies ... Some he left with their hair half dressed; with others he dressed their hair one side, and then demanded a kiss before he would do the other side. (Tallemant des Reaux cited in Cooper 1971: 164; Trasko 1994: 43)

The Church was successful in preventing any further establishments from opening on these grounds, and so moral and religious issues delayed the salon's advent until the late-nineteenth century (Cooper 1971: 164; Trasko 1994: 43; Stevenson 2001: 138). Nevertheless, as a succession of male *artiste-coiffeurs* at the French Court continued to attend the female members of the royal family it is clear that masculine involvement in female hairdressing was not entirely suppressed.

Greater control of the gendered interactions involved in hairdressing was also effectively enforced by the progressive constraints of class etiquette and strict social protocols that emerged in the nineteenth century. These became increasingly important with the cultural and political shift of power from the old aristocratic elite of court society to an emerging new urban middle class—who distinguished themselves from the lower classes by devising and enforcing stricter rules of etiquette, especially the unacceptability of un-chaperoned middle-class women's access to public places (Davidoff and Hall 1987; Rappaport 2000). As a result, ladies' hairdressing for the most part continued to be performed at home, usually by women themselves, by a maid, or in the case of wealthier women, by hairdressers.

However, from the mid-nineteenth century, changes began to occur. These were partly motivated by what were increasingly seen as the impositions of etiquette, and partly as a consequence of a growing political and social awareness of women's rights, as individuals and small groups of women became proactive in realizing social freedoms (Wilson and Taylor 1989: 25–8). The arrival of the department store, in particular, is often presented as the vehicle for nineteenth-century female emancipation, although to suggest that these stores alone facilitated the public appearance of genteel women is too simplistic. Nevertheless, they were an important contributory factor in the historical development of ladies' hairdressing. Housing a variety of 'shops' under one roof, the department store was considered a private space within the public sphere, and therefore suitable for middle-class women to visit alone (Nava 2000: 50). Amongst the perfumery and haberdashery departments there appeared hairdressing salons; the first one in England is recorded in 1876 at Whiteley's in Westbourne Grove (Durbin 1984: 28). Consequently, hairdressing within the newly sanctioned space of the department store became an acceptable, fashionable practice and other stores quickly followed. Moreover, these spaces provided training grounds for some hairdressers who later established their own salons; for example, the great Antoine of Paris began his career in the Galeries Lafayette salon in 1901 (Zdatny 1999: 6).

While the nineteenth-century department store salons provided a legitimized stepping stone to the later establishment of independent ladies' hair salons in the twentieth century, small, one-man businesses had already begun to appear. There is little surviving evidence of the type and location of these enterprises, but it can be surmised that as public spaces, they would not have been frequented by the middle or upper classes. Karen Stevenson (2001: 138) argues that Marcel Grateau was 'the only real forerunner of the feminized salons of the twentieth century'. Grateau's hairdressing salon, established in Montmartre in the 1870s, was by no means prestigious, since it served only poorer women upon whom he tried out his newly developed 'Marcel' waving technique. Replacing popular but time-consuming curls and ringlets, the Marcel was a temporary wave or *ondulation* created with heated tongs pressed parallel to a comb. It produced a cascade of ripples in less than twenty minutes, and lasted until the hair was washed (Cox 1999: 135–8). Not until Grateau 'waved' the hair of the celebrated actress Jane Hading (Stevenson 2001: 139) and attracted widespread publicity did the clientele change to those of the rich and famous who began to visit his salon instead of having their hair dressed privately (Zdatny 1999: 21; Corson 1965: 492–3).

Grateau's innovations marked the beginning of a gradual change in hairdressing experience with the balance of power tipping from the dictate of wealthy clientele to the artistic talent of the individual coiffeur. Grateau became so sought after that clients allegedly bid for appointments at the salon (Stevenson 2001: 39; Zdatny 1999: 21). Inevitably, this transformed a previously 'dubious' public space into not only an acceptable, but also a highly fashionable, place to be seen in. Stevenson (2001: 139) asserts, 'The [hair] style itself, which could easily be copied, became a less important item of consumption than the place in which one was styled'. Grateau's salon was hugely influential in establishing the links between stylistic and technological innovation and an integral relationship between salon and proprietor, becoming the blueprint for what was to develop into a middle-class, public, feminized space. That these salons, and those of department stores, were an urban phenomenon is hardly surprising since their success would have been dependent upon accessibility to capital cities such as London and Paris. Emma Gieben-Gamal's (1999: 11) study of trade literature demonstrates that there was an expansion of new salons in the inter-war period which extended to major cities and towns in Britain.

Perhaps the final consolidating factor in the expansion of the ladies' salon was the increasing importance of haircutting rather than styling and dressing. Until the 1920s, little or no cutting took place in the salon; women's stylists waved, dyed or dressed their clients' long hair with false hairpieces and padding. By then, the elaborate Edwardian hairdos were considered cumbersome and outmoded, and the 'bob'—a style that was club-cut below the ear creating a blunt-edged geometric look—became ubiquitously fashionable. While Cox acknowledges the correlative significance of the 1920s 'bob' cut as a signifier of the shift from dressing to cutting (1999: 56), it is Stevenson who analyses the cut as instrumental in the transformation of large numbers of barber shops into 'salons' to cater for the massive surge in female clientele (2001: 143). Steven Zdatny also relates the global rise in hairdresser numbers between 1896 and 1936 to the diminishing number of barbers since the demand for the bob, as it filtered from the cities to smaller towns and villages, encouraged existing barbers to adapt their premises to accommodate the more lucrative market for ladies' hairdressing (Zdatny 1999: 14, 27). By the 1930s, 'All hairdressers became of necessity ladies hairdressers, with a consequent rise in status' (Foan 1931: 5; see also Cox 1999: 57).

SALON DESIGN

Shifts in hairdressing practises and processes cannot be seen as isolated from parallel shifts in social context and the increasing accessibility of exterior physical spaces to a female clientele, but they must also be understood in relation to parallel developments within the interior spaces of the salon itself. The late-nineteenth-century consolidation of ladies' hairdressing had seen the progressive addition of 'ladies' rooms' to some entrepreneurial barber shops, which could be discreetly entered via a separate doorway in order to avoid contact with male clients (Cox 1999: 68). A cubicle system also introduced a further element of privacy for female clients (Gieben-Gamal 1999: 18) but this was not universally adopted until the inter-war period. Most turn-of-the-century interiors were 'open' salons where clients waited, and cutting or dressing took place in full view of everybody (Foan 1931: 8). Cox's (1999: 86) description of them as mostly dark and dreary places with heavy furnishings is supported by photographs of Dickensian receptions and interiors in trade publications such as the *Hairdressers' Journal*. The opulent luxury of salons such as the one opened in Harrods in 1894 stood in contradistinction to the many small salons such as Raoul's in Great Portland Street, London (Figures 5.1–5.4), that had to cope with unsuitable or cramped interiors and clumsy, old-fashioned furnishings. Pictured before and after modernization and conversion in the 1950s, Raoul's was featured in the *Hairdressers' Journal* which said, 'it bore the air of an old, well-established, conservative business where few things had been altered for half a century' (1954b: 31).

Zdatny (1999: 18) describes ladies' hairdressing salons as 'monuments to the bright new age of fashionable consumption'. Modernization incorporated new materials and technologies into the design and physical appearance of salons. Zdatny conjures up a mental picture of a typically up-to-date salon of 1920: electric lighting; marble-topped sinks with hot running water; banks of gas or electric hairdryers; recliner chairs; electric curling irons and a new linoleum floor. Women's interest in cosmetics and fashion increased, encouraged by Hollywood films and disseminated in women's magazines. This meant that hairdressing and especially the salon experience became integral to the attainment of a sophisticated and glamorous, feminine identity. Salon designs reflected this shift.

During the inter-war period the most prevalent but diametrically opposed styles were Art Deco, a highly decorative and luxurious form, and Modernism, which eschewed decoration, having a functional, pared-down appearance. Neither one was suited to the needs of ladies' salons which required a degree of glamour as well as basic functionality. The Moderne, however, was a hybridization of Art Deco and Modernism, featuring the use of new

Figure 5.1 'Look at the cluttered showcase, calendar-hung wall and file-filled alcove ...'
From 'Modern but Moderate: Old and New in One Salon', *Hairdressers' Journal*, 4 November 1954: 30–1. *Hairdressers' Journal*, www.HJi.co.uk.

materials, especially chrome, coupled with decorative elements. It is a style most frequently associated with cinema design of the period. Gieben-Gamal contends that the Moderne style 'was found to be more prominent in hair salon design than in other retailing sectors' (1999: 13–4) because it was less decorative and less costly to maintain than French Art Deco and less austere than Modernist design which often had a severe functional aesthetic. Capturing the balance between function and fashion was tricky, as an advertisement in *The Queen* in 1935 revealed: 'It is well-known that your lady clients prefer a boudoir to a power station' (cited in Corson 1965: 604). The Moderne style's appearance was able to overcome this problem. Linked to American designers such as Norman Bel Geddes, Raymond Loewy and Walter Teague who were associated with industrial styling and more particularly, the concept of streamlining with its close association to ideas of the body beautiful and hygiene

Figure 5.2 'After conversion Raoul's looks twice as large ...'
From 'Modern but Moderate: Old and New in One Salon', *Hairdressers' Journal*,
4 November 1954: 30–1. *Hairdressers' Journal*, www.HJi.co.uk.

management (Sparke 1995: 131). Salons employed new modern materials such as plastics, aluminum and chrome to give the appearance of fashionable luxury.

In his 1931 guide to hairdressing Gilbert Foan lists six key areas in modern salon design as linked to a successful business operation: the premises; shop-front; front shop (now known as the reception); hairdressing saloons; the workroom/laboratory/storeroom; offices and toilets. Throughout, Foan, himself a hairdresser, discusses fixtures and fittings as being lighter, modern, more sparsely fitted and utilitarian, signalling a masculine, scientific modernism. In contrast, he uses words like *artistic, attractive, tasteful, dainty and appealing* (Foan 1931: 643) to evoke a feminine, middle-class domesticity. This feminine/masculine juxtaposition is interesting because it also denotes the difference between the leisurely area

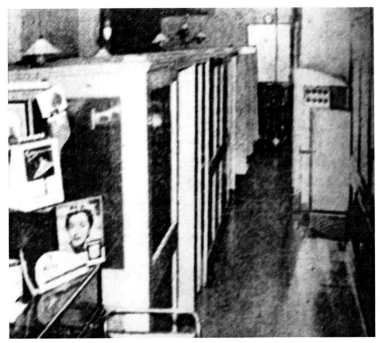

Figure 5.3 'See how the cubicles overpower the narrow space ...'
From 'Modern but Moderate: Old and New in One Salon', *Hairdressers' Journal*,
4 November 1954: 30–1. *Hairdressers' Journal*, www.HJi.co.uk.

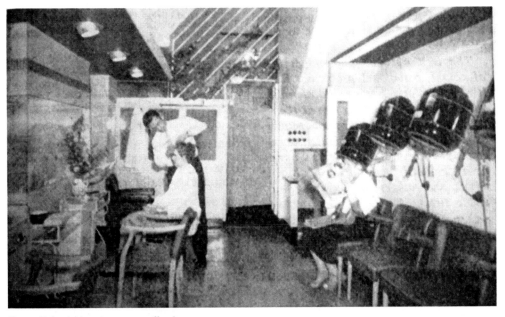

Figure 5.4 A 'drawing-room effect'.
From 'Modern but Moderate: Old and New in One Salon', *Hairdressers' Journal*, 4 November 1954: 30–1. *Hairdressers' Journal*, www.HJi.co.uk.

of reception and the functional, salon work area. In reception, Foan advocated softer, cosier furnishings, similar to those in a domestic lounge, comprising easy chairs, occasional tables, ashtrays, magazines, railway timetables, telephone directories and—the epitome of 1930s modernity—the telephone, most important not only for business convenience but also clients' use.[1]

In line with a more scientific rationale, the cubicles where hairdressing took place were functional and more sparingly furnished, but often with an integrated colour scheme (Foan 1931: 646). Foan clearly recognized the importance of a coherent, design aesthetic that created a harmonized transition from waiting to work area, through subtle differentiation. His discussion of successful salon design employs the terminology and knowledge of interior design: for example, he discusses spatiality and illusion through the use of line, form, colour and pattern to maximize large or small spaces. Furthermore, the subliminal message is that a salon should be inviting and welcoming. Foan (1931: 653) also notes the existence of children's saloons, which were just beginning to appear in Britain in 1931, although still lagging behind their American and European counterparts.

SCIENCE AND TECHNOLOGY

Throughout the twentieth century, technical and scientific advance as well as design innovation was integral to the expansion and development of the ladies' hair salon. As early as 1902, *The Queen* magazine was stressing hairdressing as a 'science' rather than a craft (Corson 1965: 604) and hairdressers assumed a scientific rationality. The application of science and its connotation of being a serious 'masculine' discipline was probably seen by many male hairdressers as a way of countering the 'feminine' aspects of hairdressing. It also repositioned the hairdresser as a professional who was the central conduit for the dissemination of scientific knowledge. No longer a simple dresser of hair, simply enough to dress hair; he had to be versed in all branches of the profession, competent in the operation and understanding of newer, complex technologies (Foan 1931: 5).

By the 1930s hair salons and other commercial enterprises actively embraced new scientific theories and technological innovations (Foan 1931: 5; Cox 1999: 60; Bowlby 2000: 143–6). Stevenson (2001: 143) has observed that 'the exclusive use of the new technology … led to a radical transformation … in terms of their décor and the services they offered'. The scarcity of clean hot water supplies had made washing and shampooing hair virtually an unknown practise before the late-nineteenth century (Zdatny 1999: 19). The installation of modern appliances and hot and cold running water evidenced a more technologically progressive approach to hairdressing, although some early apparatus and products were either dangerous or expensive resulting in a haphazard use (Cox 1999). As a result of serious investigation into hair health, the establishment of trichology, and the invention of new products and the technology with which to apply them, salon interiors were redesigned to accommodate better facilities and more hygienic surroundings.

Rationalization in design generally extended to the intense promotion of electricity as the bright, clean, healthy fuel of the future (Forty 1986: 190–2), despite being prohibitively expensive. Hair salons were undoubtedly in the vanguard of modern electrical appliance usage, but only grander salons would have installed the latest electro-therapeutic treatments, unquestionably the province of the fashionably rich (Foan 1931: 470–3). This new approach was part of a wider interest in hygienic rationalization in design which began in earnest from the 1890s, when the new germ theories were embraced as a method of eliminating disease (Forty 1986: 159). Hygiene extended into many areas of ordinary everyday life and this translated into lighter, uncluttered interiors, plainer, fitted furniture and easily cleanable loose rugs or linoleum floors. The hygiene aspect is reiterated in Foan's text, where he advocates the omission of skirting boards 'obviat[ing] the collection of dust, hair and fluff' (Foan 1931: 648).

As hairdressing establishments began to acquire the air of clinical laboratories their increasingly rationalized interiors were testament to the successful war waged on dirt and disease in the first half of the twentieth century. Foan maintained that many shops up and down the country were 'as clean and sterile as a hospital' (1931: 6). As part of this image, the wearing of salon coats emphasized cleanliness and neatness (Cox 1999: 75–8) but in a way that correlated with the doctor, surgeon and dentist (Foan 1931: 6).

Even in the 1950s the importance of science and technology is consistently underlined, and according to one article in the *Hairdressers' Journal* (1954a: 18), assumes a greater priority than a more traditional concept of craft. Describing the modern interior of the Plymouth salon of one Mr Howe as scientifically and technologically efficient, the article cites the installation of loudspeakers 'enabling [Mr Howe] to talk to and be answered by any member of the staff *while working*'. In the interview, Mr Howe reaffirms that 'Hairdressing today is more and more a scientific and chemical business'. He also stresses how greater privacy in the design of the men's hairdressing section through the incorporation of semi-private cubicles has enabled the timid male client to become 'more and more interested in treatments he would not dream of accepting in an open salon' (*Hairdressers' Journal* 1954a: 19). Rationalism and functionalism informed fundamental salon design practice and 'the application and manipulation of new materials signified a concern to represent the modernity of the salon' synthetically corresponding with the emergence of the 'new' fashionably modern woman (Gieben-Gamal 1999: 13–17). Nonetheless, such innovation clearly also both sanctioned men's increasing interest in fashion and had radical implications for future innovations in salon design.

FROM CUBICLE TO BOUTIQUE

The emergence and consolidation of the ladies' hair salon took less than a century to complete. It is no co-incidence that its advent was simultaneous with many middle-class women's pursuit of public freedom particularly, but not exclusively, through political emancipation which had consequences not only for women, but also for the industries associated with feminine fashion. These two aspects—the 'new' modern woman and the modernity of the salon—crystallized in the 1920s when fashion, design, science and hygiene converged in a mutual consensus of public, rather than private, preparation and display. While science and technology may have made the final modifications in salon design, socio-cultural issues were to influence further important developments in the nature of British hairdressing and its relative aesthetic in salon interiors.

First, in 1960 the *Hairdressers' Journal* ran an article on two Jamaican hairdressers who had set up businesses in Birmingham. The text implies that they might have been the first black salons in Britain, catering for a newly expanded immigrant population (1960: 31). While their salons followed the usual design model, black hairdressing involved very different processes, contributing to a new, more diverse salon culture. Second, with the arrival of the 'Swinging 1960s' in London, the new West End salons opened in the wake of Vidal Sassoon. These were the focus of youthful fashion and young, confident designers and hairdressers who identified themselves with a metropolitan Englishness that rejected what were seen as old-fashioned notions of sophistication. The new salons projected a fresh approach, and not unlike their counterparts, the boutiques, cultivated an aura of 'hip' rather than chic fashionability. This developing boutique style was understood by many young 1960s consumers as a metaphor for cutting-edge fashion. Young hairdressers who wanted to distinguish themselves from the older, up-market salons recognized that by copying boutique interior design and spatial styling, they would attract the more fashion-conscious customers.

By the late 1960s, open salons had virtually replaced the cubicle arrangement, which was seen as old-fashioned and inefficient, particularly at busy periods (Radford 1968: 453–4). Apart from the practical consideration, the privacy afforded by cubicles was not in step with the contemporary informal atmosphere. Open salons were conducive to another innovation of the 1960s: the unisex salon, triggered in London's trendy West End. In these highly fashionable establishments, men and women daringly had their hair shampooed and cut next to each other. Symptomatic of wider cultural trends in fashion, science and political activism, gender-differentiated design was replaced by ultra-fashionable, youth-oriented interiors, which combined pop music, fashion and art. The ladies' hair salon was a distinctly modern phenomenon that emerged and expanded in the twentieth century, but by the 1960s the very term *salon* was spurned by a new young consumer as outmoded and old-fashioned. In spite of this, the ladies' hair salon was (and still is) more than a place simply to have a haircut. As Stevenson claims, it is the public culture of 'the hair salon ... [that provides] one context in which new relationships of self and group identity-construction are developed and practised' (2001: 149).

NOTE

1. Remarkably, this notional picture of domesticity was not confined to hairdressing salons. Rachel Bowlby has found a parallel in a series of books written by Carl Dipman in the 1930s with regard to the design of early supermarkets. His suggestions for a 'women's rest corner' are almost identical to those of Foan's hairdressing reception area and the cosy, homely aesthetic combined with scientific rationalism (which is discussed later in the chapter) maps on to the model of the 1930s hair salon (Bowlby 2000: 143–9).

BIBLIOGRAPHY

Bowlby, R. (2000), *Carried Away: The Invention of Modern Shopping,* London: Faber & Faber.

Cooper, W. (1971), *Hair: Sex, Society, Symbolism,* London: Aldus Books.

Corson, R. (1965), *Fashions in Hair: The First 5000 Years,* London: Peter Owen.

Cox, C. (1999), *Good Hair Days: A History of British Hairstyling,* London: Quartet Books.

Davidoff, L. and Hall, C. (1987), *Family Fortunes: Men and Women of the English Middle Class 1780–1850,* London: Hutchinson.

Durbin, G. (1984), *Wig, Hairdressing and Shaving Bygones,* Bucks: Shire Publications.

Foan, G. (ed) (1931), *The Art and Craft of Hairdressing,* London: Sir Isaac Pitman & Sons.

Forty, A. (1986), *Objects of Desire: Design and Society since 1750,* London: Thames and Hudson.

Gieben-Gamal, E. (1999), 'Gendered Spaces: Design and Display Strategies of British Hair Salons in the 1920s and 1930s', Unpublished MA thesis, National Art, Library, Victoria & Albert Museum, London, Pressmark: THE.99.03.

Hairdressers' Journal (1954a), 'A Science, a Craft—and a Business', 21 January: 18–19.

Hairdressers' Journal (1954b), 'Modern, but Moderate: Old and New in One Salon', 4 November: 30–1.

Hairdressers' Journal (1960), 'Jamaican Stylists Cater for Coloured Clients', (Midland News, By "Colmore"), 22 September: 31.

McCracken, G. (1995), *Big Hair: A Journey into the Transformation of Self,* Toronto: Viking.

Nava, M. (2000), 'Modernity Tamed? Women Shoppers and the Rationalization of Consumption in the Inter-war Period' in M. Andrews and M. M. Talbot (eds.), *All the World and Her Husband: Women in Twentieth Century Consumer Culture,* London and New York: Cassell.

Radford, F. H. (ed) (1968), *The Art and Craft of Hairdressing* (5th edn), Vol. II, London: Sir Isaac Pitman & Sons.

Rappaport, E. D. (2000), *Shopping for Pleasure: Women in the Making of London's West End,* Princeton, NJ: Princeton University Press.

Sparke, P. (1995), *As Long as It's Pink: The Sexual Politics of Taste,* London: Pandora.

Stevenson, K. (2001), 'Hairy Business: Organising the Gendered Self' in R. Holliday and J. Hassard (eds.), *Contested Bodies,* London: Routledge.

Trasko, M. (1994), *Daring Do's: A History of Extraordinary Hair,* Paris: Flammarion.

Wilson, E. and Taylor, L. (1989), *Through the Looking Glass,* London: BBC Books.

Zdatny, S. (1999), *Hairstyles and Fashion: A Hairdresser's History of Paris 1910–1920,* Oxford and New York: Berg.

6   THE BIG SHAVE
MODERNITY AND FASHIONS IN MEN'S FACIAL HAIR

DENE OCTOBER

A young man enters the white aseptic space of his bathroom, applies a creamy handful of *Rapid Shave* to his face and neck and commences his daily depilation. As he draws the razor repeatedly over his skin, dapples of blood appear and, before long, lacerations haemorrhage into the polished, ceramic bowl. Still the young man continues the ritual, slicing strips from his face and throat, seemingly oblivious to the danger.

Martin Scorsese's student film, *The Big Shave* (1967), from which this scene is taken, was conceived as a protest against the bloodshed of the Vietnam War, yet is all the more shocking for its banal domestic setting. The *everyday-ness* of shaving provides the perfect vehicle for Scorcese's critique of patriarchal conformity. Shaving, like gender, is a repeated act that comes to feel 'right' through socialization. The film's body-horror succeeds through its clinical, aesthetic review of this familiarity, to slowly expose the young man's 'natural' performance of masculinity for what it is: highly regulated and stylized, and all the more vulnerable for it. Scorsese's film also demonstrates how the ritual's repetition eclipses the material risks of accident and infection.

This everyday repetition of the shaving ritual makes it an important site for the cultural production of masculinity (Pinfold 2000; Peterkin 2001 and also see Beechy 2004, on women's facial hair shaving rituals). Indeed, the cultural regulation of facial hair may be seen as an attempt to rein in the persistent materiality, or 'nature', of the socially significant body. This chapter examines the cultural regulation of men's facial hair in the twentieth century through a focus on the promotion of the products and processes of domestic shaving. It uses examples from popular advertising in both Britain and the United States, to explore the image and representation of shaving as a discursive rhetorical framework for the negotiation of modern masculinity, by way of inter-connecting trends rather than an exhaustive critical review or an exact chronology. In particular it examines this in relation to the imagined perils posed to the social and material masculine body by hygiene and the expanding feminized spaces of the domestic. It then considers how, in the postwar period, the ritual conformity of shaving operates within a highly regulated social and symbolic framework that nevertheless demonstrates consistent contradictions, and the potential for more nuanced accounts of masculine power and individual agency.

CLEAN-CUT CONFORMITY: THE DOMESTICATION OF SHAVING

Fashions in men's facial hair come and go in response to changes in the wider social and cultural historical environment. From the middle of the nineteenth century, the traditional beard, whilst still maintaining an iconic power which continued to be exploited to visually confer age and wisdom (Cooper 1971: 134), as well as social status and military power, was gradually superseded by various alternative fashions in facial hair. According to Peterkin, 'the 19th century proved to be a complete heyday for facial hair throughout Europe, with every variation imaginable appearing. It was a boom not unlike today's' (2001: 34–5). This stylistic shift was supported by a veritable industry in etiquette manuals and products like the moustache trainer, as well as various tonics, dyes and waxes and practical advice. For example, in the 1850s, *The Habits of Good Society* cautioned men to be wary of the foppery of twisted or curled moustaches, instructing them rather that 'Nature is the best valet' (Charles and DeAnfrasio 1970: 157). Various modes of facial hair were popular. Examples include the 'Van Dyke' goatee beard, named after the artist, and the 'Kaiser' moustache (after the German emperor). Sideburns either trailed off the face, such as 'Piccadilly Weepers', or joined up with the moustache, as with 'Burnsides' like those sported by the American Civil War general (Cooper 1971: 93–4). In turn the popularity of these styles similarly dwindled, although slowly rather than all at once, as the shaven face increasingly came to signify modern manhood. By the beginning of the twentieth century all manner of Victorian decoration was progressively considered unfashionable and unhealthy (Lears 1994) and facial hair effectively seen by some as nothing more than just another dusty ornament.

Modernity was the central trope in promoting the cult of the new in all areas of life: moral, hygienic and aesthetic. Men's hair was also short, a modern response to lice infestation, the effete styles of the late-nineteenth century and technological advance (the hairclipper was invented in 1879). Andrews (1904) reports on the case of a bank clerk who suffered *facial erysipelas* (a painful skin infection) and could not shave. Such was the importance now attached by the business world for male employees to present the 'right' sort of face at work that the clerk was dismissed. The clean-shaven look was in the ascendant and would prove ubiquitous and long-lived. Indeed by the 1920s, facial hair became so antithetical to the machine-age aesthetic that, for example, wealthy French car owners even ordered their chauffeurs to shave off beards and moustaches (Andrews 1904: 115).

Continued improvements to razor design, such as cheap, safe replaceable blades, not only pushed shaving from the barbershop into the domestic environment, but also encouraged more frequent shaving, thus boosting the market value and reinforcing the cultural dominance of the clean-cut look. As a result, much of the responsibility for the maintenance of this modern look was now shifted to the duty of the individual man, an obligation advertisers sought to remind him of and help him meet. Innovations like King Camp Gillette's modified T-shaped safety razor, introduced in 1901, however required a strong promotional campaign to shift initial public resistance. Gillette's invention was a razor that opened at the top and allowed shavers access to the sharp, double-edged disposable blade inside without fear of accident. The company only managed to sell fifty-one razors by 1903, but with publicity and an emphasis on reassurances of safety, by the following year 90,000 Americans possessed one (McKibbin 1998: 14).

One of the problems associated with shaving that needed to be overcome was the inadequacy of the domestic environment as compared with that of the barbershop, such as the lack of hot water on demand. Pairpoint's Combination Shaving Set, for example, stored utensils and water in a tray that could then be lit with a match (*Century* 1896). Companies highlighted convenience where possible: one Gillette advert depicts Father Time and promises, 'One can save at least 20 minutes a day—by renouncing the barber habit' (*Theatre Magazine,* 1905b). Gillette used technical descriptions to sell health and safety features, but also highlighted style and luxury: 'The outfit consists of one triple silver plated holder and twelve double-edged blades, in a morocco velvet lined case' (*Harper's Magazine* 1905a). Another tactic was to stress the cachet of ownership of razors and shaving sets asking, 'What kind of man are you?' suggesting that, 'The man who to-day shaves with a Gillette shaves with comfort and with safety' (*Harper's Magazine* 1905b). Thus, various visual treatments were tested out, ranging from the unexciting use of blades as a decorative motif (e.g. in Gillette's 1904 Christmas campaign, featured in *Theatre Magazine* 1904), to the more dramatic, and frequently didactic, social portraits. One very striking Gillette advert (*Theatre Magazine* 1905a) draws on melodramatic Victorian terrors such as the demon barber Sweeney Todd, and Robert Louis Stevenson's Jekyll and Hyde (1886), to contextualize

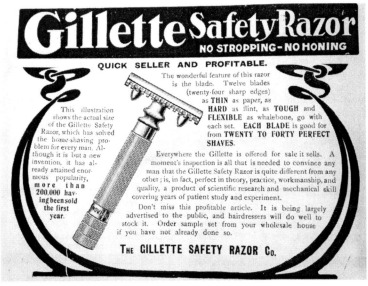

Figure 6.1 'No stropping, No honing', advertisement for the Gillette Safety Razor (1906).
By kind permission of Proctor & Gamble UK.

the great advances of technology in relation to the dark traditions being left behind. The illustration in the advert depicts a smiling model enjoying a comfortable shave while an ambiguous shadow—it could either be his, or just as easily that of a barber's—looms ominously behind him, wielding an open cutthroat razor. The copy reads, 'No shadow of doubt ever exists in the mind of the man who uses a—9 Gillette Safety Razor'. The Gillette Safety Razor campaign promoted shaving as effortless, free from the potential dangers of the cutthroat and the necessity of its honing and stropping. The invention of the safety razor 'solved the home-shaving problem for every man' by using convenient disposable blades that Gillette promoted as 'THIN as paper, as HARD as flint, as TOUGH and FLEXIBLE as whalebone … EACH BLADE is good for TWENTY TO FORTY PERFECT SHAVES' (Figure 6.1). King Camp Gillette made personal appearances in the ads, reassuring the self-shaver of the 'simple, practical and easy to use' benefits of the 'double-edged flexible blades'. So cheap are the new blades that, once dulled, the reader is encouraged to 'throw them away as you would an old pen' (*Literary Digest* 1907).

Paradoxically, however, the outmoded cutthroat razor still remained popular, although usually in the highly visible masculine spaces of the barbershop. Indeed misgivings about self-shaving owed as much to the strong tradition of the barbershop as to the perceived dangers of the blade. Since antiquity, the barbershop had been a masculine social space where beards and hair were trimmed and dressed, but also where men socialized with friends and caught up with the latest news (Cooper 1971: 154–61). Soaping up and shaving with an

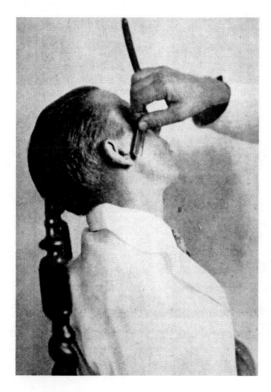

Figure 6.2   'Shaving and scraping', *Hairdressers' Weekly Journal*, 5 Oct. 1929.
From *Hairdressers' Journal*, www.HJi.co.uk.

open razor were a 'macho' part of the barbershop experience and the spectacle of the cut-throat (Figure 6.2), the sharpness of which the barber ensured by flamboyantly grinding it up and down his leather strop between customers. Furthermore, until the advent of domestic shaving products, the display of the shaven facial was associated with class and affluence: only wealthy men could afford to make frequent visits to the barber (Adams 1978: 12). A number of shaving promotions therefore attempted to mirror this homo-social world in advertisements by figuratively offering an escape from the perceived threat of feminization and domesticity manifested in increasing consumerism. At the same time, the masculine performative landscape sometimes proved difficult to people without effectively undermining the heterosexually normative values being championed and was often overcome in the historically consistent rhetoric of male bonding. A 1910 advert for Gillette, for example, depicts a group of four men on a camping trip—while one shaves, the others catch fish, prepare the frying pans and look on (*Saturday Evening Post* 1910).

HEALTH AND SAFETY

The clean-cut look prevailed thanks to shaving promotions that capitalized on the reported dangers of facial hair and the moral influence of the hygiene movement of the late-nineteenth and early-twentieth century. For example, at the turn of the century, it led to the enforced shaving of hospital patients (Tomes 1998: 103–4), while in 1907 an unsuccessful American bill sought to tax beards on the basis of health (Peterkin 2001: 157). In 1916, a campaign against tuberculosis demanded that men 'Sacrifice Whiskers and Save Children' (Tomes 1998: 127). There was a belief that the beard hid germs at a microscopic level and shaving advertisements seized upon the aseptic to make claims about products and insinuate relationships between the social and material body. In the new age of the microbe, danger was perceived as lurking everywhere so that even shaving off these germ-filled whiskers introduced a possible risk of infection. A *William's Shaving Soaps* advert of 1899 warns against microbes penetrating the pores of the skin, which were 'always open' and required shoring up by the joint 'force' of consumer and product intervention (*Illustrated London News* 1899).

One of the hazards of the barbershop was a condition known as 'barber's itch' (*folliculitis*), a fungal infection transmitted via unhygienic blades. In reporting the danger, advertisers deployed scare copy, or 'negative appeal' according to the trade jargon. This tactic 'sought to jolt the potential customer into a new consciousness by enacting dramatic episodes of social failures and accusing judgements' (Marchand 1986: 14). One William's Shaving Soap advert (1902) uses a travelling salesman to highlight both the convenience of domestic shaving and the hygienic safety offered by a clean blade and a familiar clean environment. In the advert, the traveller is not only subject to the dangers of visiting an unknown barber and an inadequate range of brands stocked, but also the unreliability of using products and practitioners of dubious quality. A mock testimonial from the pictured salesman complains of immediate sensations of burning: 'I consulted a physician and he pronounced the trouble a bad case of barber's itch' (*Harper's Weekly* 1902).

The management of the modern body also meant engaging with the 'tough beard problem', as adverts frequently referred to it, via the appliance of science and design. One advert for Vibro Shave Electric Razor promised a man can 'shave with or against the wiry bristles simply by gliding the razor at an *astonishing* speed' (*Literary Digest* 1929). The 'beard problem' seemed to cover a wide range of physical and social malaise, and in tackling it advertisers dramatized the relationship between self and the social environment. Modern masculinity, it was suggested, made demands like staying up all night dancing, or doing the paperwork, which the material body struggled to achieve and was even imperilled by. Although you might 'rob yourself of sleep' new products such as Gillette razors promised to iron out signs of tiredness and restore those of modernity and health (*Asia* 1929). Technological advances were treated as important breakthroughs in the battle: in another Gillette Razor advert (Figure 6.3) the construction of the razor and its blades was analysed with scientific precision and promised '6 vital improvements' (*Asia* 1930).

Advertisers debated the value of modern methods, such as psychology, to put 'human scale' and emotional weight behind their messages, which frequently meant highlighting social benefits as much as product function, befriending the reader and interpolating him to 'play a vicarious, scripted role as protagonist in the ad' (Marchand 1986: 12). A Shumate Razor advert (1920) guarantees 'To Keep My Face Smooth For Life' (*The Outing* 1920) and demonstrates it by an admiring stroke of the hand from the model's attractive female

Figure 6.3 '6 vital improvements', advertisement for new Gillette Blade (1930). By kind permission of Proctor & Gamble UK.

companion. A later Gillette ad from 1937, which adopts the popular medium of the comic strip, depicts a white train passenger stripped to his vest in mid-shave, compromised by his poor choice of blade. George, a black porter, dispenses advice about blade loyalty, his lowly status presumably offsetting the intimacy of the scene. The passenger's reappearance in a suit and tie in the second image restores the masculine social hierarchy, while the service relationship is mirrored below with cartoon versions of a razor and (feminized) blade talking: 'George knows we were made for each other' (*Life* 1937).

CLEAN-CUT CONFORMITY: CULTURE AND COUNTERCULTURE

In the aftermath of the Second World War, the social and physical landscape was a contrast of old and new that was to some extent paralleled in the rhetoric of shaving. Wilkinson Razor nostalgically used prewar imagery and its traditional crossed-sword emblem to reinforce the advertisement's copy, emphasizing the skills of industrial workmanship and robust masculinity in the figure of the steel worker. Other brands, however, stressed the ultra modern: one Gem advert (*Life* 1952), for example, depicted the efficiency of a shave as monitored by 'light tracking', mixing scientific jargon and photographic effect to demonstrate the benefits of the 'Duridium' blade. Technological advance continued to inform both product development and promotion, and the era of the new space age clearly influenced the introduction of Gillette's 'Rocket Set' in the early 1950s. The set offers 'Superspeed Shaving' and references the important place space and space age technology occupied in the popular imagination at this time and its role in bringing about advances in design and technology (*Hairdressers' Journal* 1954). Facial hair, however, also increasingly offered a more confrontational medium for different constructions of young masculinity, even if conformity to traditional masculine rituals such as shaving were still implicitly assumed, and the rhetoric of health and hygiene still discursively deployed in the promotion of facial hair's spectacular management, its products and its processes.

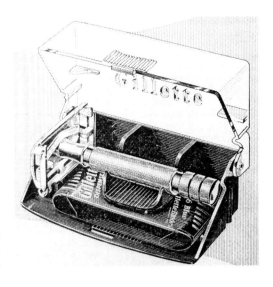

Figure 6.4   'Superspeed shaving', advertisement
for the Gillette 'Rocket Set' (1954).
By kind permission of Proctor & Gamble UK.

By the 1950s, advertisements were targeting the new male 'teenager' by offering tailored products and lifestyle messages, particularly, for example, in the polarized American constructions of 'the Jock' and 'the Nerd'. The Jock was the clean-cut 'health nut, the fitness addict, the man who participates fully in the games of life'; the nerd on the other hand, was 'the egghead, the intellectual, the outsider' in 'limbo' (Martin and Koda 1989: 7). The Jock could be said to exemplify a narcissistic individual, who is 'excessively self-conscious; and constantly monitoring his body for 'flaws and signs of decay' (Lasch 1979: 33), which made him an easy target for advertising strategies. In contrast, the nerd's careless grooming was at odds with more popular imagery, 'suggesting a lack of self-assessment or a failure to look in the mirror' (Martin and Koda 1989: 35).

Cold War relations between Russia and the West were particularly frosty in the 1950s and creative teams relied upon an assumed anxiety to conform, making links between the social and physical body that, to a contemporary audience, now seem unsubtle and rather absurd. An advert for the Remington Super 60 Deluxe electric shaver promised to expose the menace of the 'hidden beard' (*Life* 1957). Although shaving promotions depended on his narcissism, advertisers needed to assure the male reader not only of the importance of looking, but also the acceptability of male-on-male looking. Rugged sports stars, like the American footballer Sam Huff, were enlisted to provide masculine reassurance. An advert for 'Afta' after-shave lotion, by Mennen, deploys a visual formula typical of this period: a head-and-shoulder shot of Huff to meet the reader's gaze, while an idealized link to his sporting success is depicted above. In the ad, the star reflects on being 'indestructible' on the sports field yet scorns 'unnecessary roughness' in the context of grooming hygiene (*Look* 1963).

The good-looking, sporty figure appeared frequently in American advertising of the 1950s and early 1960s, and was considered patriotic and even heroic, particularly in comparison to the frowned-upon intellectualism of the nerd. In a television commercial for Gillette *Blue Blade* razors, Sharpie-the-Parrot cajoles a Jock to 'Look Sharp! Feel Sharp! Be Sharp!' (1952). The Jock's compliant and agreeable demeanour is characterized by his foam beard, referencing an older and more traditional patriarchal authority. The social status of such rituals is evidenced in representations of youths shaving that appeared even in adverts unrelated to shaving products—like those by Munsingwear for Hawaii shorts (illustrated in Powell and Peel 1988: 47). Conformity meant shaving younger, but equally functioned to differentiate an older target market adopting ever more prestigious and expensive symbolism. A Remington cordless electric shaver advert asks, 'Why give it to a fellow just beginning to shave?' The answer, in the copy, emphasizes the cachet both of the product and a clean-cut maturity (*Look* 1964).

Nevertheless, the figurative duality of the Jock and Nerd also provides a consistent conceptual framework within which to situate the fertile space of experiment and nonconformity that was increasingly a dominant narrative of the postwar era. A new generation of young men progressively challenged the heterogeneity and conformity of traditional masculinity and the ideology of its patriarchal socio-political power. They particularly drew on the symbolic potential of dress and appearance to make their point, their creative use of style representing 'a symbolic violation of the social order' (Hebdige 1979: 19). Integral to this was arguably facial hair, both its growth and its removal. For example, the emergence of the narcissistic figure of the bachelor playboy extolled the virtues of fun and spending and a new male subjectivity entirely compatible with postwar affluence and its discourses of leisure and hedonism. This construct of the single fun-loving man was a popular reference for advertisers and offered, for magazines such as *Playboy*, the 'button-down, Aqua-Velva look our readers wanted' (*Playboy* executive editor, Ray Russell, quoted in Osgerby 2001: 184). In one Aqua Velva advert, featuring a Norman Rockwell illustration, the after-shave product is described without irony as 'A luxury that actually does you good' (*Life* 1953).

Belying the conformist world described by these advertisers, however, alternative imagery had also begun to bubble up into the mainstream; something both anticipated and seized upon by reforming forces in fashion. Although the un-cool Nerd appeared in public with five-o'clock-shadow this did not represent an attempt to formulate a coherent image. The Beat, on the other hand, sought to demonstrate more radical ideas through appearance, dressing in black, with sandals, turtle neck sweaters, straggling French haircuts and beards. The poet Allen Ginsburg, and his compelling appearance—'[t]he hair, the beard, the costume, the mischievous grin' (Roszak 1971: 129)—that encapsulated the figure of the Beat, swiftly became a visual shorthand for the creative outsider and artist. The Beat symbolized an anti-establishment ethos and an alternative political voice that also offered an alternative to the ubiquitous shaven facial of traditional masculinity. It was an offer seized upon by the upcoming middle class, particularly those deploying careers in the expanding boom industries of media, fashion and advertising. Facial hair had become a symbol that set creativity apart from more mundane business.

CONCLUSION: CUTTING IT BOTH WAYS

Just as at the end of the nineteenth century the beard had progressively been seen as 'old fashioned', so by the mid 1960s, clean-shaven conformity and short barber-cut hair was now associated with the older generation and as a consequence was perceived as 'hopelessly tired and "square"' (Osgerby 2001: 18). However, it would clearly be too simplistic to reductively equate the wearing of a beard and long hair with a wholesale disregard for both shaving and traditional tropes of masculinity. Indeed, Ehrenreich (1983) argues that the playboy, like the Beat, equally shared a 'rejection of convention ... virtues of masculine independence, nonconformity and (often misogynistic) sexual expression' (cited in Osgerby 2001: 183). The rhetoric of facial hair and its shaving therefore rather demonstrates the consistent ambiguities of the ritual and its performance.

The 'new advertising', managed by smaller teams of creative individualists, deployed concepts of youth and facial hair as a metaphor for 'hip' consumption. Far from fearing the counterculture, the menswear and advertising industries increasingly welcomed it as an ally in their struggle against the 'dead-weight procedure and hierarchy that had accumulated over the years' (Frank 1997: 8). The success of facial hair as a symbol of political resistance and anti-materialism therefore makes its use as a part of mainstream consumption and mass popular culture much more problematic. Such ambivalence is aptly satirized in a 1967 cartoon in the magazine *Madison Avenue*, which depicts the professional evolution of a young man from art director to a bearded, scowling executive, 'his middle finger raised in defiance' (in Frank 1997: 112). As facial hair gradually began to lose its direct association with radicalism, so advertisers explored and promoted stylistic diversity rather than conflict.

In 1966—one year earlier than Scorcese's *The Big Shave*—the Swedish glamour model Gunilla Knutson appeared in an American commercial for Noxema Medicated Shave. In the ad, a young man shaves to the beat of 'The Stripper' theme, with Knutson offering the lewd voice-over: 'take it off, take it off'. The ad's unrepentant portrayal of hetero-normative masculinity has a hip swagger that is suggestively anti-establishment, cocking a snoop at stuffiness and dull conformity. Alongside Knutson's endorsement of the pleasures of the clean-shaven look, the Beatles, and other rock stars like Jimmy Hendrix and their followers, were contemporaneously 'growing their hair, cultivating moustaches and beards' but also 'wearing flamboyant jackets, trailing scarves ... high-heeled boots, kipper ties and hats with wide, floppy brims' (Wilson and Taylor 1989: 171–2). The American magazine *Newsweek* announced, 'the American male is submitting his body to perfume and his hair to stylists'; the cover of the same issue depicted a younger man with a moustache, surrounded by almost a 'cut out and dress' array of patterned shirts, ties, jeans and footwear that, along with the model's suit, reflect the interchangeable wardrobe suggestive of a new fashion peacock (*Newsweek* 1968).

In the 1960s, promotions, advertisements and fashion editorials presented manifestations of the new man in much more ambiguous terms, proclaiming a new dandyism while at the same time reassuring him of his inherent masculinity. This concept of interchangeability and the mix and match of both stylistic and social conformity and nonconformity is not something that is lost in the discursive rhetoric of facial hair. Products like Hollywood Joe's Beard-and-Mustache Wig, for example, encouraged business types to 'let it all hang out at the weekend' (*Time* 1968), presumably so that they could put it all back in again Monday to Friday. Peter Blake's album cover for *Sgt Pepper's Lonely Hearts Club Band* (1967) ironically included cardboard moustaches inserted into the sleeve to match those of the Beatles themselves. Hairstylist John Raynes instructed trainees, '[T]here is no reason ... why a client should not have a long beard as well as long hair,' although this meant cleaning and shaping it in line with the customer's career needs and lifestyle: '[W]hat is intolerable is for either [long hair or beard] to consist of lank, badly shaped wisps or tangles' (Raynes 1972: 5) so typical of the hippy. A 1968 fold-out advert for Schick Razor (Peter 1969: 70) depicting a long-haired, bearded hippy morphing into a clean-shaven James Bond figure announces the 'clean-cut look is here'. Meanwhile, the Remington electric shaver is promoted as a tool to 'Break your beard in right', more ambivalently promoting the styling and trimming rather than the total elimination of facial hair (cited in Peter 1969: 67).

This dilution of subversive and sub-cultural styles in facial hair should be considered in the context of earlier debates around shaving that anticipated symbolic nonconformity as an opportunity to accelerate men's consumption. At the beginning of the twentieth century, the move to self-shaving at home drew on the long tradition of the barbershop to give a new visual identity to traditional rituals of conformist masculinity. Technical innovation in shaving processes and products, and the resulting spatial shift from the commercial to the domestic, were promoted through the ambiguous rhetoric of modernity. But there was also a focus on the social body and the proclaimed perils posed by both poor hygiene and the masculine negotiation of the traditional spaces of femininity. In the postwar period, it is the emergence of a new, more narcissistic masculine identity more comfortable with the spectacular display of the material body that is now being exploited. Fashions in facial hair are never entirely exhausted; their cultural capital rather dwindles slowly. However, shaving and its historical promotion demonstrate the cultural consistency of conformity and the rituals of its everyday masculine performance; these remain a potent strategy of fashionable and social status.

BIBLIOGRAPHY

Adams, R. B. (1978), *King C. Gillette: The Man and His Wonderful Shaving Device,* Boston: Little, Brown.

Andrews, W. (1904), *At the Sign of the Barber's Pole: Studies in Hirsute History.* Cottingham, Yorkshire: J. R. Tutin.

Asia (1929), October.

Asia (1930), May.

Beechy, D. A. (2004), *How Facial Hair Influences Women's Everyday Experiences,* Unpublished PhD thesis, Centre for Humanistic Studies, Farmington, Michigan.

Century Magazine (1896), March.

Charles, A. and DeAnfrasio, R. (1970), *The History of Hair: An Illustrated Review of Hair Fashions for Men throughout the Ages,* New York: Bonanza Books.

Cooper, W. (1971), *Hair: Sex, Society, Symbolism,* London: Aldus Books.

Frank, T. (1997), *The Conquest of Cool: Business Culture, Counterculture and the Rise of Hip Consumerism,* London: University of Chicago Press.

Hairdressers' Journal (1954), 29 April.

Harper's Magazine (1905a), July.

Harper's Magazine (1905b), November.

Harper's Weekly (1902), 22 February.

Hebdige, D. (1979), *Subculture: The Meaning of Style,* London: Methuen.

Illustrated London News (1899), 1 April.

Lasch, C. (1979), *The Culture of Narcissism: American Life in an Age of Diminishing Expectations,* New York: W. W. Norton & Company.

Lears, T. J. (1994), *Fables of Abundance: A Cultural History of Advertising in America,* New York: Basic Books.

Life Magazine (1937), 8 March.

Life Magazine (1952), 23 June.

Life Magazine (1953), 1 June.

Life Magazine (1957), 9 December.

Literary Digest (1907), 9 November.

Literary Digest (1929), 2 November.

Look Magazine (1963), June.

Look Magazine (1964), June.

Marchand, R. (1986), *Advertising the American Dream: Making Way for Modernity 1920–1940*, London: University of California Press.

Martin, R. and Koda, H. (1989), *Jocks and Nerds*, New York: Rizzoli.

McKibbin, G. (1998), *Cutting Edge: Gillette's Journey to Global Leadership*, Boston: Harvard Business School Press.

Newsweek (1968), 'Male Plumage 1968', 25 November.

Osgerby, B. (2001), *Playboys in Paradise: Masculinity, Youth and Leisure-style in Modern America*, London: Berg.

The Outing, (1920), April.

Peter, J. (ed) (1969), *48th Annual of Advertising and Editorial Art and Design of the Art Directors Club of New York*, New York: Farrar, Straus & Cudahy.

Peterkin, A. (2001), *One Thousand Beards: A Cultural History of Facial Hair*, Vancouver: Arsenal Pulp Press.

Pinfold, M. J. (2000), ' "I'm Sick of Shaving Every Morning": or, The Cultural Implications of "Male" Facial Presentation', *Journal of Mundane Behaviour*, 1 (1) (February): 75–88.

Powell, P. and Peel, L. (1988), *50's and 60's Style*, London: Quintet.

Raynes, J. (1972), *Men's Hairdressing*, London: Heinemann.

Roszak, T. (1971), *The Making of a Counter Culture: Reflections on the Technocratic Society and Its Youthful Opposition*, London: Faber & Faber.

Saturday Evening Post (1910), 18 December.

Theatre (1904), November.

Theatre (1905a), November.

Theatre (1905b), December.

Time Magazine (1968), 'Beards, Boards and Brushes', 12 April.

Tomes, N. (1998), *The Gospel of Germs: Men, Women and the Microbe in American Life*, Cambridge, MA: Harvard University Press.

Wilson, E. and Taylor, L. (1989), *Through the Looking Glass: A History of Dress from 1860 to the Present Day*, London: BBC Books.

PART 2
HAIR AND IDENTITY

7 HAIR AND MALE (HOMO) SEXUALITY
'UP TOP AND DOWN BELOW'

SHAUN COLE

Gender, according to Judith Butler (1990a), is a performance. She proposes that we do not have any fixed or given gender identity that informs our behaviour; rather that behaviour *is* our gender. Butler argues: 'There is no gender identity behind the expressions of gender ... identity is performatively constituted by the very "expressions" that are said to be its results' (Butler 1990a: 25). Gender, therefore, is what one does rather than who one is, a performance through which one constructs a gender character while at the same time creating the illusion that such a character is somehow primary. Nevertheless, Butler also posits that the ways in which an individual performs or presents his or her own body are unique, so that, despite seeming similarities between predecessors, contemporaries and successors, no two bodies are ever actually the same (Butler 1990b: 272). Therefore, following Butler, David Gauntlett states:

> since identities are not fixed—neither to the body nor to the 'self'—we can perform gender in whatever way we like. Although certain masculine and feminine formations may have been learned, these patterns can be broken ... the mass media can serve a valuable role in shattering the unhelpful moulds of 'male' and 'female' roles which continue to apply constraints upon people's ability to be expressive and literate beings. (Gauntlett 2002: 150)

A range of factors, including any and all features, ornamentation and adornment of the physical body, such as weight, height, body modification, choice of clothing and hairstyle have an impact upon an individual's self-identity and presentation to the world.

McCracken (1995: 15–16), significantly, places hair within this context of 'self-invention' suggesting that, 'our lives are now a constant succession of selves' in which 'we move from one to the next, as if they were so many rocks in the stream'. Hair, McCracken continues, is used to 'audition and annex new selves, to seek out new versatility and variety' in defining who 'we are' and is the 'best instrument of self-invention, our best solution to the problem of constant change'. This chapter examines gay men's intimate relationship with their hair—on their heads, faces and bodies—in the twentieth and twenty-first centuries. This relationship is marked by personal and public attitudes formed through the observation, representation, production and consumption of the styling, growth and removal of hair. How has this been influenced by, and reflected in, gay men's changing and developing identities; and how has this impacted upon the choices, definitions and changes made in the presentation of gay male sexuality and identity?

'IS HE OR ISN'T HE?'

The French philosopher Michel Foucault (2000: 137–8), speculated on whether it was possible to create 'a homosexual mode of life.' He said, 'A way of life can be shared among individuals of different age, status, and social activity. It can yield intense relations not resembling those that are institutionalised. It seems to me that a way of life can yield a culture and an ethics. To be "gay", I think, is not to identify with the psychological traits and the visible masks of the homosexual but to try to define and develop a way of life.' This notion interested Foucault because homosexuality does not necessarily come with ready-made patterns of lifestyle in the same way that heterosexuality does, but presents a freedom and challenge to create a meaningful lifestyle. This is particularly important when understood not just in terms of stylistic choice but as a fundamental part of gay subjectivities, and following Judith Butler, their performative expression.

Such behaviours clearly have an influence on the articulation of gay fashionable identities and stylistic choice, integral to which are a range of head and body hairstyles and grooming practices. Sociologist Martin P. Levine (1998: 21) has identified three strategies that gay men use to 'manage' their identities: 'passing, minstrelization and capitulation'. Passing involves dressing and behaving in such a way as to become 'invisible' as a gay man in order to negotiate the wider 'straight' world under a disguise of heterosexuality. Minstrelization is the adoption of cross-gendered behaviour through feminine dress, behaviour and speech, described by many participants and observers, both gay and straight, as 'camp'. Capitulation arises from the sense of guilt and self-hatred about one's homosexuality resulting from the belief that homosexuality is a form of gender deviance. Within the tensions of Levine's strategies of managed identity, questions arise both in terms of individual self-image and sexual attraction: 'is my/his hair too long, too short, too fey, too butch?' Binaries of male/female, gay/straight, masculine/feminine continue to exist in practice. However, just as there has traditionally been a tension between masculinity and femininity, so there has been a tension between *individuality and conformity* expressed through hair. Gay men have wanted to either conform to heterosexual ideals (Levine's passing strategy) or revel in their difference from heterosexuals. By utilizing such strategies a gay man can, through his hair and hairstyling strategies, appear and 'be' as 'gay' or 'straight' as he chooses.

For many gay men up to the advent of gay liberation in the late 1960s, it was, for example, critical not to stand out or be easily identifiable as gay within straight society. Thus, most gay men conformed to the fashions of the day, and followed Levine's passing strategy. Peter Robins recalls that most gay men in the 1950s and early 1960s had a 'very ordinary short back and sides,' unless 'one was in an artistic profession' when it was acceptable for a man's hair to be 'a little longer' (Robins 1997). Hair in the 1950s, McCracken (1995: 49–52) observes, was 'anti-transformational,' with both men and women treating hair as if it 'were a dangerous substance' noting that, as 'opposed to women's "fastidious discipline", men reacted by treating their hair with "fastidious disregard'"; men in barber shops were 'proceeding with care' in the presence of 'this strange, powerful, transitional and terribly female substance called hair'.

It could be argued that for gay men such fastidious disregard was itself an essential part of the fastidious discipline inherent in careful and studied strategies of conformism. However, this must also be situated in relation not just to the norms of heterosexual hair dressing, but also the stylistic traditions of 'gay hair' itself. Long hair on men has for many centuries had associations of effeminacy and this has manifested itself in the burgeoning identities and dress choice of men engaged in same-sex activity (see Trumbach 1989). In the late-nineteenth century, unconventional signifiers of bohemian men—including long hair, colourful dress and an interest in art—led to associations with homosexuality, particularly after the Oscar Wilde trials of 1895 (Figure 7.1). Subsequently, long hair became prevalent in homosexuals with an aspiration to an aesthetic leisure-class image. In the first half of the twentieth century some effeminate homosexuals manifested their identities through the adoption of visibly female characteristics, which along with plucked eyebrows, rouged lips, and powdered faces, included long, styled, and frequently, coloured hair, exemplifying Levine's strategy of minstrelization. Bleached or peroxide hair was a typical indicator of homosexuality to the extent that a blond-haired gay protagonist famously gave one novel its name: *Goldie* (Bruce 1933). *Goldie* is the story of athletic, handsome Paul Kameron, who dyes his hair, embarks on a part-time career as a New York hustler and whilst working in a Greenwich Village restaurant organizes, what in today's terminology

Figure 7.1   Oscar Wilde receiving a haircut in prison.
Illustration entitled: 'The locks that fall have been
admired and admired by society, alas!
how they have fallen'.
Image taken from *The Illustrated Police Budget*. Originally
published/produced in London, 1895. Copyright © 2008
The British Library Board. All rights reserved.

would be called, a gay liberation club. Goldie constantly fears policemen will recognize him as 'degenerate [because of] the unusual hue of his hair', and consequently wears a cap, taking it off 'only to attract the attention of his prospect', a potential sexual partner equally aware of the hair colouring's significance (Bruce 1993: 102, 119).

Expressions of both transgression and conformity in relation to both gay and straight hair dressing and styling practices are therefore always a dynamic that produce and reproduce gay men's attitudes to their individual and, increasingly, collective identities. With the rise of gay liberation, gay men made a concerted effort to distance themselves from previous conformist and effeminate stereotypes. Many young gay men were also involved in wider counter-cultural movements which they found to be liberating, as John Fraser described 'growing my hair long and wearing beads. That was great. Now that was liberation, you know, to have hair down to your shoulders and wear bright clothes ... it was very open but it was very political' (quoted in Hall Carpenter Archives, 1989: 133–4). Journalist Laud Humphreys (1971: 41), too, noted the appearance of new masculinities amongst young gay men based on a 'youthful masculinity of bare chests and beads, long hair, mustaches and hip-hugging pants'.

By the 1970s gay men self-consciously adopted manly attire and demeanour as a means of expressing a new sense of self-worth. The figure of 'the Clone' (as this new masculine gay man became known) looked to icons of American working-class masculinity and created a new hypermasculine gay identity. Gay men abandoned as role models the dapper, groomed and clean-shaven stereotype of the upper-class aesthete, as well as the long hair of the hippie and the historical effeminate 'fairy'. They appropriated blue-collar signifiers such as the costumes and workday clothing of lumberjacks, cowboys and construction workers (Levine 1998; Cole 2000), and visibly displayed their body hair, cropped their head hair and adopted the facial hair of the archetypal 'Marlboro man' (Figure 7.2). The moustache became one of the key signifiers of Clone styling to such an extent that some men who could not grow a sufficiently impressive moustache resorted to a (convincing) fake stick-on variety (Weller 1997). Clark Henley's tongue-in-cheek guide to clone style and behaviour *The Butch Manual: The Current Drag and How to Do It* (1982) offered advice on the styling of both head and facial hair: 'There is no right look for Butch hair ... There are however, lots of possibilities ... Receding hairlines, thinning hair, and baldness are all great Butch hair because they make you look distinguished', adding, 'The Butchest possible combination is a decorative moustache and a two-day old beard, which suggests that you have just come back from shooting the rapids on the Salmon River or from a long weekend at the baths' (Henley 1982: 52).

Closely cropped hair communicated qualities of masculinity and working-classness that appealed to many gay men. Reinforced by associations of criminality and delinquency, the values of the subcultural straight Skinhead were based on traditional concepts of male dominance and solidarity and offered a pared down masculine anti-fashion statement. Whilst the subculture was notorious for its aggressive stance towards homosexuality, and was renowned for its acts of violence against gay men (pejoratively known as *queer bashing*),

Figure 7.2   Hairy gay masculinity, San Francisco, 1970s.
Photo by Crawford Barton. Courtesy of the Gay, Lesbian, Bisexual, Transgender
Historical Society, San Francisco.

the image was nevertheless popular with many gay men and led to an emerging gay skin-head culture, charted in Murray Healy's book *Gay Skins* (1996). It was the very qualities of masculinity and hardness, and also a lack of effeminate frivolity apparent in a more stereo-typical gay image, that attracted many gay men to shave their heads. Gay skinhead Jamie Crofts described the appeal of the haircut in his adoption of skinhead image and lifestyle: 'I've always thought short hair was sexy anyway. When I grew up, my teen years were all in the seventies, and long hair didn't turn me on at all … I suppose it's a natural thing you get into, the shorter the better' (Healy 1996: 106).

The look was gradually softened in the late 1980s, with a fashion for a longer tuft at the front reminiscent of the cartoon character 'Tin Tin', or by its conversion into the 'Nero cut' where the fringe was 'cut short and brushed forward producing a short cropped effect'

(Cox 1999: 252). This softened skinhead look became associated with a new queer political image identity that grew up around AIDS protest. Dubbed by American journalist and
activist Michelangelo Signorile 'the new clone', this style constituted a crucial part of the
'uniform' of political radicalism for both lesbians and gay men. The Nero, worn by 'out'
gay pop star George Michael subsequently became associated with lad culture in Britain.
Young gay men adopted the clothes and hairstyles of sporty heterosexual lads to visibly signify their working-class roots, if they had them—and if they didn't equally employed them
as a way of attracting those who did. As Paul Hardy noted 'gay men fancy the whole "lad"
image because it represents "real" masculinity' (Hardy 1996: 23; see also Cole 2008).

SMOOTH PEOPLE: THE RISE OF THE MUSCLE MAN

Anthony Synnott (1993: 12) suggests that the theory of hair can be called the theory
of opposites, summarized in three propositions: (*a*) Opposite sexes have opposite hair;
(*b*) Head hair and body hair are opposite; (*c*) Opposite ideologies have opposite hair. He
notes that men conventionally *minimize* their head hair and face hair—they shave their
faces and generally keep their scalp hair relatively short, unstyled, and undyed. In contrast
they *maximize* their body hair, neither cutting nor shaving their body hair and Synnott
concludes that therefore the head hair and body hair are opposite. However, Synnott's
generalizations, while largely valid across much of straight Western culture, nevertheless
make a heterosexist assumption that fails to consider how gay men may or may not follow
these conventional practices. Synnott ignores both the associations of effeminacy and the
attention and 'control' that gay men might differently exercise over the presentation and
representation of their head, facial hair and body hair. What Synnott's work does highlight
is how male head and body hair are always intrinsically linked. Styles and trends in gay
head and facial hair are constantly shifting, mirroring and moulding trends in straight
hairstyling. But equally growth and removal of hairy gay and straight male bodies have a
symbiotic relationship and a fluidity of influence and adoption.

It is worth noting that Synnott was writing at the point (the early 1990s) when many
gay men were completely removing (minimizing) their body hair in the pursuit of a smooth
muscular ideal inspired by the homoeretoic illustrations of cult artist Tom of Finland, who
was a hugely influential part of gay visual culture in the late-twentieth century. This image
runs counter to many of the 1970s images of gay masculinity, which emphasized hairiness, as a symbol of masculinity. However for both gay *and* straight men at any one time,
idealized masculinity is always confounded by shifting complex understandings of 'the
conventionally rugged, super-independent, extra-strong, macho man [that] circulate in
popular culture' (Gauntlett 2002: 250). For gay men this has proved particularly important
as they attempt to identify and negotiate their social and sexual identity and position, both
within and outside of the dominant hegemony of heterosexual, white bourgeois culture.
The experience of 31-year-old gay San Francisco resident, John Welton, is typical and illustrates the extent to which some gay men will go to achieve a hairless ideal. Over thirteen
years Welton spent more than $7,000 on hair removal procedures to strip his back, shoulders

and upper arms. The impetus came from the overriding predominance of hairless imagery delivered to gay men: 'In gay magazines, on TV, everywhere I looked, I saw smooth people' (Ryan 2006).

The gay muscle man was very much the offspring of historical shifts that occurred in gay visual culture in the postwar period, linked to the opening up of new spaces of masculine consumption such as 'Vince Man's Shop' on the fringes of London's Soho (Cole 1997).

Figure 7.3   Physique photograph by Vince (Bill Green), early 1950s.
By kind permission of Walter Wilkins.

The 1950s saw the development of a mass market for muscle magazines and physique photographs, such as those taken by Vince, that equally offered a template for a redefinition of the gay body (Figure 7.3). In the 1950s, the predominant stereotypes of a gay man were the limp-wristed sexless 'sissy' and the effeminate cross-dressed pseudo woman. Much of the gay sexual iconography in the 1950s therefore was an attempt to break away from, or modify, the sexual stereotypes of gay men. As Daniel Harris notes: 'If the stereotype was the 90 pound weakling of the Charles Atlas body-building ads, then the 'real' men had to be muscular and well built' (Harris 1997: 170). While ostensibly offering bodybuilding tips and moral guidance to young men the world over, such representations equally operated as a form of specifically gay pornography by allowing gay men to view other men's bodies as objects of desire, whilst simultaneously wanting to be the very object of such desire (Bronski 1984: 165).

STRIPPED, SHAVED AND SHORN

Gauntlett (2002: 254–5) observes that in contemporary society, the media disseminates a huge number of messages about gendered identity and acceptable forms of self-expression and lifestyle. He suggests, 'We lap up this material ... because the social construction of identity today is the *knowing* social construction of identity' (2002: 247–8). In the 1950s, the majority of the models in magazines such as *Vim* and *Physique Pictorial* were young (assumed) heterosexual, white, muscular and smooth-skinned. However, such magazines offered an acceptable means for gay men to look but also functioned as 'the site and occasion for the production of bodily knowledge of the body' (Dyer 2002: 140). The subsequent progressive advance of gay liberation and the gay rights movement, and the simultaneous growth of the male beauty industry, stimulated a 'self-pampering narcissism' amongst gay men that led to the publication of *Looking Good* (1977). This 'bible' of grooming, peppered with homoerotic photography by Bruce Weber, represented 'the very summit of the gay obsession with hygiene that fundamentally altered the look of our bodies in the years following Stonewall' (Harris 1997: 92). However, as photographer David Bergman points out, it is not just that hairless male bodies facilitate aesthetic physical definition but that 'hair is a deeply psychological symbol of both sexuality and mortality ... body hair especially is part of the abject—part of the dirty, smelly, detachable parts of the self that are associated with being mortal', particularly significant for a gay culture 'torn by its feelings about its mortality' (quoted in Peterkin 2001: 136).

It is important, therefore, to consider how the representation of a sexualized gay identity functioned in the era of AIDS. The 'shaved face, chest, legs, genitals and anus on muscled bodies ... reassured men of the object's (or partner's) purity, youth, and by extension, freedom from disease' (Peterkin 2001: 136). Safer sex advertising utilized images of hairless, muscular, tanned bodies to reinforce the stereotype of the smooth, *healthy*, gym-toned gay body. Such a body came to predominate in gay visual culture and manifested itself in the almost fetishistic ritual shaving of heads, chest and genital areas amongst gay men. Harris (1997: 127) charts this changing image of the gay male body within the context of

Figure 7.4 Hairless gay muscle men.
Photo by Chris Geary, 2006. www.ChrisGeary.com

contemporary masculinity and consumption, noting that 'To compare the actors of old pornography, whose bodies were scrawny, hairy, sallow, untanned, pimply, scarred, wrinkled, and buttless, with the groomed, buffed, tanned, shaven, oiled, tattooed, and pierced adonises of contemporary films, is to see the entire history of the last 25 years of the commercialization of gay culture summed up in the most tangible way possible' (Figure 7.4).

Turner (2006: 224) has proposed that 'representations of cultural identities matter because they are among the raw materials from which we construct our own sense of "who we are" at any point in time.' In 1982, the American designer Calvin Klein famously erected an enormous billboard in New York's Times Square advertising his men's white briefs. Photographed by Weber, it was an overtly sexual image of a perfectly formed, smooth skinned, muscular man wearing nothing but white underwear. The nods towards homoerotic imagery were overt. However, on being questioned about the homoerotic appeal of its advertising, a spokesperson for Calvin Klein stated, 'we did not *try* to appeal to gays. We try to appeal, period. If there's an awareness in that community of health and grooming, then they'll respond to the ads' (Stabiner 1982: 34). Klein's billboard has been credited with heralding a new era in the imagery of men in advertising. This campaign preceded the revolution in men's magazine production and advertising which resexualized the male form as a hairless muscular object of sexual desire for both men and women through consumption (see Jobling 1999; Mort 1996; Nixon 1996). The heterosexual male body in the 1980s became smoother, more commodified and invitingly aestheticized in popular cultural and advertising images that all served to create a new heterosexual ideal that by the early 2000s had become 'simultaneously a cliché and de rigueur' (Simpson 2002).

Boroughs, Cafri and Thompson (2005) ground their study in the belief that both heterosexual and gay men are similarly subject to the effects of exposure to media on their body image. Their study of 118 male participants (2 homosexual, 9 bisexual and 107 heterosexual) attempted to 'confirm the numerous anecdotal accounts and preliminary data that suggest that body hair removal is indeed a new and potentially important component of body image for men' (2005: 638). Their findings indicated that seventy-five respondents had recently shaved or trimmed any body hair below the neck; the primary areas for depilation were the groin, chest, and abdomen; body image issues were key factors for body hair reduction and removal; the most significant reasons for depilation included: cleanliness, sex appeal, and body definition/muscularity. The increasing popularity of 'back, sack and crack' hair removal for both aesthetic and hygiene reasons would appear to indicate that the new ideal of masculinity is a man who is in control of his hairy masculine attributes, very much exemplified in the figure of the contemporary 'meterosexual' man.

First identified by Mark Simpson (1994), the metrosexual is a 'single young man with a high disposable income, living or working in the city (because that's where all the best shops are)' and 'perhaps the most promising consumer market of the decade'. There was increased pressure on men to take better care of themselves and look more attractive, alongside the sales strategies of companies seeking to increase profits from a previously untapped market. This promoted an increase in hair-related production and consumption of, for example, gels and waxes and products for the control and removal of facial and body hair, amongst young hetero/metrosexual men. While Simpson's original meterosexual was defined in terms of consumption as much as sexuality, the description gave rise to a concept of a heterosexual man embracing products and processes previously seen as both feminine and effeminate. The boundaries between gay and straight masculinity, therefore, appeared to be more blurred through the more sexually ambiguous repertoire of the perfectly coiffured, obsessively groomed and manicured late-twentieth-century male consumer.

HAIRY BEARS

Since 2005 a fashion for cropped head and facial hair, where the head and beard are clipped to the same length, has been worn by both gay and straight men, and become equally popular amongst 'celebrities'. Pop singers Shane Ward, Justin Timberlake and Mike Skinner (The Streets) all combine the masculine attribute of facial hair clipped and controlled with a certain wide-eyed youthful innocence that counteracts the working-class 'hardness' of cropped hair's previous incarnations. Two journalists, one gay and one straight, who write for *The London Paper* both have this same hairstyling, marking a certain unconcern about sexual orientation in their appearance whilst at the same time demonstrating the performative role of hair and hairstyling. 'Guy about Town' Kevin Braddock discussed his style, ironically noting that, 'I cropped it back to a compromise between five o'clock shadow and louche three-day stubble–a whiskery, laissez-faire look that takes no more than three hours of tending every day' (Braddock 2007); while 'Gay Guy about Town' Joshua Hunt, focussed on the colour of his hair and beard (ginger) in relation to his appearance and sexual attractiveness, and the increasing trend for gay men to dress in 'scruffy,' 'straight-acting fashion' (Hunt 2007). This blending and crossover between gay and straight styles would suggest an increasing ambivalence about the role that sexuality has to play in an individual's hair presentational strategies.

In the age of meterosexuality, gay and straight men's styling and grooming practices have seemingly moved increasingly closer together and become progressively almost interchangeable. Straight metrosexuals and 'strays' (gay-acting straights) appear equally comfortable in adopting and articulating performative subjectivities that would once have been understood as 'camp'. This poses the question, is it any longer necessary for gay men to follow Levine's strategies of capitulation, minstrelization and passing? Gay men's responses to such changes and their consequent body and head hair styling strategies certainly seems to suggest a new autonomy—but significantly one that also challenges the proscriptive hairless ideal of both contemporary gay *and* metrosexual masculinity. A 2007 campaign for Armani underwear features the hairless muscular, passively reclining epitome of metrosexuality, footballer David Beckham. The emphasis appears to be on his fabric-encased genitals and smooth muscular six-pack. His hairy (but neatly trimmed) face is cast to the background of the image. However this image of sometime gay icon, Beckham now runs counter to images of muscular but hairy torsos that are increasingly appearing in gay media. The year 2006 saw designers such as Gaultier, Dolce and Gabanna, and DSquared—incidentally designers who are either gay or draw inspiration from gay culture—sending hairy models down catwalks. A study of one edition of *Boyz* magazine from January 2008 also reveals twelve photographs of hairy torsos (not including those in the escort advertisements) in both advertisements and editorial photographs. Adam Mattera (2007), editor of gay magazine, *Attitude,* believes that David Beckham is no longer included in the top five of most sexy males in the magazine's reader polls because he is 'too over-groomed' for current gay tastes.

This new hairy gay aesthetic has been most visibly manifested in the emergence over the last ten years of 'bears' who celebrate what they perceive as 'real' masculinity—hairiness, big bulky bodies, work-toned muscle (rather than gym-induced), and a belly (in direct response to washboard stomachs). Organizer of New York's annual 'Bearapolooza', Freddy Freeman explains: 'A bear is what you are meant to look like, not a construct to attract others. Men lose the hair from the top of their head as they age. They grow hair on their bodies. They get a little chubby around the waist' (quoted in Flynn 2003: 68). Alongside the rise in 'bear culture' there was simultaneously a call for images of hairy and big men to be portrayed in gay magazines and pornography, which magazines such as *Drummer* and *Bear* attempted to fulfil. Laura Kipnis identified a growth in images that focus on 'bodies in the 250 to 300 pound range ... beefy, barrel-chested, potbellied, and most important, hairy ... carpets of chest hair, back hair, full beards' (1999: 114).

PERFORMATIVITY AND THE GAY MALE BODY: 'UP TOP AND DOWN BELOW'

To return once more to Butler (1990a) and her theories of gender as a series of performed actions and behaviours, it is clear that gender and gendered identity is constantly negotiated and performed in relation to internal and external pressures. 'Gayness', therefore, is constantly produced and reproduced through numerous images and practices. In this sense, in strategies for the affirmation *and* negation of gay identity, the body and its presentation are never fixed and, for example, are always both conforming to and challenging the idea of what it is to be a man, gay and straight. The cyclical adoption and adaptation of gay and straight styles by the one and the other exemplifies Butler's notions around the 'constructed status' of all gendered identities that disrupts any concept of a 'heterosexual original'; as she argues, 'gay is to straight *not* as a copy is to an original, but rather, as a copy is to a copy' (1990a: 41).

Since the 1970s, the appropriation of traditionally 'macho' clothes and styles of dress, body, and a variety of face and head hair dressing, grooming and styling practices opened up radical and transgressive possibilities for many gay men. Some appropriated the extreme stereotypes of both male and female dress in a style known as 'gender-fuck' that combined workmen's boots, beards and moustaches with very feminine dresses and full make-up. John Lloyd described the clothes he and his friends wore to achieve such a look: 'Colam would be wearing a very short white dress with boots and his beard and a badge ... and David would have a long flowing black gown and a long beard as well' (Birch and King 1988: 31). Many men utilizing 'butch' signifiers did so with a sense of play, inherited from a traditional gay 'camp' sensibility. It was both a self-conscious, almost parodying, reference to traditional stereotypical images of masculinity and a self-conscious embracing of those same stereotypes. However, in adopting such 'macho' images and identities, the 'masculine' gay man must also walk a tightrope between the old strategies of 'straight' imitation and the powerful potential of their re-interpretation that could identify them not only as real men but as real *gay* men.

Gregg Blachford argues that 'it is to the uniforms of the oppressor that the oppressed run in the hope of safety' (1981: 203). From the beginnings of modern gay culture, the images gay men have of their bodies have been haunted by a sense of weakness, and unattractiveness, and 'of sexual subordination to the heterosexual Übermensch' (Harris 1997: 90). Consequently the gay body has been vulnerable to a variety of cosmetic and surgical treatments to overcome this sense of physical inadequacy. 'Male homosexuals seem to be inextricably linked to an exaggerated respect and contempt for masculinity—rather like male heterosexuality toward femininity' (Simpson 2002). This has all, Gilad Padva (2002: 282) suggests, resulted in the queer body being 'marginalised by the straight bourgeoisie but also controlled, commodified, and commercialised by the gay media itself.' For gay and straight body alike, the social 'cost' of idealization is difficult to sustain: 'attempts to aestheticise hairy, out of shape bodies are in part motivated by fatigue with the amount of energy required for the onerous maintenance of the bourgeois body, which can be kept at its deodorised peak of svelte perfection only through back-breaking regimens of diet and exercise' (Harris 1997: 106). If gay liberation and modern counter-cultures were intended to provide an alternative approach to the male body, then the emphasis on youth and the perfectly developed, hairless musculature consistently promoted within the gay media are not in fact liberating but rather operate as an alternative form of normative body fascism.

David Gauntlett argues that within queer theory 'the point of the celebration of diversity and difference is that *everybody* is a little different from everybody else (and that we are happy about that)' (2002: 148). Gay liberation advocated that there should be a freedom of expression for gay people and that gay and lesbian identities should not have to be bounded by traditional ideals of male and female, masculine and feminine, in order to provide an alternative approach to the presentation and representation of the gay body. However, discussing concepts of real and perceived masculinity within gay men's strategies of identification and representation, Padva (2002: 288) suggests 'the popularity of muscular, non-camp bodies in gay communities in the 1980s, from smooth, shaved bodybuilders to the new clone of the hairy 'bears' ... does not signify any 'real' masculinisation of gay men, but a new masquerade that is no less artificial and manipulative, and even parodic in a way, than the camp/effeminate performance.'

This recognition of the impossibility of the 'authenticity' of gender and sexuality is nevertheless always grounded in real bodies, gay or straight, and real actions that reveal both the potential power of individual agency and the structures of ideological constraint that proscriptively define and describe it. One 32-year-old gay man, Graham Tansey (2008), has moved away from a time-consuming sculpted beard—'artistic goatee with no moustache'—to the more 'bearish rugged look' of a full beard. 'Basically I felt like a change', he said. 'I suppose because I am into the bear scene and think that men with full beards are very attractive, and I am getting a bit older! Also it's quicker to have a shave too but that's just an advantage not a reason why I changed'. This also links to his strategy for his body hair: 'I do nothing with my body hair. I suppose it's the same reason as for my beard really in the fact that I like men with plenty of body hair so I don't feel the need to do anything with it' (Tansey 2008). Tansey's pragmatic approach reflects the observation made by John, a 34-year-old gay man, 'You've got some who are hairy and do nothing about it, some who are almost obsessive about being clean-shaven, and some who just keep their facial hair neatly trimmed—and what goes on up top is usually a good indication of what goes on below' (quoted in Em and Lo 2006). Even the most mundane hairy strategies are the site of complex negotiations that shape and are shaped by the performance of a self-conscious gay male identity.

BIBLIOGRAPHY

Birch, K. and King, M. (1988), 'The Nancy Revolution', *Square Peg*, No 20: 30–2.
Blachford, G. (1981), 'Male Dominance and the Gay World', in K. Plummer (ed), *The Making of the Modern Homosexual*, London: Hutchinson.

Boroughs, M., Cafri, G. and Thompson, J. K. (2005), 'Male Body Depilation: Prevalence and Associated Features of Body Hair Removal', *Sex Roles: A Journal of Research,* 52: 637–44.

Boyz (2008), Jan.

Braddock, K. (2007), 'Call It Beard Magnetism: Facial Hair as a Sexual Weapon', *The London Paper,* 13 February: 29.

Bronski, M. (1984), *Culture Clash: The Making of Gay Sensibility,* Boston: South End Press.

Bruce, K. (1933), *Goldie,* New York: William Godwin.

Butler, J. (1990a), *Gender Trouble: Feminism and the Subversion of Identity,* London: Routledge.

Butler, J. (1990b), 'Performative Acts and Gender Constitution: An Essay in Phenomenology and Feminist Theory', in S.-E. Case (ed), *Performing Feminisms: Feminist Critical Theory and Theatre,* Baltimore: Johns Hopkins University Press.

Cole, S. (1997), 'Corsair Slacks and Bondi Bathers: Vince Man's Shop and the Beginnings of Carnaby Street Fashion', *Things,* 6 (Summer): 26–39.

Cole, S. (2000), '"Macho Man": Clones and the Development of a Masculine Stereotype', *Fashion Theory,* 4 (2): 125–40.

Cole, S. (2008), 'Butch Queens in Macho Drag: Gay Men, Dress and Subcultural Identity', in S. Coseby and A. Reilly (eds.), *The Men's Fashion Reader,* New York: Fairchild Books.

Cox, C. (1999), *Good Hair Days: A History of British Hairstyling,* London: Quartet Books.

Dyer, R. (2002), *Only Entertainment,* London: Routledge.

Em and Lo (2006), 'Stubble Theory: What Your Facial Hair Is Really Saying', *New York,* 6 Aug., http:/www.Nymag.com/relationships/mating/18852, accessed 26 April 2008.

Flynn, P. (2003), 'Bear Up', *Attitude* (September): 66–70.

Foucault, M. (2000), *Essential Works of Foucault 1954–1984: Ethics,* P. Rabinow (ed), London: Penguin Books.

Gauntlett, D. (2002), *Media, Gender and Identity: An Introduction,* New York and London, Garland.

Hall Carpenter Archives Gay Men's Oral History Group. (1989), *Walking after Midnight: Gay Men's Life Stories,* London: Routledge.

Hardy, P. (1996), 'Glad to Be Lad', *QX* (March): 23–5.

Harris, D. (1997), *The Rise and Fall of Gay Culture,* New York: Ballantine Books.

Healy, M. (1996), *Gay Skins: Class, Masculinity and Queer Appropriation,* London: Cassell.

Henley, C. (1982), *The Butch Manual: The Current Drag and How to Do It,* New York: New Amer Library Trade.

Humphreys, L. (1971), 'New Styles in Homosexual Manliness', *Trans-Action,* 8 (5/6): 38–40.

Hunt, J. (2007), 'Why Gay Men Act Straight', *The London Paper,* 9 May: 25.

Jobling, P. (1999), *Fashion Spreads: Word and Image in Fashion Photography since 1980,* Oxford: Berg.

Kipnis, L. (1999), *Bound and Gagged: Pornography and the Politics of Fantasy in America,* Durham, NC: Duke University Press.

Levine, M. P. (1998), *Gay Macho: The Life and Death of the Homosexual Clone,* New York and London: New York University Press.

Mattera, A. (2007), *Attitude* (December): 2.

McCracken, G. (1995), *Big Hair: A Journey into the Transformation of Self,* London: Indigo.

Mort, F. (1996), *Cultures of Consumption: Masculinities and Social Space in Late Twentieth-Century Britain,* London: Routledge.

Nixon, S. (1996), *Hard Looks: Masculinities, Spectatorship and Contemporary Consumption*, London: UCL Press.

Padva, V. (2002), 'Heavenly Monsters: The Politics of the Male Body in the Naked Issue of *Attitude* Magazine', *International Journal of Sexuality and Gender Studies*, 16 September (11): 22.

Peterkin, A. (2001), *One Thousand Beards: A Cultural History of Facial Hair*, Vancouver: Arsenal Pulp Press.

Robins, P. (1997), Personal communication with author, 3 September.

Ryan, B. (2006), 'Getting Physical: Hairy Situations', http://www.planetout.com/health/mental, accessed 26 April 2008.

Simpson, M. (1994), 'Here Come the Mirror Men', *The Independent*, 15 November, http://www.marksimpson.com/pages/journalism/mirror_men.html, accessed 26 April 2008.

Simpson, M. (2002), 'Meet the Metrosexual', http://www.salon.com/story/ent/feature/2002/07/22/metrosexual, accessed 26 April 2008.

Stabiner, K. (1982), 'Tapping the Homosexual Market', *The New York Times Magazine*, 2 May, 34.

Synnott, A. (1993), *The Body Social: Symbolism, Self and Society*, London: Routledge.

Tansey, G. (2008), Personal communication with author, 14 January.

Trumbach, R. (1989), 'The Birth of the Queen: Sodomy and the Emergence of Gender Equality in Modern Culture, 1660–1750', in M. Duberman, M. Vicinus and G. Chauncey (eds.), *Hidden from History: Reclaiming the Gay and Lesbian Past*, New York: Penguin Books.

Turner, B. S. (2006), 'Body', *Theory, Culture and Society*, 23 (2–3): 223–9.

Weller, R. (1997), Personal communication with author, 24 April.

8   HAIR, GENDER AND LOOKING

GERALDINE BIDDLE-PERRY

'TRESSES CARRIED LIKE FLAGS ...'

Across cultures, hair is one of the most powerful symbols of our individual and collective identities. But historically and culturally it is arguably the *sight* of hair that makes its styling, cutting and dressing significant. Hair is our unique 'species signal' that in prehistory made us 'visible from afar.... our great bushy heads on top of our smooth naked bodies identified us immediately as human. Our extravagant tresses were carried like a flag' (Morris 1987: 21). The human species continue to 'flag' remnants of the hair display rituals of our hairier ancestors and mammalian relatives, particularly during hostile encounters. We may no longer raise our hackles, or fan out spectacular crests, but nevertheless, at times of crisis our hair stands on end, and we still toss our manes in annoyance. A gesture, known in French as *La Barbe* (the beard), consists of waving the fingers under the chin at an enemy and survives as a stylized form of more animalistic masculine display, as Desmond Morris (1978: 229) would have it, 'hair erection'.

Human hair is essentially all about looking: at ourselves, at other hairy people, and at other hairy people looking back at us. It is one of the first visible markers of who we perceive others to be (Hallpike 1969; Synnott 1987) and triggers an immediate and fundamental either/or response: male or female, friend or foe, good or bad, danger or safety. Powell and Roach argue:

> Surveying any terrain, the eye of the beholder seeks out the highest feature as focal point for its gaze, marking all the head as a stage, and the features on it only players. More intimate than clothing and yet more reliably prearranged than countenance, hair represents a primary means of staking a claim to social space on the occasion of first impressions. (2004: 79)

This chapter explores head and body hair as a constant (and historically consistent) means of spectacular gender identification. However, rather than focussing on what is looked at and looked for, it is the power of looking that is under scrutiny here—the modes and parameters of surveillance, classification and performative expression that the *sight* of hair offers to men and women. Using Foucault's regulatory schema and Freudian understandings of fetishized disavowal, this chapter analyses the presentational and representational symbolic potential of this spectacular dynamic. More crucially, it situates the sight of human hair or its visible absence as pivotal to the articulation of gendered looking.

CONDITION, CONTROL, CORRECTION

The French philosopher Michel Foucault (1977, 1979, 1985, 1986) uses the term *discourses* to describe the shifting systems of power and knowledge that operate according to the competing interests of a society at any given time. Discourses are multiple, and function as the automatic and anonymous apparatus of social and institutional control; they are systems of knowledge and power that condition the way in which people understand themselves and the world around them. For example, in *Discipline and Punish* (1977) Foucault examines the discourses on criminality that expanded and developed in the eighteenth century. New ways of thinking about, talking about and classifying criminal behaviour emerged alongside new ways of managing and punishing the individual and collective criminal 'body'. The spaces of new modern institutions and buildings like the prison were now organized through a vast network of surveillance, definition and regulation. The prisoner's body became the object of punishment and control exercised through observation. This physical and psychological structure of watching and being watched is used by Foucault as a metaphor for modern society as a whole and further explored in his work in relation to schools, religious institutions, asylums and hospitals.

According to Foucault (1977: 177), power 'is not possessed as a thing, or transferred as a property; it functions like a piece of machinery'; it does not need to operate by explicit proscription, nor by violent physical compulsion, but uses an equally forceful spectacular system of regulatory looking, worked through the social body. Foucault maps out the authority of what he describes as a 'normative gaze'. This gaze enables us to constitute ourselves as subjects, and separate ourselves from the 'other' against which gendered and idealized normality is measured. Structured like a form of language through which our bodies are individually and collectively both watched and problematized, we look at ourselves and at others, and determine the gaps between the two.

Foucault's theoretical framework has been applied to a range of critical analyses of the body as a vehicle of subjectivity and its performative expression (e.g. Butler 1992; Hall and Du Gay 1996), and of the ways it is experienced in contemporary consumer culture (e.g. Featherstone, Hepworth and Turner 1991). However, to date, academic enquiry into hair and hairy bodies using Foucauldian concepts of the discursive apparatus of self have been subsumed within these wider understandings of the gendered body. Nonetheless, Foucault (1997: 177) might have had hair in mind when explaining the mechanisms of disciplinary power: a pyramidal system with a 'head' at the top, but within which power is distributed between 'individuals in this permanent and continuous field ... and uninterrupted play of calculated gazes'. Thus, hair, according to its length, colour, style or absence might be the crucial looked-for indicator of sex, race, age, sexuality, religion, ethnicity, gender and even class. But such observation then creates a 'physics' of power through a whole moral universe of arbitrary and highly complex shifting meanings. Hair on the body and the head is part of a vital system of gender identification and representation that makes cultural and social distinctions between the sexes, but in ways that do not unequivocally make one either male or female. All human bodies are, after all, hairy bodies, but hair's visible absence or presence operates to make clear the boundaries of normative gender identity at any one time.

In Western culture while abundant head hair is perceived as the essential visual marker of idealized femininity, and as a trope for female sexuality itself, feminine body and facial hair must be removed or rendered invisible (Synnott 1993). Women with facial hair, or those with unshaven hairy bodies, are condemned as inherently unfeminine, even masculine, or as monstrous social and cultural deviants; such accusations are also levelled at women with very short hair or shaven heads who equally disrupt conventional understandings of appropriate feminine hair display (see Lesnik-Oberstein 2006). Men's head, body and facial hair equally functions as a form of performative display to differentiate not only between the sexes but within them. For example, in the 1860s, pamphlets were distributed warning men of the dangers of shaving: a clean-shaven face was seen as effeminate and ungodly and this 'fatal fashion' was linked to growing immorality, the spread of disease and rising rates of murder and suicide (Middleton 2006). A hundred years later, young men with long hair provoked a similar moral panic: it was not just that their long hair was seen as effeminate, but that sight alone could no longer immediately identify them as men at all. With hair, it is always the 'show' as much as the 'shave' that is significant.

Negative publicity continues to surround Hollywood actress Julia Roberts's appearance in 1999 at the premiere of the film *Notting Hill,* in which she had a starring role (*London Metro* 2006). Immaculately made-up, wearing a glitzy designer dress and her hair swept up in a classic *chignon,* Roberts appeared the picture of celebrity A-list sophistication. That is until she lifted her arm to wave at the crowds to reveal a very visible growth of dark armpit hair. Julia Roberts did not offer a coherent narrative of what a female body on public display should look like. The exposure of her 'inky tufts' (Knight 1999) revealed a dissonance between psychic fantasy and physical reality. This celebrity body crossed the symbolic dividing line between privileged spectacle and erotic concealment upon which both aesthetic distance and masculine psychological composure depend.

In modernity, Foucault argues that self-control, self-discipline and self-regulation became a substitute for historical systems of public corporeal correction and punishment worked through individual bodies and their display. We individually and collectively hold up a real or metaphorical mirror to survey and scrutinize our hairy heads, faces and bodies, and understand them not just in terms of what constitutes 'good' and 'bad' hair but also a gendered self. Such processes follow Foucault's regulatory schema: an 'examination' and its mechanisms of classification precede a regime of corrective action—in relation to hair a repertoire of plucking, brushing, waxing, cutting, curling, purging, bleaching and colouring—through which Foucault's idea of the 'docile body-as-project' is performed (1977: 135–7). Hair and its management references and reproduces the gendered body as a whole in relation to specific and culturally legitimated acts of gendered looking; the *sight* of hair serves as the ambiguous vector of the power relations through which the gendered subject is constituted.

VOLUME AND SHINE

According to the traditions of fine art, the unclothed body is represented through a whole series of classical codes, conventions and contexts formalized in relation to vision. The *sight* of this particular sort of body—luminous, smooth and hairless—is realized through what art historian Kenneth Clark terms the 'transmutation of matter into form' (1956: 23). The painterly act of hair removal is the starting point for a work of art and the aesthetic separation of the merely 'naked' from the idealized 'nude'. Drawing on Clark's analysis of this distinction, John Berger's (1972) seminal essay *Ways of Seeing* polemicizes how the female nude is arranged to present herself to an invisible male viewer through a range of visual strategies that emphasize her sense of being surveyed, of being naked not in her own right, but as an 'object of vision: a sight' (Berger 1972: 47). In fine art representations such as Rubens' *The Judgement of Paris* (1639), the visible absence of body hair functions as an elemental part of this specifically female aesthetic body made (imaged) flesh (Figure 8.1). The very nature of the naked female body, 'the surface of one's own skin, the hair of one's own body is turned into a disguise in order to be put on display' (1972: 54).

However, Berger's analysis neglects to emphasize the crucial role played by the removal of body hair within this visual dynamic, and in the constitution of *all* nudes, both male and female. Berger notes only in parenthesis how the European fine art convention of not painting a woman's body hair constitutes a powerful hairy equation: 'Hair is associated with sexual power, with passion. The woman's sexual passion needs to be minimised so that the spectator may feel that he has the monopoly of such passion' (1972: 54–5). Daniela Caselli (2006: 21–2) points out that this highly ambivalent and 'extraordinary' statement is bracketed off from Berger's overall analysis of women's bodies in painting, and reduced

Figure 8.1   Peter Paul Rubens (1577–1640), *The Judgement of Paris*, 1639 (oil on canvas).
Prado, Madrid, Spain/The Bridgeman Art Library.

to a mere self-evident aside. This only further marginalizes the discursive potency of female body hair and the highly problematic nature of its 'exposure'. As Caselli very forcefully argues, it is not so much a case of whether the absence or presence of female body hair is either natural or unnatural, but rather that 'women cannot simply show their body hair, but are forced to expose it' (2006: 20). What Caselli's feminist analysis underscores is how the sight of female body hair—and such exposure in a range of literary and cultural texts as inherently masculine—reveal the mechanisms of gender identification which define the very condition of femininity and masculinity.

It is important to acknowledge therefore that Berger's discussion does not address how the aesthetic transition from subjective physical presence to objective symbolic abstract is not one solely confined to the representation of the unclothed female body (Bryson 1994; Solomon-Godeau 1997). Furthermore, how since the fifth century BCE, the representation of the physically developed male body has equally conformed to a (necessarily different) schematic formula of depilation, which has dominated the history of Western attitudes to the male body (Dutton 1995: 63). Given the significance of facial and body hair as the traditional symbolic marker of masculinity, it might be expected that such idealized 'he-men' be pictured as heavily bearded and hirsute. However, like their female fine art counterparts, these too are bodies 'to-be-looked-at', constituted through strictly formalized concepts of depilated physical beauty. The stakes are not quite the same as sexual difference but are equally high. Hairless, highly developed, super-muscular male bodies become the metaphor of masculine sexual power and its self-transcendence through the symbolic language of High Classicism—and the means by which the naked male body is viewed, interpreted and understood (see Dyer 1988).

THE MEDUSA'S HEAD

The hairless male body, one way or another, diverts or, in Freudian terms, 'sublimates' desire through such traditional aesthetic strategies. Attention is shifted from 'the genitals on to the shape of a body as a whole' by offering 'a possibility of directing some proportion of their libido on to higher artistic aims' (Freud 2001: 156–7). This substitution of a part for a whole, so fundamental to any understanding of the psychodynamic of human hairiness, is also the characteristic mechanism of Freud's idea of the fetish. The powerful psychological and symbolic potential of the fetish hinges on looking, and the 'glance' or sight of something—shiny, hairy, furry, hard—with the capacity to stand in for something else: for Freud, women's castration and, in effect, sexual difference itself.

One of the key symbols invoked by Freud in working through the relationship between sight and unconscious sexuality is the Medusa's head, which is clearly not without significance for this chapter. In the ancient myth, Medusa is famous for her luxuriant long hair. The goddess Minerva, jealous of her rival's superior claim to beauty, converts Medusa's hair into snakes and makes any man who looks at her 'stiff with terror' and turned to stone (Freud 2001: 273). Hair in the form of snakes, according to Freud, effectively mitigates the horror of castration by standing in for women's absence of a penis, and by extension (pun intended) safeguarding the male spectator's possession of one. Medusa's symbolic hair 'offers consolation to the spectator: he is still in possession of a penis, and the stiffening reassures him of the fact' (Freud 2001: 274).

The sight of hair, therefore, assumes a pivotal role in the circulation of sexual power through the aesthetic mechanisms of fetishistic disavowal. In Greek mythology, Medusa is finally conquered through the deflection of her deadly gaze by the reflective surface of Perseus's shield. Richard Dyer highlights the comparative strategies of naked male models whose hairless, pumped-up bodies take on the glossy sheen of polished bronze or marble statuary to ward off the dangers posed by earthbound, but equally potentially threatening, male gazes. These are masculine bodies 'to-be-looked-at', but only through a subconscious process of denial and disavowal: 'The male model looks either off or up … his look suggests an interest in something else that the viewer cannot see' (Dyer 1988: 200). Images of men's heads and hairstyling techniques in barbershop windows or advertising similarly exploit such figurative and spatial strategies (Figure 8.2). Male-on-male looking is isolated and distanced (crucial to Freudian disavowal) through a labyrinth of angled looks and excessive technical detail, or the reassuring presence of classical symbolism in the form of modern-day sporting heroes who are frequently the promotional face of male hair and grooming products.

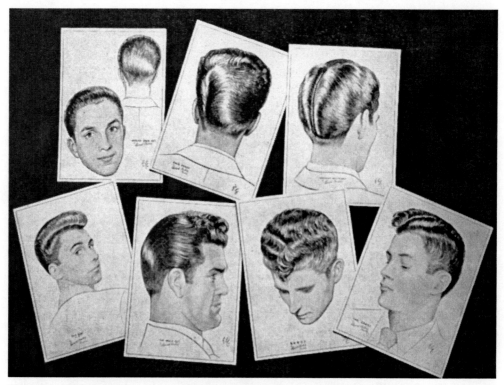

Figure 8.2   Deflecting the gaze: Men's hairstyling for display.
From *Hairdressers' Journal*, 8 April 1954, 11. *Hairdressers' Journal*, www.HJi.co.uk.

Sport and the sporting arena offer the opportunity for men to dissect other men's bodies in fetishistic detail (Miller 1998). In the legitimizing context of gyms and changing rooms and amidst the sporting camaraderie of communal baths and showers the parameters of inter-male surveillance are made clear: just 'Wash N Go' with a single bottle of shampoo; 'Get the Dry Look ... and don't be a stiff' exhorts a Gillette advertisement of the 1970s, the all-too-obvious *double-entendre* emphatically demonstrating hair's fetishistic capacity to serve as the embodied psycho-sexual go-between in ambiguous and potentially threatening visual encounters.

The representation of the naked 'body-as-object' is achieved through the systematic balance between the *knowledge* of hairy physicality and the *sight* of its suppression: in classic Freudian terms, 'I know ... but all the same'. In the depiction of idealized female nudes, the strategic placement of the women's hands, tendrils of her curling or profuse head hair (often emphatically snake-like), small furry domestic animals, shadows, fur and feathers all equally offer the means of fetishized displacement (see MacDonald 2006 for a contemporary discussion of such strategies). This is typified throughout the Western art tradition by the Venus pudica, which originated in Praxiteles' *Knidian Aphrodite* c. 340 BC but was reworked in the revival of classical antiquity in the Renaissance. The female nude covers her pubis in a gesture of shame and modesty but as Nanette Salomon (1996: 73–4) remarks: 'In any reading, the hand that points also covers and that which covers also points. We are, in either case, directed to her pubis, which we are not permitted to see ... We yearn to see that which is withheld. The viewer's shameful desire to see matches the sculpture's "modest" desire not to be seen'. The sexual significance of hair as fetish is not lost but rather emphasized in such ambivalence. Shaved or hairy, the female body as fetish functions as denial, 'produced as the absence of a potential presence' (Lesnik-Oberstein 2006: 9).

'BEHOLD ESAU MY BROTHER A HAIRY MAN ...' (GENESIS, 27:11)

Gendered identity is produced by systems of power and knowledge, and the codes of looking that embody, protect and sustain them; it is defined not necessarily by who is looking at whom, but the conditions under which a gendered repertoire of allowable looking is produced and patrolled. In this way, the sight of hair on the head and on the body continues to reinforce the spectacular power relationship implicit within certain representations by maintaining the illusion of a stable and fixed identity. However, hair's inherent capacity for instability and disruption constantly undermines a subject's sense of a coherent psychic self. Hairy bodies and heads constantly threaten to break out of the closed contextual frames upon which any sense of performative reassurance rests.

Writing in the early 1970s, John Berger argued that the representation of the female nude had essentially remained unchanged for more than 400 years and put forward his now-familiar radical dynamic: 'men act; women appear' (1972: 47). However, since the 1970s there has been a rapid and conspicuous expansion of images of idealized and eroticized male bodies in the media and popular culture (Jobling 1999; Nixon 1996). Such bodies and their representation disrupt Berger's conception of an 'ideal spectator', who can no longer be assumed to be male, nor his gaze solely understood as one confined to a voyeuristic relationship between an active male viewer and a passive female viewed (Berger 1972: 661–4). Significant changes have occurred to challenge traditional 'ways of seeing' and the gender assumptions that went along with it, and can be seen as evidence of a much more ambiguously empowered gendered gaze. And, whilst hairlessness remains the norm, hair has also begun to sprout as if to symbolically register the emergence in popular culture of an erotic body moving towards at least the suggestion of actual rather than symbolic sexual relations.

Courting controversy, Yves Saint Laurent's (YSL) advertisement for the new aftershave M7 appeared in *Vogue* in France in 2002 (Carrell 2002). Shot in black and white, it featured not just a reclining male nude but a very hirsute one with his legs apart and his penis very clearly visible. Yves Saint Laurent's hairy male visual exposure caused uproar—the image was cropped by most of the world's leading magazines—but was followed in swift succession by an image of female pubic hair in Gucci's spring/summer 2003 campaign, photographed by Mario Testino. Referred to as 'the ultimate in branding' by YSL's artistic director Tom Ford (McDowell 2003), the model Louise Pedersen with a young man kneeling at her feet is pictured *flagrante delicto,* with Pedersen pulling her underwear down to reveal her pubic hair shaved into the letter 'G'. Added to this, over the last five or so years a host of young female celebrities have been similarly 'caught' without their knickers (in the current vernacular termed 'going commando'), self-consciously exposing their genitals to the watchful lens of the paparazzi, but with any hint of public hair or genitalia in their resulting photographs concealed by their prepublication pixellation.

The sight of these hairy and not-so-hairy but more explicitly sexualized bodies has generated much media discussion and been seen by some as heralding a new era of spectacular gendered display. For example the YSL ad was hailed as the antidote to the progressive feminization of the male body in contemporary culture: 'the waxed, buffed and manicured male body is *démodé,* and the rough, hairy beast is back … that reeks of nothing more than testosterone and Brut' (Sherwood 2004). Gucci's ad too, supposedly 'hit the G Spot' of the contemporary female consumer; Colin McDowell (2003) writing for *The Sunday Times* described it as not only a rare example of irony in advertising, but also one of female sexual empowerment: 'even at a glance she is the one in charge'. Barbara Ellen (2006) calls the new female celebrity flashers the 'Daughters of Sharon', after Sharon Stone's famous 'flash' in the film *Basic Instinct* (1992), and similarly finds such acts 'interesting and powerful'. Ellen's particular focus is the pop star Britney Spears, 'freshly liberated from her duff marriage, swanning around … in what appeared to be a frontless dress teamed with no knickers'. For Ellen, the two are inextricably linked: Spears's emancipation from the need to wear knickers somehow symbolizes freedom from the shackles of (failed) marriage and contemporary feminine independence in general.

BETES NOIRS AND PIXELLATED PUDICA

It is, however, perhaps premature to equate the profusion of more explicitly sexual bodies of both sexes, and a few stray hairs, as an indication of a new sexual equality in the field of vision. Foucault (1977, 1979) argues that seeing, or looking, and the pleasures involved in looking, are always historically contingent and part of a whole system of socially legitimated, culturally coded discursive strategies. As much as any radical advance, the controversial ads for YSL and Gucci, and the female celebrity 'shaves and shows' (and non-shows) arguably offer only further demonstration of the historical continuity of traditional visual paradigms—and additional reinforcement of the consistency of hair's spectacular regulation in relation to gender. Such forms of hairy display are not without aesthetic significance—nor historical precedent.

In classical antiquity the depiction of hairier, more animalistic fauns, and 'sleeping' satyrs or well-built rural youths 'caught' in naturalistic repose, were always characterized by a 'more openly carnal treatment' (Figure 8.3); these figures marked 'the entry into the senior art of sculpture of a frank sexuality' and are frequently imitated in gay iconography (Dutton 1995: 42). In the M7 advertisement, YSL's use of the unknown martial arts champion Samuel de Cubber, with his hairy body and splayed legs, 'discovered' on the beach by Tom Ford (*Hello*, 2002), clearly references this aesthetic repertoire of erotic gestural poses and their more contemporary refiguration. The objectified narcissistic male body is one that has arguably been 'progressively queered in fashion photography' (Jobling 1999: 145), but an explicitly hairy one also takes on new meaning with the expanding spectacular social spaces of contemporary gay male culture (see also Chapter 7). Web sites and message boards celebrate hirsute gay men known as 'bears'. These sites offer descriptions with detailed scientific precision of a range of classes and sub-classes of bears, differentiated according to age and/or build ('Cubs, Daddy Bears, Polar Bears, Grizzlies'); ethnicity ('Black Bears'); body size (thinner hirsute men—'Otters and Wolves') that all offer an alternative embodied gay male identity (Monaghan 2005).

Yves Saint Laurent's advertisement purports to push the boundaries of contemporary taste and offer up a new visual schema of masculinity. However, just like the smooth muscle-bound heroes of antiquity, the sight of de Cubber's hairy body and suggestive attitude is not one that can be unequivocally assigned as a site of visual pleasure for an active heterosexual female gaze. Fashion journalist James Sherwood (2004) on the one hand celebrates the return of 'the chest rug' and its progenitor Tom Ford (himself equally 'displaying impressive chest-hair cleavage'), but on the other compares the 'shock of seeing major chest hair on a 50ft billboard in Times Square' with that of seeing 'underarm hair displayed in *Vogue*'. But perhaps that is the point. The new celebration of the former but continued vilification of the latter only underlines the unequal sexual equation that still constitutes the gender politics of hairy vision.

Differently culturally constituted hairy bodies continue to symbolically broker the visual deal between explicit signals of earth-bound sexuality and their gendered embodiment. The sight of Pedersen's supposedly ironically shaved bush and the growing band of female commandos, like that of the hairy Samuel de Cubber and his appendage, offers at least the possibility of an alternative trajectory of female looking, both straight and gay (Lewis and Rolley 1997). However, with their roots, like de Cubber's, equally secured in traditional

Figure 8.3   *Sleeping Satyr,* Roman copy of a Hellenistic original of the third century BC (bronze).
Museo Archeologico Nazionale, Naples, Italy/The Bridgeman Art Library.

visual paradigms as well as the continued understanding of the hairy female body as the literal and metaphorical *bete noir* of idealized feminine sexuality (Casseli 2006), sight and knowledge once more disrupts any such easy equation being made. The figure of the Venus pudica came to define femininity and feminine sexuality through the implicit 'sight' of the visibly absent genitals (Salomon 1996) and the collusive knowledge of their concealment.

This functioned as the ambiguous mechanism of fetishistic and aesthetic displacement. Sadly mistaking new forms of digital manipulation for sexual potency, Gucci's carefully crafted pubes, and the pixellation of the new commandos, only succeed in constituting a post-modern Venus pudica: directing the gaze to the non-sight of female pubic hair—in Freudian terms decisive affirmation in itself of the nonthreatening nature of their symbolic power and the annulment of any risk of castration (Benson 1994: 111).

The current focus in contemporary visual culture on the transgressive potential of hairier and more explicitly sexualized naked bodies obscures the dynamic process of objectification that literally en-genders such looking in the first place, with very different implications for men and women. It is the hairy female body that remains a cultural taboo (Lesnik-Oberstein 2006), the site not of 'natural' femininity but its proscriptive lack. Pumped up and hairless or satyr-ically hairy, the naked male body remains a symbol, not just of the idealized sexual subject, but of the psychic boundaries that allow it to be visualized in the first place, and the asymmetrical masquerade of gender and gendered looking that the masculine imagination patrols and proscribes.

As further reinforcement it is interesting to note the even greater media furor that greeted Britney Spears's shaving of her own head in a Los Angeles hair salon (the professionals refused to carry out the cut). Amidst media speculation on her career decline, allegations of substance abuse and her very acrimonious divorce and custody battles, Spear's shaved head was pathologized as a form of mental illness, the external physical marker of her internal psychological turmoil (see for example Harris 2007). Spears's earlier going without underwear symbolized, for some, female emancipation; but the press coverage of her drastic tonsure revealed the proscriptive boundaries of idealized femininity articulated in hair conformity—and the price to be paid for their mutual betrayal.

PROBLEM HAIR

Always potentially beyond control, sexuality and its hairy embodiment remains an ambivalent mix of internal and external, psychical and physical, that must constantly be regulated to be sustained. In the nineteenth century, the philosopher John Ruskin reputedly fainted at the sight of his wife's pubis on their wedding night. Overwhelmed by the reality of an obviously hairy sexual body, quite different from those inhabiting the Elysian groves of his aesthetic imagination, the marriage was never consummated (Cooper 1971: 88). The hairy female body reveals the enduring and always potentially threatening nature of a lack of aesthetic qualities and consequential loss of male composure. Its historically consistent disavowal reveals what ultimately must never be seen: the power of transgressive female sexuality, and the impossibility of the phallus. John Rajchman, in his discussion of Foucault argues that:

> Foucault's hypothesis was that there exists a sort of 'positive unconscious' of vision which determines not what is seen but what can be seen. His idea is that not all ways of visualizing or rendering visible are possible at once. A period only lets some things be

seen and not others. It 'illuminates' some things and so casts others in the shade. There is much more regularity, much more *constraint,* in what we can see than we suppose. (Rajchman 1988: 391)

Hair and hairless-ness are not just the effect of a psychically and socially produced 'look'; the sight or concealment of hair functions to sanction such looking in the first place by providing a masculine comfort zone of aesthetic pleasure. Whoever is looking at whomever, hair remains the performative focus of a highly fragile and uncertain masculine subjectivity. The sight of hair, therefore, continues to function as a vital catalyst in the gendered politics of vision, and the enduring relationship between hair, gender and looking signals the very tenuous nature of its idealized negotiation.

BIBLIOGRAPHY

Benson, P. (1994), 'Freud and the Visual', *Representations,* 45 (Winter): 101–16.

Berger, J. (1972), *Ways of Seeing,* London: Penguin Books.

Bryson, M. (1994), 'Gericault and Masculinity' in N. Bryson, M. A. Holly and K. Moxey (eds.), *Visual Culture: Images and Interpretations,* Middletown, CT: Wesleyan University Press.

Butler, J. (1992), *Gender Trouble: Feminism and the Subversion of Identity,* New York: Routledge.

Carrell, S. (2002), 'YSL Ad to Feature Britain's First Full-frontal Male Nude', *Independent on Sunday,* 10 November, 11.

Caselli, D. (2006), '"The Wives of Geniuses I Have Sat With": Body Hair, Genius and Modernity', in K. Lesnik-Oberstein (ed), *The Last Taboo: Women and Body Hair,* Manchester and New York: Manchester University Press.

Clark, K. (1956), *The Nude,* London and New York: Penguin Books.

Cooper, W. (1971), *Hair: Sex, Society, Symbolism,* London: Aldus Books.

Dutton, R. (1995), *The Perfectible Body: The Western Ideal of Male Physical Development,* London: Cassell.

Dyer, R. (1988), 'Don't Look Now', in A. McRobbie (ed), *Zoot Suits and Second-hand Dresses: An Anthology of Fashion and Music,* Boston: Unwin Hyman.

Ellen, B. (2006), 'Female Celebrities Going Commando', *The Observer,* 3 December, 5.

Featherstone, M., Hepworth, M. and Turner, B. (eds.) (1991), *The Body: Social Process and Cultural Theory,* London: Sage Publications.

Foucault, M. (1977), *Discipline and Punish,* Harmondsworth: Penguin Books.

Foucault, M. (1979), *The History of Sexuality,* vol. 1; *Introduction,* Harmondsworth: Penguin Books.

Foucault, M. (1985), *The History of Sexuality,* vol. 2; *The Uses of Pleasure,* New York: Vintage Books.

Foucault, M. (1986), *The History of Sexuality,* vol. 3; *The Care of the Self,* Harmondsworth: Penguin Books.

Freud, S. (2001), 'Fetishism', in *Three Essays on the Theory of Sexuality,* London: Pelican Freud Library, vol. 7.

Hall, S. and Du Gay, P. (eds.) (1996), *Questions of Cultural Identity,* London and Thousand Oaks, CA: Sage Publications.

Hallpike, C. R. (1969), 'Social Hair', *Man,* 4: 256–64.

Harris, P. (2007), 'Months of Wild Partying. And Now Britney Shears in Public', *The Observer,* 18 February, 2.

Hello. (2002), 'YSL Causes a Stir with Full-Frontal Nude', 24 October, http://www.hellomagazine. com/fashion/2002/10/24/tomford/.

Jobling, P. (1999), *Fashion Spreads: Word and Image in Fashion Photography since 1980,* New York and Oxford: Berg.

Knight, I. (1999), 'Winning by a Whisker', *The Sunday Times,* May 2, 7.

Lesnik-Oberstein, K. (2006), 'The Last Taboo: Women, Body Hair and Feminism', in K. Lesnik-Oberstein (ed), *The Last Taboo: Women and Body Hair,* Manchester and New York: Manchester University Press.

Lewis, R. and Rolley K. (1997), '(Ad)Dressing the Dyke, Lesbian Looks and Lesbians Looking', in M. Nava, A. Blake, I. Macrory and B. Richards (eds.), *Buy This Book: Studies in Advertising and Consumption,* London: Routledge.

London Metro (2006), 'Ugly Side of Dating', 14 May, 9.

MacDonald, A. (2006), 'Hairs on the Lens: Female Body Hair on the Screen', in K. Lesnik-Oberstein (ed), *The Last Taboo: Women and Body Hair,* Manchester and New York: Manchester University Press.

McDowell, C. (2003), 'Fashion Hits the G Spot, and the Funny Bone', *The Sunday Times,* 19 January, http://www.timesonline.co.uk/tol/news/article813869.ece.

Middleton, J. (2006), 'Bearded Patriarchs', *History Today,* 56 (2), February, 26–7.

Miller, T. (1998), 'Commodifying the Male Body, Problematizing "Hegemonic Masculinity"?', *Journal of Sport and Social Issues,* 22: 431–46.

Monaghan, L. F. (2005), 'Big Handsome Men, Bears and Others: Virtual Constructions of "Fat Male Embodiment"', *Body and Society,* 11 (2): 81–111.

Morris, D. (1978), *Manwatching: A Field Guide to Human Behaviour,* London: Triad Panther.

Morris, D. (1987), *Bodywatching: A Field Guide to the Human Species,* London: Grafton Books.

Nixon, S. (1996), *Hard Looks: Masculinities, Spectatorship and Contemporary Consumption,* London: UCL Press.

Powell, M. K. and Roach, J. (2004), 'Big Hair', *Eighteenth Century Studies,* 38 (1): 79–99.

Rajchman, J. (1988), 'Foucault's Art of Seeing', *October,* 4 (Spring): 88–117.

Salomon, N. (1996), 'The Venus Pudica: Uncovering Art History's "Hidden Agendas" and Pernicious Pedigrees', in G. Pollock (ed), *Generations and Geographies in the Visual Arts,* London and New York: Routledge: 69–88.

Sherwood, J. (2004), 'Hair's Looking at You Kid: The Chest Rug Is Back', *The Independent,* 18 February, 2.

Solomon-Godeau, A. (1997), *Male Trouble: A Crisis in Representation,* London and New York: Thames and Hudson.

Synnott, A. (1987), 'Shame and Glory: A Sociology of Hair', *British Journal of Sociology,* 38 (3): 381–413.

Synnott, A. (1993), *The Body Social: Symbolism, Self and Society,* London and New York: Routledge.

9 MEN'S FACIAL HAIR IN ISLAM
A MATTER OF INTERPRETATION

FAEGHEH SHIRAZI

In many cultures beards are sometimes treated with great care and veneration. Men's facial hair in Islam falls within a host of issues related to Muslim masculinity. These include defining cultural and religious markers that signal 'masculine' identity and behaviour, as well as determining the consequences of these markers. Although a paucity of scholarship exists in Muslim masculine topics relative to those on Muslim femininity and women's rights (Moghadam 2007; Kamrava 2006; El-Azhary Sonbol 2005; Mir-Hosseini 1999; Beck and Nashat 2004), Muslim masculinity is gaining more attention.

Peter Hopkins's (2006) study of young Muslim masculinities uses narratives and generational relationships of Pakistani men living in Scotland, revealing how young Muslim men's masculinities are not only influenced by markers of social differences, but also by locality, making their masculinity multifaceted. Vivinder Kalra (2005) focuses on the *pagh* (Sikh turban) and the beard as a symbol of manhood that is mistaken for Muslim identity. Kalra

Figure 9.1 A young man's fashionable hairstyle and beard in the 1980s.
This example is from the album of a barber in Tehran, Iran. 1986.

Figure 9.2   Two Iranian officials in accepted and typical beards and moustaches. 2005.

demonstrates how Balbir Singh Sodhi, a Sikh man, was murdered because his outward appearance (beard and turban) associated him with the destruction of the World Trade Center in September 11, 2001. My own study of beards and turbans also examines how in contemporary Iran, the historical influences of Shi'i Islam affect male grooming habits that are filled with symbolic messages. 'Like other visual signifiers, a man's facial hair as well as his clothing often carries certain non-verbal cues that may be more meaningful than actual words exchanged in conversation' (Shirazi 2007: 161) (Figures 9.1 and 9.2).

This chapter examines the issue of men's facial hair within the context of Islam. I will be looking at historical and contemporary influences, and also briefly addressing the practices and beliefs of other religions regarding this issue to demonstrate that men's facial hair is of importance in most religious practices and is not exclusive to Islam. However, the primary interest of this chapter is to explore how societal rules and Islamic traditions regarding facial grooming impact the experience of Muslim men. Examples will be drawn from Iran, Afghanistan, Pakistan, Turkey and Uzbekistan in order to explore the underlying significance of this issue.

A CULTURAL MARKER

In different religious groups, the presence or absence of facial hair holds distinct meanings. For example, among the Amish, beards indicate marital status. Amish men are not allowed to grow moustaches. Married Amish men must wear full beards known as 'the chin curtain' and dress in black (Hostetler 1995: 218). The Amish read Psalm 133:2 as a sure sign that the beard is associated with godliness. Mennonites strictly regulate men's facial hair. For the Mennonite, pacifism is all-important and is characterized by a bare upper lip, and Anabaptist Mennonites are decidedly opposed to beard cutting (Umble 1953). In the New Testament, the apostle Paul teaches that it is shameful for men to wear long hair; neither are women to cut their hair (Corinthians II). In Mosaic law (the law of Moses), one is admonished (as a matter of conscience) not to mar the corner of one's beard. Mosaic law, regarding the cutting of one's hair and beard, is based upon the fundamentals of nature. This means that if God did not plan for man to have a beard he would not grow one. The beard is also a major aspect of Hasidic Judaism as are the forelocks. Following an Old Testament interdiction not to shave the sides of the face, most Hasidic males wear long, uncut sideburns called *payoth*[1] (Ashkenazi Hebrew *peyos,* Yiddish *peyes*). The Torah states, 'You shall not round off the *peyos* of your head' (Leviticus 19:27).

Members of the Sikh community also place great importance on both facial and body hair. Because hair is among God's creations, it should be preserved, maintained and respected. Most male adult Sikhs never cut their long hair and wear a peaked turban as a partial covering. Devout Sikhs also eschew trimming their beards, preferring instead to comb, twist and tuck facial hair into their turbans. Sikhs consider the beard to be intertwined with the nobility and dignity of manhood.

When a boy experiences the first growth of facial hair, it is universally acknowledged that he is leaving childhood behind and moving towards maturity. Facial hair presents the young male with multiple options. He may choose to shave completely, shave partially, shape, dye or divide his facial hair into different sections, or even add objects of adornment such as beads, rings, ribbons or rubber bands (I have seen young men tying their bushy beards with rubber bands at the University of Texas). The choices made in grooming one's facial hair may indicate social or personal status, religious or sect practices, or affiliation with a particular political, cultural or social group.

Social cognition studies demonstrate that people tend to judge others on physical appearance, coupled with previous knowledge (including cultural stereotyping) (Kaiser 1990). For example, during the 1970s, men wearing 'beards and long hair were associated with a liberal world view ... [And] were perceived as not only more open-minded, but also more educated, intelligent, outgoing, and reckless than a clean-shaven male' (Pancer and Meindl 1978: 1328).

In one culture, to be clean-shaven may equate with a strong work ethic while in another, clean-shaven faces may be identified with Satan. For Muslims, there are various opinions on the issue of the beard. These range from traditions of the Prophet of Islam that one must follow, to the view that the Prophet's sayings on beards are merely recommendations that are not obligatory (Syed [2008]). Still others stress the importance of historical context in the origins of the Islamic beard issue, when the Prophet Mohammad may have been seeking to visually distinguish Muslims from the surrounding non-Muslims (Al-Qaradawi 2002). Therefore, with *hadith* (recorded sayings of the Prophet), fundamentalist interpretations are pitched against contextual readings in the arguments surrounding the growing of facial hair.

ISLAMIC INTERPRETATIONS

Islamic scholars, clerics and experts on *sharia* (Islamic religious law) do not agree on the issue of shaving. Those who argue against shaving refer to the following Qur'anic verse (*Al Nisa* 4: 119) in which God curses Satan. In response, Satan promises to take revenge on human beings:

> I will mislead them,
> And I will create
> In them false desires. I will
> Order them to slit the ears
> Of cattle, and to deface
> The (fair) nature created by God ...

The key phrase here is 'to deface the (fair) nature created by God.' In other words, one is not to change or alter what God has created. Shaving facial hair, then, is interpreted as entrapment in Satan's web. This ultra-orthodox interpretation is used to forbid both men and women from removing facial and/or body hair. As I will discuss later, other equally important sources such as *ahadith* (plural of *hadith*) tend to contradict this conservative Qur'anic interpretation.

Hassan Safavi argues against the conservative interpretation and challenges the assertion that any changes made in God's original creation is *haram* (forbidden by Islam). If this were so, how could one justify the act of circumcision, the cutting of umbilical cords, clipping nails or ritually shaving a man's hair during the holy *hajj* (pilgrimage) to Mecca? Thus Safavi concludes that the orthodox interpretation is illogical; removing hair from one's body can hardly be an example of dishonouring God's creation (Safavi 1961: 21). Safavi (1961: 26) further explains that during the Persian Sassanid Empire[2] (226–651), an era in which Zoroastrianism prevailed, strict religious rules required men to wear facial hair and to keep it clean and well-groomed. When a man committed a crime, he was 'paraded' or exposed in public with a shaven face. In time, Muslims adopted this same strategy of shaming, so that a man's facial hair became synonymous with his masculinity, integrity and power. A man's beard eventually came to symbolize honesty. One could swear by his beard or pledge it for the payment of a debt. Even today one can refer to a bond of kinship or family member using the Persian expression *ham rish,* meaning 'from the same beard.'

Persian culture dates to the earliest periods of human civilization. Around 650 CE, the Arab conquest carried Islam to Persia (including what is now the Islamic Republic of Iran). Ancient coins and engraved archaeological monuments dating from this era all point to the fact that in pre-Islamic Persia, men not only wore shoulder-length hair but also had full beards and moustaches. Thus the tendency of men to grow facial hair was already set, centuries prior to the introduction of Islam into Persian culture.

In today's patriarchal Iranian culture, following the example of Ayatollah Khomeni, all of the clergy are bearded. In contrast to the Shah's clean-shaven regime, which ended in 1978 and which is now vilified as effeminate, the conservative bearded clerics set the stage for a hyper-masculine culture. According to Shahin Gerami, 'the revolutionary ideologies and the Republic leaders glorified new masculinity types: the mullahs became the leaders of revolution, martyrs its soul, and men its beneficiaries' (Gerami 2003: 264).

Carol Delaney (1994: 159–72) points to the symbolic meaning of hair in relationship to the religious ritual of *hajj* (the Muslim pilgrimage to the holy city of Mecca). She notes that during the actual *hajj* men let their beards grow. However, the male pilgrim, called *hajji*, must participate in prerequisite grooming activities to prepare for *ihram* (a state of sacredness in which a Muslim performs *hajj*). This is essentially a beautification for God and includes the male cleaning himself (*ghusl*), dying his nails with henna and putting on non-alcoholic perfume. Finally, he will shave his head, have his beard trimmed, and nails cut. Grooming the beard at this point is usually suspended for the next fourteen days, or until he finishes the *hajj*. To engage in further grooming of facial hair would imply that one's mind remains absorbed in worldly matters instead of being focused entirely on Allah (God). Normal life resumes for all pilgrims upon their return home.

At this point men can once again let their beards grow. However, they are obligated to stay balanced in their grooming habits; they must not pay too much or too little attention to the maintenance of facial hair (Figure 9.3). This insistence on moderation has always been a safe practice, as evident in the writings of Mohammad Baqir Majlisi (1993: 87–90), a sixteenth-century Shi'i cleric from Iran who confirms that shaving one's hair was considered shameful in early Islam. Pre-Islamic Arabs were not used to shaving, having associated the practice with punishment for a crime and subsequent public humiliation. Majlisi's texts

Figure 9.3　A religious scholar in the typical style of beard and moustache.
Note how well-kept and trimmed the facial hair is. 2007.

contain a wealth of detailed information on the subject of hair, including references to various types of combs. He even recommends the specific number of times a man must comb his beard or hair in order to keep it neat and presentable.

The following are my translations from Majlisi's *Huliyat al Motaqin* (1993: 87–90) of the sections related to hair and facial hair. The reader should keep in mind that sixteenth-century superstitions and curative remedies were often intermixed with popular religious practices. I am including this important document because the Islamic Republic of Iran tends to follow Majlisi's norm as a recommended model for men in contemporary Iran.

On the matter of shaving hair and its etiquette

Imam Musa stated: I shave my hair every Friday ... if one shaves the back of his hair he will feel happy. If a man's hair grows too long it may affect his eyesight [weaken it]. As long as hair is kept short, the eyes will twinkle. When shaving, it is recommended to face the Qibla [direction towards Mecca]; begin shaving from the front of the forehead towards the back of ears.

If a man wants to let his hair grow, it is best to train the hair to part in the middle. He must wash his hair regularly, comb it to keep it neat and maintain a short length by regular trimming.

On the matter of trimming a moustache and its etiquette

The term *sharp gereftan* means to trim the hair that grows on a man's upper lip [trimming very close to the skin]. This is the tradition of the Prophet of Islam. Prophet Mohammad said do not let your moustache grow long because Satan may hide in it. Trimming one's moustache should be done every Friday [once a week].

On the matter of growing a beard and its etiquette

A proper beard should not be too long or too short. The *ulama* [religious scholars] claim that shaving one's beard is *haram*, religiously forbidden. However, to shave both sides of the lower lip is religiously sanctioned, although not so closely that the skin becomes smooth. It is said that any beard that is too long [exceeding the length recommended by the Prophet] will be burned in the fire of hell on the Day of Judgement. It is recommended to clip one's beard in order to reduce the bush effect but be careful not to clip too much. It is recommended to clip the long beard from the sides to make it neat in appearance. It is believed that when Adam repented and asked forgiveness from God, he asked God to make him look more pleasing in appearance. Since God accepted his repentance and became pleased with him, God gave him a black beard. Since Adam had not had a beard before, he was surprised and asked God, 'My Lord, what is this [facial hair]?' God said: 'This is your ornament, as well as the ornament of your men and your children until the Day of Judgement' ... It is also said do not touch your beard too much while in public. This bad habit will detract from a man's good behaviour and presentation.

Those Muslims who believe that *sharia* (Islamic law) requires a man to wear a beard also base their argument on another set of writings, the *hadith* of the Prophet in the Al Bukhari collections known as *Sahih Al Bukhari*. In Volume VII one reads the following regarding the beard and moustache:

#780. Narrated Nafi: Ibn 'Umar said, 'The Prophet said, "Do the opposite of what the pagans do. Keep the beards and cut the moustaches short"'. Whenever Ibn 'Umar performed the Hajj or 'Umra [Muslim's pilgrimage to holy city of Mecca], he used to hold his beard with his hand and cut whatever remained outside his hold.

#776. Narrated Ibn 'Umar: The Prophet said, 'To cut the moustache short is characteristic of Fitra' [Literally translates to 'human nature' but religious scholars agree that here it means a pattern and tradition of the Prophet].

#779. Narrated Abu Huraira: I heard the Prophet saying, 'Five practices are characteristic of the Fitra: Circumcision, shaving pubic hair, cutting the moustache short, clipping the nails, and depilating armpit hair'.

Chapter 60, Book VII. Ibn 'Umar used to cut his moustache so short that the whiteness of his skin (above the upper lip) was visible, and he used to cut (the hair) between his moustache and beard.

#781. Narrated Ibn 'Umar: Allah's Apostle said, 'Cut the moustache short and leave the beard (as it is)'.

Depending on the geopolitics and cultural traditions of various Muslim factions, these recorded statements can be interpreted differently at different times even within the same region. As noted in *hadith* #780, ''Umar used to hold his beard with his hand and cut whatever remained outside his hold'. I interpret this statement to be a clear indication of what was religiously allowed in terms of the length of a man's beard: no longer than the width of a man's fist (holding the beard).

If so, then one questions how extremist Muslim groups like the Taliban can justify ignoring this recommendation? How do Taliban members conclude, based on the *ahadith* (from *Al Bukhari*), that men's moustaches and beards should remain intact and that grooming facial hair is an irreligious act? It is possible that the radical Islamists who insist that no man should trim his beard are confused between Islam as religion and Islam as culture, insisting on what is cultural as a religious requirement. Ayatollah Shaykh Mohammad Redha Tabasi (a twentieth-century Shi'i scholar) states the following regarding the issue of shaving. '[The] beard is man's facial decoration, which gives him a higher status than that of a woman' (Tabasi 1974: 41). Tabasi believes that shaving facial hair not only goes against the tradition of Islam, but is in fact considered *haram* (religiously forbidden). Sheik Yusuf Al-Qaradawi,[3] for example, discusses three different religious opinions on the beard issue, while Sheik Ahmad Kutty believes that one can be a good Muslim without a beard (Al-Qaradawi 2002; Syed [2008]). It is important to remember that in most patriarchal societies, facial hair is a sign of manhood—something that a woman is not blessed with—thus shaving this blessed sign perhaps signifies a departure from 'manhood'.

FUNDAMENTALIST OPINION ON BEARDS

Presently, in Muslim countries such as Iran and Pakistan, and in North African Muslim nations, the beard has become synonymous with Islamic fundamentalism. Young men wear beards to express their piety and religious commitment to Islam. The beard may be useful as a marker of authority regarding Islamic knowledge. This phenomenon emerged particularly after fundamentalists seized power in the Islamic Republic of Iran. The younger male generation began to wear facial hair in support of the new Islamic regime. It is not unreasonable to assume that many young men joined the 'bearded bandwagon' to secure their own physical safety, and to avoid being accused or labelled as *un-Islamic.*

Today the beard is considered mandatory among radical Islamists. After sweeping to power more than four years ago, the Taliban announced that growing a beard was compulsory for all males. To coerce Muslim men to their way of thinking, Mullah Mohammad Omar[4] of the Taliban issued an extraordinary decree in 2005 which was pasted at the gates of government buildings in the Afghan capital of Kabul. The decree stated that all male citizens without beards would *not* be considered as applicants for jobs and would be denied services. Afghan citizens were also intimidated by the following *fatwa* (religious decree) displayed as graffiti on walls throughout Kabul: 'Growing a beard is the tradition of Islam's Prophet Mohammad and must be followed by Muslims'.

The primary objective of radical movements such as the Taliban is to 'purify' Islam. These movements, emerging from religious schools or *Madressahs* primarily in Pakistan, have drawn criticism not only from the West but also from some Islamic countries for their unreasonable policies, restrictions on the activities of women and fear-based techniques in the manipulation of Muslim men's appearance. Not only has Afghanistan tangled itself in this 'bearded web' but neighbouring Pakistan has also followed suit. In 2007, at Khar, along the Pakistan-Afghanistan border, barbershops were targeted with bombs when their owners refused to follow Taliban orders and stop shaving beards. A regular customer was reported as saying: 'I am a Muslim and I know that no one can force me to shave or not to shave. This should be my decision ... But I was threatened. They asked if I will obey the new laws; I will obey because I am afraid' (Yusufzaim and Grisanti 2007).

Another news report by the *Pakistan Daily Times* (2007) included the following:

> After Dir and Bajaur, barbers in Mardan have also received letters from a purported jihadi outfit to stop shaving beards. Sana hairdresser, a barbershop in the Par Hoti area, has received a letter from an organisation called Tanzeemul Mujahideen NWFP, warning barbers that they should stop shaving beards, otherwise their shops would be set on fire or bombed. The letter reads: 'Our beloved Muslim brothers, listen and listen attentively and then think over it that shaving off beards is a great sin.

This (beard) is the Sunnah of our beloved Prophet (PBUH), but regretfully we have
been shaving it off and throwing these blessed hairs at dirty places, which is a shame.'

Pronouncements such as this, elevating a man's beard to such a lofty position, miss the
original intent of the Prophet Mohammad's *hadith*. Thankfully, the fundamentalist
interpretation is not the only one accepted among Muslims. When Al Bukhari's *hadith*
is placed in historical context, the reader more easily understands why Muslims needed
to distinguish themselves clearly from non-Muslims. The beard was an easy and quick
visual marker. In that particular place and at that specific time in the early Islamic era, the
Prophet faced significant opposition from various Arab tribes. These tribes were in constant
battle with the Prophet and his followers. Perhaps restrictions regarding a man's beard and
moustache grew out of security concerns, a need for quick identification of friend or foe,
and not from any specific religious precepts. Indeed, the Qur'an does not seem to concern
itself with hirsute issues regarding men or women.

The majority opinion of the four major Sunni schools of jurisprudence states that growing a beard is mandatory for every man, unless he can produce a medical justification
for not doing so. The exception is the Shafi'i branch of Sunni Islam, which includes two
equally valid opinions: one stating that a beard is required and one stating that a beard is
Sunnah Mu'akadah (an example set by the Prophet, but not required). Minority opinions
exist in all four schools declaring that the beard is optional, yet virtuous.

Today it is not uncommon for practising male Muslims in both Islamic nations and
Western countries to grow beards or moustaches, and to consider doing so an act of piety
and religiosity. Naturally Muslims want to follow the Prophet's actions; here was a man
proclaimed as the 'walking Qur'an' (he knew the entire Qur'an by heart). Muslims try their
utmost to follow the teachings of the Qur'an as well as to emulate the Prophet. Since the
Prophet wore a beard, many Muslim men choose to do the same.

Each Islamic sect sanctions different religious opinions regarding facial hair. For example, one sect may sanction the use of henna to dye one's beard. Another may proscribe the
required length of a man's beard down to the most elaborate details. Such details assume
greater significance under the dictate of Islamic fundamentalists, as previously noted from
reports in Pakistan and Afghanistan.

In most Muslim cultures, a properly groomed beard signifies authority in religious matters, as well as authority that comes with wisdom, maturity and age. Many elderly members
of Muslim communities feel they have earned this right; it is their prerogative to wear a
beard. Young males in these same communities who also wear beards may be too quick to
assume a prestigious status; as a result, they are sometimes viewed as disrespectful, rebel-
lious and engaging in a sacrilegious practice (Delaney, 1994).

Contrary to fundamentalist Islam are those Muslim nations pursuing secular political agendas. Nations such as Uzbekistan and Turkey face very different challenges regarding the issue of men's facial hair. The Republic of Uzbekistan, a former Soviet satellite
nation, placed limits on Uzbek religious freedom following independence. The secular

government's legislation restricts any activities considered Islamic, and the activities of the police in forcing men to shave off their beards has become a matter for human rights organizations (Simpson, 1989: 135).

In Turkey, especially, the moustache is a social, cultural and political mainstay, as journalist Chris Morris (1998) reveals:

> [in Turkey] you don't wear your politics on your sleeve here. There's no need. It's right slap bang in the middle of your face. Take the full-grown moustache, for example, with down-turned ends at the corner of the mouth. The owner is definitely a right wing nationalist. Then there's the classic small brush moustache, apparently struggling to survive on the lip. It has to belong to a follower of political Islam, like the former Prime Minister Necmettin Erbakan, who's now been banned from politics. The goatee, as you might expect, is reserved for intellectuals, while a longer moustache, drooping over the upper lip to touch the lower one, well, that's the sure sign of an old-fashioned leftist.

According to Morris, facial hair is a reliable signifier of political affiliation. From the urbane Istanbul-style moustache 'which barely touches in the middle' to the nostalgic 'twirly-ended [moustache that symbolizes] a yearning for the Ottoman past,' a Turk's moustache reveals much about the man and his perspective.

Turkey's secular government, opposed to outward shows of Islamic fervour, has provided civil servants with detailed instructions as to how to trim facial hair. These legislative guidelines clearly forbid government employees from wearing the type of beard and specific style of moustache identified with Islam. The officially sanctioned moustache has to be clipped straight and must end above the upper lip. The official governmental restriction on shape, length and style of moustache also extends to Turkey's university students. Male students are forbidden to grow 'a beard altogether. It's just too Islamic' (Morris, 1998). Quite expectedly, such personal grooming dictates are resisted by many. Morris records that thousands of Istanbul University students demonstrated against these governmental facial hair restrictions.

In addition to the significance of shaving in terms of religious piety, or political affiliations, it is obvious that the beard also carries symbolic meanings in terms of sexuality in both the historical setting as well as at the beginning of the twenty-first century. The social issue of prostitution had created a dilemma for the Turkish government, following the fall of the Soviet Union when numerous prostitutes began pouring into Turkey. After many failed attempts on the part of the Turkish government to control prostitute trafficking, one Turk began thinking 'outside the box'. Recalling how criminals had been punished in pre-Islamic days, the governor of the eastern province of Igdir announced that: 'Any man caught having sex with a prostitute will get his beard and mustache shaved off, and then be exposed for all to see in the city's main square' (Boulware, 2000). It is interesting to note that beards in both fundamentalist and secularist perspectives are used to regulate a man's behaviour, to punish or to reward.

CONCLUSION

In Islam and in other religions, a man's facial hair is an object of preoccupation, providing clues to his godliness and revealing much about the extent of his religious beliefs. Although at times the significance of facial hair may be transcultural, more frequently, it is culturally specific. Like every other religious group, Islam tends to be partially defined by its fundamentalist members who represent extremist positions, often interpreting sacred texts to support male patriarchy and dominance. For example, the Afghanistan Taliban's interpretation of Islamic religious texts and recorded opinions of religious scholars in relation to men's facial hair is based on its own patriarchal and contemporary cultural understanding of this symbol of manhood. When taken out of historical context, the Prophet's teachings and traditions on male facial hair practices lose their socio-cultural meanings.

Hair is almost universally used as a marker to signify membership, status, authority or a degree of religious piety. However, nowhere in the religious literature is it stated that every Muslim man must grow a beard. The moderate Islamic perspective holds that while growing a beard is generally considered a virtuous act, it is *not* mandatory. Thus Muslims who *do* shave recognize that Islam lies deep in the heart of a man rather than hidden in between the locks of his beard.

NOTES

1. *Payot* (or *payos, peiyot, pei'ot, Hebrew:* פאות), variously translated as 'corners', 'sides' or 'edges' (of the head and face), denote 'side-locks' and also the male sideburns and beard according to the teachings of the Book of Leviticus as understood and practiced within Orthodox Judaism. Amongst Yemenite Jews they are called *Simmonim* and in the Yiddish language it is pronounced *payos*.
2. Sassanids are the fourth Iranian dynasty, and the second Persian Empire in Iranian history. The Sassanians came to power in AD 224. The Sassanids named their empire Erânshahr (*Iranshæhr*) 'Dominion of the Iranians (Aryans)'.
3. Sheikh Yusuf Al-Qaradawi is an Egyptian Muslim scholar and preacher best known for his popular al Jazeera program; his views and opinions are followed and respected by a large audience globally.
4. Mullah Mohammad Omar is known as the brain behind Osama bin Laden's support for Al Qaeda.

BIBLIOGRAPHY

Al-Qaradawi, Y. (2002), 'Islamic Guidance on Growing Beard?' Living.Shariah, http://www.islamonline.net/servlet/Satellite?pagename=islamOnline-English-Ask_Scholar/FatwaE/FatwaE&cid=1119503545028, accessed 7 April 2008.

Beck, L. and Nashat, G. (eds.) (2004), *Women in Iran from 1800 to the Islamic Republic,* Champaign: University of Illinois Press.

Boulware, J. (2000), *Coming Clean: A Governor in Turkey Says He'll Remove the Beards and Mustaches of Any Men Caught with Prostitutes* (16 October), http://www.uri.edu/artsci/wms/hughes/ukraine/turbrd.htm, accessed 7 April 2008.

Delaney, C. (1994), 'Untangling the Meanings of Hair in Turkish Society', *Anthropological Quarterly,* 67 (4) (October): 159–72.

El-Azhary Sonbol, A. (ed) (2005), *Beyond the Exotic: Women's Histories in Islamic Societies,* Syracuse, NY: Syracuse University Press.

Gerami, S. (2003), 'Mullahs, Martyrs, and Men: Conceptualizing Masculinity in the Islamic Republic of Iran', *Men and Masculinities,* 5 (3) (January): 257–74.

Hopkins, P. E. (2006), 'Youthful Muslim Masculinities: Gender and Generational Relations', *Transactions of the Institute of British Geographers,* 31 (3) (September): 337–52.

Hostetler, J. A. (1995), 'Dress as a Language of Protest', in M. Roach-Higgins, J. Eicher and K. Johnson (eds.), *Dress and Identity,* New York: Fairchild Publications.

Kaiser, S. (1990), *The Social Psychology of Clothing, Symbolic Appearances in Context* (2nd edn), New York: Macmillan.

Kalra, V. S. (2005), 'Locating the Sikh *Pagh*', *Sikh Formations,* 1 (1) (June): 75–92.

Kamrava, M. (ed) (2006), *The New Voices of Islam: Reforming Politics and Modernity: A Reader,* New York: IB Tauris.

Majlisi, M. B. (1993), *Huliyat al Motaqin,* Tehran: Nas publication.

Mir-Hosseini, Z. (1999), *Islam and Gender,* Princeton, NJ: Princeton University Press.

Moghadam, V. M. (ed) (2007), *From Patriarchy to Empowerment: Women's Participation, Movements, and Rights in the Middle East, North Africa, and South Asia,* Syracuse, NY: Syracuse University Press.

Morris, C. (1998), 'Moustaches under Threat', *BBC News* (17 June), http://news.bbc.co.uk/1/hi/programmes/from_our_own_correspondent/112759.stm, accessed 7 April 2008.

Pakistan Daily Times (2007), 'Mardan Barbers Warned Not to Shave Beards' (23 March), http://www.dailytimes.com.pk/default.asp?page=2007\03\23\story_23-3-2007_pg1_3, accessed 7 April 2008.

Pancer, S. M. and Meindl, J. R. (1978), 'Length of Hair and Beardedness as Determinants of Personality Impression', *Perceptual and Motor Skills* 46: 1328–30.

Safavi, S. H. (1961), *Tahqiq dar yek mas'leh fiqhi: Rish Tarashi* (in Persian). Tehran: Chapkhaneh Bank e Keshavarzi. Farvardin, 1340 HS.

Shirazi, F. (2007), 'Manly Matters in Iran: From Beards to Turbans', in M. M Khorrami and M. R. Ghanoonparvar (eds.), *Critical Encounters, Essays on Persian Literature and Culture in Honor of Peter J. Chelkowski,* Costa Mesa, CA: Mazda.

Simpson, E. S. (1989), 'Islam in Uzbekistan: Why Freedom of Religion Is Fundamental for Peace and Stability in the Region', *Journal of Arab and Islamic Studies,* 2, http://www.uib.no/jais/v002/simpson.pdf, accessed 15 December 2007.

Syed, I. B. ([2008]), 'Growing a Beard: Is It Mandatory in Islam?' Islamic Research Foundation International, http://www.irfi.org/articles/articles_201_250/growing_beard_is_it_mandatory_in_islam.htm, accessed 7 April 2008.

Tabasi, M. R. (1974), *Tarash e Rish az Nazar e Eslam,* Mohammad Eshtehari (translated to Persian). Qum: Chapkhaneh Mehr e Ostovar. 1394 HQ.

Umble, J. S. (1953), 'Beard', *Global Anabaptist Mennonite Encyclopedia Online.* http://www.gameo.org/encyclopedia/contents/B4362.html, accessed 7 April 2008.

Yusufzaim, M. and Grisanti, C. (2007), 'In Tribal Pakistan, a Shave May Cost Your Life', *NBC News World Blog,* http://worldblog.msnbc.msn.com/archive/2007/03/06/79810.aspx, accessed 7 April 2008.

10 RESOUNDING POWER OF THE AFRO COMB

CAROL TULLOCH

A GIFT WITH RESONANCE

'The Afro Pick' T-shirt featured in the accompanying photograph (Figure 10.1) was given to me as a gift in November 2004 by the black arts institution, the Studio Museum in Harlem.[1] It was a limited edition design by David Hisa, commissioned by the museum in 2004. I was mesmerized then, as I am now, by the strong graphic impact on the front of the garment: a black-fisted afro comb and the word *beautiful*. The latter runs the width of the Afro Comb, as if it has been carved out of the prongs of the hair tool. This integrated design of the comb and the word *beautiful* suggests an indivisible relationship—black-fisted Afro comb/beautiful. The image, produced in dense black flocking, lends a bold quality to the graphic design. This is made more powerful by the vibrant viridian green of the T-shirt that allows the image to sing. The design is compounded by 'studio museum in harlem' printed in lower case letters, in black flocking, on the back of the T-shirt. The presentation of the garment followed a conversation I had at the museum on black style with the African-American fashion stylist and writer Lloyd Boston. We discussed, in front of a black and white audience, the impact and meaning of black style in different parts of the world. Our shared views illustrated the empathic diasporic connection between us, based on the cultural, social and political relevance of dress and beauty, and the objects that have embodied and reflected this aspect of black cultural history. Therefore, there was no fear that the graphic imagery of the T-shirt would not be understood by me.

My immediate reading of the components of the image—the Afro comb, the black fist, the word *beautiful*—made reference to the emergence of the Black Power and Black Consciousness movements in the 1960s. To me, they are instant iconic symbols of the political activism associated with this pivotal period of African-American and African diasporic political history; symbols and ideas I was able to witness in the 1960s and 1970s, and incorporated into my sense of self whilst growing up in Britain (Tulloch 1999: 73–75).

I have only worn the T-shirt a couple of times. With each wearing I felt less comfortable. I feared the strength of the vivid green of the T-shirt would fade with use and washing, and thereby lose the intensity and meaning of the original design. By preserving this T-shirt, I feel

The inclusion of the hyphen in the term 'African-American' will be used throughout this essay to underwrite the integral connections between the two cultures for black people in America; in this instance, through the cultural exchange and critical dialogue engendered in the use and development of the Afro comb.

Figure 10.1   Limited edition 'Afro Pick T-shirt', 2004. Designed by David Hisa. The T-shirt was commissioned by the Studio Museum in Harlem to underwrite the identity of the museum. The Black Fist Afro Pick and the word *beautiful* were chosen because of 'their iconic status in the community—Black *is* Beautiful, Black Power, black hair *are* Harlem', Ali Evans, PR Manager and editor at the Studio Museum in Harlem.
© Carol Tulloch, courtesy of Carol Tulloch.

that I am contributing to the collection of objects that help to chart African diasporic history, and that will underwrite their historical and cultural value. This T-shirt is a valuable item for me, as a memento of a particular period of my professional life; it is also material evidence of the significance of the Afro comb and the word *beautiful* in African diasporic cultural heritage. This chapter will present a 'reading' of the visual communication of this T-shirt.

A defining aspect of graphic design is its intent to persuade, inform or instruct the viewer (Livingston 1998: 90) by 'making or choosing marks and arranging them on a surface to convey an idea ... They are signs whose content gives them a unique meaning, and whose positioning can lend them a new significance' (Hollis 1997: 7). This latter point, that the positioning of the elements of a graphic design can lend new significance, is a framework applied here in order to unlock the significance of the black-fisted Afro comb/*beautiful* T-shirt. 'Scanning' and 'seeing' (Vischer, Mallgrave and Ikonomou 1994: 94) a conscious act of looking at an object in close detail by separating the elements, analysing each segment and then 'reconnecting them' will be used to explore what these signs and symbols of 1960s black American activism meant then, and what they mean now in the first decade of the twenty-first century.

Essentially, a comb is an everyday object with the primary function to tidy, care for and style hair. Therefore a comb is part of personal grooming and simultaneously contributes to the construction of a range of personal and group identities through hairstyling (Unger 1989: 8). Yet a comb can become used as an accessory to adorn the body, as 'an object of cultivation, something that wants to be seen and admired, perhaps more than being used' (Seuren 1989: 16). For example, during the heyday of the Afro, the black-fisted Afro comb was placed into the hairstyle of young black men. Thus, the Afro comb has had a particular cultural resonance on an equal footing with the hairstyle it was used to create, the natural hairstyle, the Afro. This hair statement had fallen out of vogue by the end of the 1970s, and was being replaced by other black consciousness-inspired hairstyles such as cane rows and dreadlocks. Why then, in 2004, was the black-fisted afro comb with the word *beautiful* still able to reverberate? The comb is also known by a range of other names in the United States that include Afro Pick, Afro Pic, Afro Rake, Hair Pick and Hair Pik. *Afro comb* will be used as the general reference here to retain the interdependent relationship between the Afro hairstyle and the comb, and as an appropriate umbrella term for all the combs that have been invented or designed to lift, extend and shape the Afro hairstyle.

CAN YOU DIG IT?: BLACK POWER

In the black-fisted Afro comb/beautiful T-shirt design, the word *beautiful* is part of the Afro comb and underlines the Black Power fist. To underline is to make a statement of fact, to emphasize, to reinforce. The teeth of the hair tool do not go through the word *beautiful*, but frame it; one could even say the black-fisted Afro comb protects the word *beautiful*, as the militancy of Black Power advocated and cherished the aesthetic sensibilities and personal empowerment of being black *and* beautiful.

On 16 June 1966, Stokeley Carmichael (Kwame Turé)[2] led the shout for 'Black Power' as part of a Civil Rights protest march and consequent arrests, in Mississippi. The rallying call was an urgent galvanization of black people in America to take control of their sense of self and their social, economic and political positions in their home country. Its strident philosophy was to underpin black activism and was a continuation of political concerns amongst black Americans, such as Malcolm X, about their unequal social status, their lack of visibility, economic and political power in America and the need to engage in self-determination and group improvement (Bennett 1966: 27). This was a situation that went beyond the borders of America and dated back to slave revolts. Thus this interminable situation led to a 'psychological struggle in this country' (Carmichael 2008). In light of this, a concern for Carmichael (2008) was 'how can white society begin to move to see black people as human beings? I am black, therefore I am':

> Black People must redefine themselves, and only *they* can do that. Throughout this country, vast segments of the black communities are beginning to recognise the need to assert their own definitions, to reclaim their history, their culture; to create their own sense of community and togetherness ... The black community will have a positive image of itself that *it* has created ... From now on we shall view ourselves as African Americans and as black people who are in fact energetic, determined, intelligent, beautiful and peace-loving. (Carmichael and Hamilton 1969: 51–2)

Self-image was fundamental to the success of Black Power. At the first National Conference on Black Power, held in Newark, New Jersey, on 20–23 July 1967, Professor Robert S. Browne outlined how Black Power would unify black Americans and inaugurate 'an era in

which black people will set their own standards of beauty, conduct and accomplishment'
(Browne 1968: 231–2). This, of course, was a means to erase the psychological impact of
the standard of American beauty as 'a milk-white skin and long, straight hair' (Browne
1968: 231). The curly nature of black hair[3] had long been a target of racial stereotyping and
denigration of the black body since the time of slavery. The hair texture of slaves was often
referred to by the derogatory term *wool,* that on the one hand referenced the texture of
black hair and on the other suggested the 'animality' of slaves (White and White 1998).

The only way forward, according to the ideologies of Black Power, was through black
nationalism, and for black Americans to become 'part of a larger international community
of black-skinned, kinky-haired people who have a beauty of their own, a glorious history
and a great future. In short he [and she] can replace shame with pride, inferiority with dignity … The growing popularity of this viewpoint is evidenced by the appearance of "natural" hair styles among Negro youth and the surge of interest in African and Negro culture
and history' (Browne 1968: 231). To promote and protect the fact that 'Black is Beautiful'
is to acknowledge and protect black presence in America. The Afro comb—the axis of my
T-shirt's design (Triggs 1995: 81)—simple though it may appear, *was* an axial power in the
practice of Afro hair creation, and *the* tool that in theory would liberate black hair into a
hairstyle that encompassed black self-determination and self-definition. Ron Karenga consolidated Browne's points in the black middle-class magazine *Ebony.* In December 1968 he
explained that 'the act of self-determination and self-definition' was achieved through 'the
choice of the language one speaks (like incidentally, the choice of an "Afro-hairstyle", African dress or African name)' (Poinsett 1968: 163). The natural Afro hairstyle, then, was an
aesthetic marker of self-redefinition and commitment to the black nationalist cause of Black
Power—an aesthetic counter-narrative to 'White Power' and white beauty standards.

Black hair care specialist and writer Willie Lee Morrow's book *Curly Hair: A Specialized
Text on Styling the Natural Afro and Straight Hair* (1973) marks the Afro as an art form.
Morrow viewed it as a marker of modern black hairdressing that would see the rise of
the 'new' barber and 'new' beautician (Morrow 1973: 19, 21). These specialists, Morrow
believed, had to come to terms with the popularity of the Afro, and must be proficient in
the new techniques required to style and care for Afros worn by adults and children, and
the styling and fitting of Afro male toupees and women's wigs: 'This Afro natural is not a
fad—it is here to stay. It reflects the recovery of black pride, and is in no danger of fading
away. There is more knowledge of handling the natural hair on the streets today than in
schools, barber shops or beauty shops' (Morrow 1973: 15). These remarks were also aimed
at white hair specialists who, in the main, had not shown an interest in the phenomenon,
but which Morrow hoped would now be addressed in the teaching institutions (Morrow
1973: 20). In his book, he explained the correct usage of combs in styling the Afro, for the
professional and for the general public (Morrow 1973: 28–34).

In the choice of Afro comb, Morrow asks the reader to consider the ergonomics of the
handle, that it 'balances well' so 'the fingers do not come into contact with the hair … [and]
the principle weight naturally points the teeth downwards' (Morrow 1973: 27). The teeth

of the combs should be strong, rounded and smooth, with even, untapered spaces between them, and preferably made of steel to provide a rust-proof strength. For the general public, Morrow suggested a portable comb, and perhaps with men in mind, a comb that fits well in the pocket. On the issue of cleanliness, combs should be able to withstand sterilization in the salons, or washing in the home. In this respect the specialist advised against the use of wooden combs in professional hair salons, as sterilization would cause the wood to split and splinter (Morrow 1973: 27).

Morrow identified another type of comb used by black Americans that had been labelled the 'Afro Comb' (Morrow 1973: 28). This was originally the shampoo comb, used to untangle shampooed Caucasian hair due to the wide space between the teeth, yet had been appropriated by African Americans to create the Afro. Here was a fine example of bricolage, where a 'white comb' became the symbol of 'Black Power'. Due to its popularity this comb was often carried on the body with the handle on view. A case in point was the caption used below a photograph of William Brown, a 22-year-old black man with an impressive Afro, published in the December 1969 edition of *Ebony* magazine. Brown was part of the crowd who witnessed the presidential inauguration of Richard Nixon. Visible in his back jean pocket is the handle of a comb, of the design associated with the 'shampoo comb'. *Ebony* assumes, through the link between the handle and Brown's hairstyle, that this is an 'Afro-comb' for his '"Black Pride" hair' (*Ebony* 1969: 42). Interestingly, Brown also carries two small American flags in each pocket, a comment on the reality of being both black and belonging to America.

Significantly, the Afro, along with African-inspired clothing and accessories built on black pride and cultural heritage, was one of the few areas of consensus that linked the diverse perspectives on Black Power (Verney 2000: 77). One year earlier, in the same issue of *Ebony* in which Karenga had qualified the cultural relevance of the Afro, an advertisement appeared for 'BLACK AND BEAUTIFUL African Designs By Blackfashion' (Ebony 1968: 166). These included three different styles of 'Hand carved wood combs perfect for natural hair styles worn today' (Ebony 1968: 166), and representative of 'authentic' African culture. Although of plain design, the combs were based on the standard components of an African comb: a number of prongs or teeth, a body and handle in a vertical profile. The other items available from Blackfashion were an 'Authentic Buba Dress' for day or evening wear; a 'Men's Shirt', which had matching head wear; an 'African Styled Evening Gown'; and wooden medallions and earrings. Thus the natural wood comb was a key component of pan-African ensembles which formed part of the redefinition process suggested above. Ironically, in the same issue there were three advertisements for Afro wigs 'that give that young "with it" look' (Ebony 1968: 124, 155, 182).

Regardless of whether the natural hair statement made was through one's own hair or provided by a wig, the Afro comb was the requisite tool to create and maintain the style. The advertisement does not indicate which part of Africa these designs came from or represented. What appears to be of upmost importance were the references to natural sources, such as wood, or the 'authenticity' of Buba dresses made of 'wild imported African designs'. In this fervour, to be 'part of a larger international community of black-skinned, kinky-haired people who have a beauty of their own' and to 'know their roots' (Carmichael and Hamilton 1969: 52), there was a lack of reference to the original cultural meaning of objects associated with different parts of Africa.

UN-PIK THIS: AFRICAN COMBS, AFRO COMBS AND AMERICAN COMBS

Traditional African combs are generally imbued with cultural memory and regional references. Janet Adwoa Antiri's 1974 study of Akan combs of the Ashanti, Fanti, Asin and Denkyira communities provides an example of the immense cultural value and skill of these cultural artefacts. The 'diverse shapes and designs, as well as the combs' function, are connected to the life and traditions of the Akan and all the people of Ghana' (Adwoa Antiri 1974: 32). Akan combs were produced for different social groups for various reasons. They were created by men for their mothers or girlfriends, but women were known to carve their own combs. Examples produced by apprentice carpenters could be acquired at markets, whilst commissioned carvers supplied women of royal families with ornate combs appropriate to the high status of their family.[4] Every aspect of the design and production of an Akan comb carried cultural value and symbolism: 'To carve a comb, the craftsman first purifies the tools by sacrificing a fowl, or at least an egg, upon them … The comb will usually have a minimum of seven teeth, as seven is a sacred number in Akan rituals' (Adwoa Antiri 1974: 32–33).

The handle of the comb is reserved for the creative expression of the carver, with the aid of specific tools: 'sekan mma, a small sharp knife; akuntuma, … a bent blade for shaving and smoothing corners; and a sharp chisel called bowere for carving and incising the designs and motifs.' More significantly, the 'shape of the comb, particularly the handle and its incised design, can be distinguished according to tribe, as each has its own myths, proverbs, symbols and spirits which are revered in the community' (Adwoa Antiri 1974: 33). Essentially Adwoa Antiri stresses the cultural importance of the Akan comb as a 'verbal art'; they are 'the medium of communication of the people … and serve as philosophical guides to action' (1974: 35).

This introduction to a specific, geographically located African comb provides an understanding of how an African comb can translate and underwrite the cultural and social philosophies of a particular cultural group. One then wonders how Afro comb designs developed in America to represent the political and cultural definition process of African Americans in the 1960s and 1970s.

To date there is no clear indication of when the Afro comb first appeared in the United States, although the general consensus suggests that it was during the 1960s. As Robin D. G. Kelley (1997: 340–1) has outlined, the forerunner of this genre of hair statement, the au naturel, a medium to short style emerged in the 1950s. However, the United States Patent Office does not hold examples created specifically for natural black hairstyles during that decade. Yet between 1970 and 1980, thirteen Afro comb designs and inventions were granted patents.[5] The designs were being submitted from all over the United States, with one submission from the Bahamas. They ranged from the traditional upright, manual African comb with a series of prongs, a body and handle, to electric models such as the 'Afro Pic and High Speed Cold Air Blower Combination' by John E. Ford of New York, which 'fluffs' natural hair 'simultaneously shaping and teasing the hair' with a rotating, detachable Afro Pic which could be used in the salon, home or conveniently on the beach (US3730190). There were also retractable designs which comprised only of prongs and a body (US39774290). Undoubtedly the granting of thirteen design patents in just ten years indicates the intense popularity of the Afro hairstyle across the United States during the 1970s. Three examples are of particular interest in the development of the Afro comb in America.

Patent number USD217997, 'Comb' (Figure 10.2), was designed by African Americans Samuel Henry Bundles Jr and Henry M. Childrey, of the black hair company Summit Laboratories Inc. of Indianapolis.[6] The design, originally filed on 4 April 1969, was patented on 7 July 1970. It is based on the traditional form of an African comb with even-length prongs, a body and handle. A sleek neck extended from the body of the comb, fanning out into a diamond shape to become the head of the comb. The design was to some extent a reflection of the creativity channeled into the handle as discussed by Adwoa Antiri above. Yet there is no indication that this handle design had a symbolic cultural meaning other than being based on an African or 'natural' comb to be used on black hair. One could argue that 'Comb' indicated a development of generic African combs for the black American market.[7]

'Comb' was followed by 'Styling Comb and Method of Making' (Figure 10.3), Patent US3646945, filed on 1 March 1971 and patented on 7 March 1972. This invention rejected the traditional upright African comb design for a horizontal profile, more in keeping with the conventional comb of the West—'a U-shaped tooth carrier and U-shaped teeth formed of metal for strength' (US3646945). The inventor, Anthony R. Romani, gave detailed information outlining why this comb was a new invention. The following extract is represented at length, as these are the first registered details which state, categorically, that in the United States a new comb had been produced specifically for a 'new' hairstyle, the Afro:

> BACKGROUND Recently there has developed a fashion trend toward hair styles reflecting the natural genetic characteristics of race. For example, just as many persons of Caucasian heredity seek to promote hair styles requiring curls or waves, many people of the Negro race have ceased to emulate such hair styles in preference for styles more natural to their genetic characteristics. Among such styles is the so-called "Afro" style wherein the hair on the head is permitted to grow quite thick and is combed about the head in such a manner as to stand out from the scalp in the manner of a bushy halo or cap. Because of the natural tendency of the hair to curl into tight ringlets, it is necessary to style the hair by means of a comb to produce the desired compact yet bushy effect. Again, because the length of hair is substantial, any comb used must have teeth of quite substantial length and hence such "Afro" styling combs have come to resemble cake cutters ... having a handle and a tooth holder of stepped shape. The teeth are quite long, in order of 2½ to 3 inches and the handle lies in an axis which extends through the teeth about midway of the length from tip to backing.

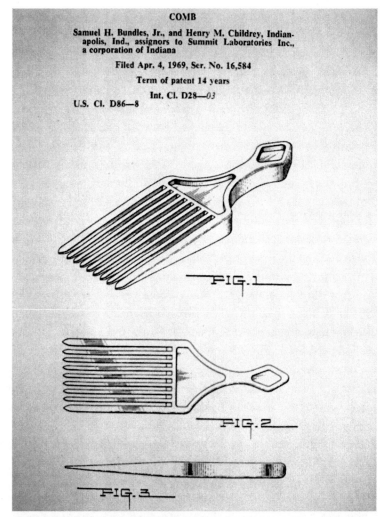

Figure 10.2   Design of 'Comb' (USD217997) submitted by Samuel H. Bundles and Henry M. Childrey to the United States Patent Office on 4 April 1969. A patent was granted on 7 July 1970.
Courtesy of United States Patent Office.

The comb, which became known as the 'Afro Rake Comb', was mass-produced by Romani from 1972, after he founded Antonio's Manufacturing Inc., Hollidaysburg, Pennsylvania, in December 1971. It also acquired the soubriquet 'Cake Cutter' due to its close resemblance to the popular American kitchen utensil used to cut the white-frosted angel food cake.[8] Therefore Romani's comb drew on American cultural heritage as a solution to styling the Afro, and thereby inhabited a localized cultural reference and meaning. In the same vein, Morrow invented a version of the 'Afro Comb' (Figure 10.4), based on the white shampoo comb, mentioned above. It was patented on 31 May 1977 as 'Afro Comb'

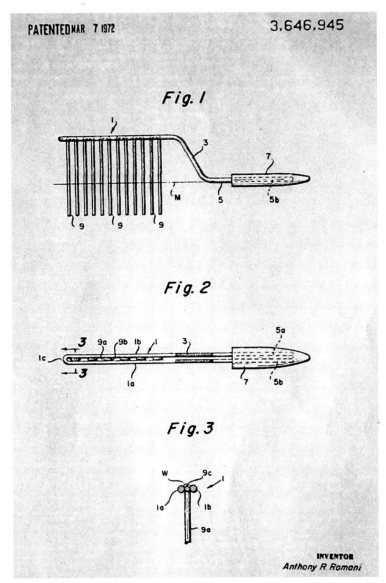

Fig. 1

Fig. 2

Fig. 3

INVENTOR
Anthony R. Romani

Figure 10.3 'Styling Comb and Method of Making' (US3646945). Devised by Antonio R. Romani specifically for the creation of the Afro hairstyle. It was patented on 7 March 1972, and mass-produced under the name 'Afro Rake Comb'. The tool was known as the 'cake cutter' due to its close resemblance to the American cake cutting tool.
Courtesy of United States Patent Office.

and 'combined the advantages of the long-toothed Afro comb with the compactness of the conventional comb' in order to be an effective tool for 'kinky' hair. (USP4026307).

Other patented Afro combs incorporated heated mechanisms or 'blow-out' facilities (USP3742964) to help soften and lengthen curly hair, yet grated with the positive black

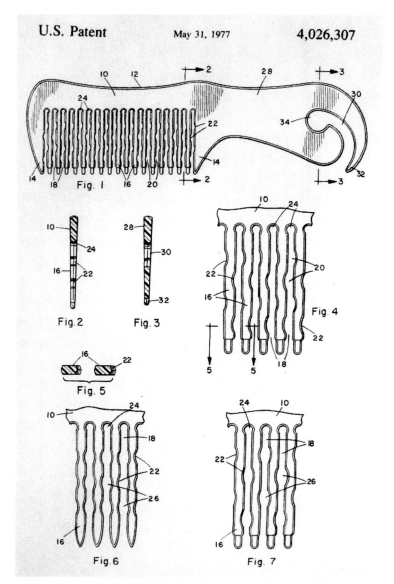

Figure 10.4 'Afro Comb' (US4026307) invented by Willie L. Morrow. It was submitted to the United States Patent Office on 26 March 1976, and granted a utility patent on 31 May 1977.
Courtesy of United States Patent Office.

pride philosophy. Through these systems the Afro shape, its halo, was created through the intervention of not only the Afro comb, but of warm pressing, chemical blowouts or diluted sodium hydroxide to soften and lengthen (but not completely straighten) the curls of black hair (Morrow 1973: 62). In addition, electric hair clippers could be used to shape the halo of male and female Afros and to perfect the hair line, while hair rollers provided the basis for an Afro of large, softer curls, suitable for men and women (Morrow 1973: 74, 79). As cultural historian and critic Kobena Mercer has stated in his seminal study on the politics of black hair, the Afro was not natural. The style did not just appear, but required grooming tools, pomades or night-time preparations such as plaiting to help 'stretch' the hair, to achieve the best length and condition. Thus, as Mercer has pointed out, rather than having links with 'Africa', the Afro in its 'rejection of artifice … embraced a "naturalism" that owed much more to Europe than it did to Africa' as a mirror of natural beauty (Mercer 1995: 256). This is further evident in the references to, and development of, combs produced specifically for Caucasian hair or everyday utensils for the Afro alongside fundamental black political messages. Therefore, Afro combs in the United States *are* embued with cultural memory, references and status particular to America, and specifically to the African American's 'double conscious' existence as African *and* American. At this point in their history, African Americans were not seeing themselves 'through the eyes of others' (Du Bois 1994: 2), but through their own African-American eyes.

In 1975 Romani purchased Ajax Comb Co. of Morrisville, and moved Antonio's Manufacturing to Cresson, Pennsylvania (Antonio's [2008]).[9] The company currently trades under two product lines: Antonio's for 'Antonio Afro Piks', styling and electric and non-electric straightening combs; and Ajax for a wide variety of 'conventional-type combs',[10] which also carries Afro combs such as the Ajax Pick n' Lift. Antonio's currently offers twenty-three different Afro combs, including six black-fisted handle Afro combs, and proudly states on its Web site that its black-fisted CND Pik design has been donated to the National Afro-American Museum and Cultural Centre in Wilberforce, Ohio (Antonio's [2008]).[11] Such a range of black-fisted Afro combs, available today, confirms the continued popularity of this design and its historical resonance where politics and hair aesthetics are conjoined.

1968 WAS ALL THAT: A CULTURAL MEANING OF THE BLACK FIST

The Black Power Salute of a clenched fist was the public performative signature of various factions of the movement. For example, it was a signature of the Student Non-Violent Coordinating Committee (SNCC),[12] and of course the Black Panther Party, reflecting group cohesion driven by the ideologies of Black Power (Figure 10.5). The fist's association with such radical groups gave the salute its uncompromising vigour. But on Wednesday 16 October 1968 the black fist salute was personalized, and expressed on the world stage of the 1968 Mexico City Olympics. Black American sprinters Tommie Smith and John Carlos won gold and bronze medals, respectively. As they stood on the victory podium, as the American flag was raised and its national anthem played, with their heads lowered towards the ground, the men thrust one arm each above their heads in a black-leather-gloved fist salute. Smith explained:

Figure 10.5   Olympic Games, Mexico City, 1968, men's 200-metres award ceremony. Gold medallist
Tommie Smith (centre) and bronze medallist John Carlos raise a black-leather-gloved fist salute as a
protest to the unequal rights of their fellow black Americans.
TopFoto/AP.

My raised right hand stood for the power in black America. Carlos's left hand stood for the unity of black America. Together, they formed an arch of unity and power. The black scarf around my neck stood for black pride. The black socks with no shoes stood for black poverty in racist America. The totality of our effort was the regaining of black dignity. (Smith 2007: 173)[13]

Smith was incredibly proud to have made it to the Olympic games,[14] but also knew that to win a gold medal and to become a world record champion at the Olympics would not deter the racial segregation that he, his family, friends and fellow African Americans continued to endure. Smith is adamant that this moment of militancy was not a 'Black Power' or a 'Black Panther' stand but 'a human rights stand' (Smith 2007: 39, 161). The meticulous premeditated design of his black-leather-gloved fist salute encodes the cultural significance of dressing a part of the body in leather in this context. This can refer to the arming of oneself for a specific action. Thus the visual activism of the salute intensified the emphatic timbre of the action.

Although Smith and Carlos were suspended from the games, and feared for their lives back in the United States, their activism had a resounding impact on like-minded individuals, as evidenced in a double-page spread in the December 1968 (160–1) issue of *Ebony* magazine with a full-page photograph of the Smith/Carlos salute. *Ebony* was not viewed as the magazine of choice by some militant black 'revolutionaries', yet the magazine had a powerful outreach with a circulation of one million in 1968 (Wolseley 1990: 142).

The salute was also empowered by the aims and objectives of the Olympic Committee for Human Rights (OCHR), an arm of the Olympic Project of Human Rights (OPHR). Smith and Carlos were members of both organizations. The OPHR's goal was to galvanize a boycott by black athletes of the 1968 Olympics games as 'another phase of the Black Liberation Movement' (Edwards 1969: 38). In November 1967, Smith, OPHR founder Harry Edwards and other OPHR supporters held a workshop at the Los Angeles Black Youth Conference, where Martin Luther King Jr was the guest speaker. The organization was driven by shared goals amongst black Americans and between 'all Africans', and this was reflected in one of the OCHR posters designed to generate support for the boycott of the games in Mexico City. The graphic image was dominated by a pair of ungloved black fists. One extended out of America, the other was raised out of Africa (Edwards 1969). The pair of hands linked with the 'arched' black fist unit created by Smith and Carlos, a symbol of transnational unification and empathy between black people of the African diaspora. The black-fisted bond between black America and black Africans also signified the historical links between the two places; the redefinition of black Americans from 'Negro' to 'African-American' 'means a long history, beginning on the Continent of Africa' (Carmichael 1969: 51–2).

LEST WE FORGET

During a speech in London in 1967, C.L.R. James, the historian and champion of black politics, celebrated and redefined Black Power as 'a banner' rather than a political slogan

(James [2008]).[15] Such a reclassification of what Black Power can be brings this study back to the graphic meaning of my viridian green T-shirt as a rallying call, a flag and a standard. In light of this, I suggest that the black fist Afro comb/beautiful T-shirt commissioned by the Studio Museum in Harlem is a banner that symbolizes the crystalizaton of African-American political and cultural heritage under the ideologies of Black Power in the 1960s and 1970s.

I also suggest that this banner T-shirt be viewed within the fashion context of 'Struggle Chic'. This term has been given to T-shirts produced by South African fashion designers who depict 'past political heroes', including South Africans Steve Biko and Nelson Mandela, and the African-American former heavy-weight champion Mohammad Ali. This genre of popular culture comes under the umbrella fashion term *Afro Chic*—clothing and accessories produced by black and white South African designers who want to reflect, for themselves and their customers, who they are and their heritage (Kirkham Simbao 2007: 66). The Afro comb, the black fist and the word *beautiful* are part of this acknowledgement of African diasporic cultural and political heritage. The anti-apartheid movement used the fist as part of its activism. And who can forget the raised fist of Nelson Mandela on his release from prison on 11 February 1990. These historical moments, marked by the raising of a fist alongside the transnational meaning of the Afro comb as a symbol of self-determination, solidarity, activism and general Black Pride, have also been drawn on by the black South African designer Themba Mngomezulu. The Afro comb and a fist are logos of his fashion label 'Darkie'. Mngomezulu's design approach is partly influenced by the history engrained in fabrics and objects (Jacobs 2003: 58) and his T-shirts often feature the Afro comb and/or fist.

Susan Stewart (1993: xi–xii) suggests that 'narrative ... seeks to "realize" a certain formulation of the world. Hence we can see the many narratives that dream of the inanimate-made-animate as symptomatic of all narrative's desire to invent a realizable world, a world which "works"'. Therefore, the black-fist Afro comb/beautiful T-shirt is a graphic narrative on the struggle of the Black Power movement and its various political, cultural and aesthetic actions. This T-shirt is just one, seemingly small, contribution that provides a contemporary narrative on a pivotal moment in African diasporic political and cultural history. Graphic design is 'the visualisation of ideas in two dimensional form' (Shelton 2008). Therefore, the black-fist Afro comb on this T-shirt reflects a further meaning of what a comb can be—to be proud, to hold one's head high—I am black, therefore I am. In spite of the legacy of the Black Power movement, in 2004 the Studio Museum in Harlem recognized that this still needed to be expressed.

NOTES

1. The Studio Museum in Harlem was established in 1968. In the Annual Report of 2006, the museum outlines its mission statement: 'The Studio Museum in Harlem is the nexus for black artists locally, nationally, and internationally, and for work that has been inspired by black culture. It is a site for the dynamic exchange of ideas about art and society', http://www.studiomuseum.org/about/annual-report/.

2. Stokeley Carmichael was the Chairperson of the Student Non-Violent Coordinating Committee (SNCC) in 1966. Originally born in Trinidad, he immigrated to Harlem, New York in 1952. He founded the Loundes County Freedom Organization, the logo of which was a black panther. In 1968 he became prime minister of the Black Panther Party. Carmichael changed his name to Kwame Turé in 1978.

3. This is one of a diverse range of black hair textures, but tight, so-called kinky hair strands that result in a dense mass has been the prime target of unwelcomed denigration.

4. Female royal combs were usually made of soft woods such as mahogany, sese or wawa, whilst examples reserved for ceremonies and festivals could be made of ivory, bone or metal, and be worn as decorative pieces.

5. These dates refer to the year a patent was awarded and do not reflect the date when the item was filed. This can be a time lapse of up to two years.

6. In 1973, Samuel Henry Bundles Jr and Henry M. Childrey established Suzanne International (Journal of the House 2001). Bundles, who was president of Summit Laboratories, was the husband of A'Lelia Mae Bundles, the great-granddaughter of Madam C. Walker, the creator of 'Madam C. J. Walker's Wonderful Hair Grower'. Walker is also credited with the popularization of the pressing comb amongst black American women. For a period, the Bundles ran the Madam C. J. Walker Manufacturing Company, which was originally established by Madam Walker in Indianapolis in 1906 (Bundles 2001: 17).

7. Interestingly, an assymetrical design for an Afro Comb was submitted by Arthur Rogovin of Yonkers, New York, to the United States Patent Office on 17 June 1970, and received a patent on 6 July 1971. Rogovin's plain asymmetric handle design makes reference to Bundles and Childrey's 'Comb' patented in 1970, as a development of the latter, and to a 'handle of comb in center block' featured in 'Hair Do magazine, June–July 1961' (USD221114).

8. I am grateful to Professor Susan Kaiser for this information. Angel food cake is incredibly white, because it does not include egg yolks, and is so light and fluffy that it cannot be cut with a 'regular' knife (Kaiser 2008). I would also like to thank Susan Kaiser for reading and commenting on this chapter.

9. Anthony R. Romani died in December 1977. Antonio's continued under the guidance of his widow, Gina Maria Romani, and their son Anthony Romani II.

10. http://www.antoniosmfg.com/am_about.html

11. No. 530 Afro Fist Pik (Metal), No. 531 Afro Fist Pik (Antomite), No. 532 Metal, No. 533 Antomite, No. 542 Afro Fist Fan Pik 12 Steel Teeth, No. 542S Pocket Fist Fan Pik Steel Teeth.

12. H. Rap Brown became the head of the SNCC following the departure of Carmichael in1967. Brown changed the name of the organization to the Student National Coordinating Committee.

13. In his recollection of the event, Tommie Smith said that it was his first wife, Denise, who bought the leather gloves (Smith 2007: 280).

14. Tommie Smith has kept most of his running outfit, and the hat, coat and trousers he wore for the opening ceremony of the games (Smith 2007: 28).

15. C.L.R. James viewed the 1960s Black Power Movement as the culmination of a gradual development of political thinking amongst black men in America, the Caribbean, France and Britain such as Booker T. Washington, W.E.B. Dubois, Marcus Garvey, Frantz Fanon and George Padmore.

BIBLIOGRAPHY

Adwoa Antiri, J. (1974), 'Akan Combs', *African Arts,* 8 (1) (Autumn): 32–5.

Antonio's ([2008]), 'About Us', *Antonio's Manufacturing, Inc.,* http://www.antoniosmfg.com/am_about.html, accessed 2 April 2008.

Bennett Jr., L. (1966), 'Stokeley Carmichael: Architect of Black Power' *Ebony Magazine,* 21, 11 September, 25–32.

Browne, R. S. (1968 [1967]), 'The Conference on Black Power Adopts a Momentous Resolution', in Bradford Chambers (ed), *Chronicles of Black Protest,* New York and Toronto: Mentor.

Bundles, A. (2001), *On Her Ground: The Life and Times of Madam C. J. Walker,* New York: Washington Square Press.

Carmichael, S. (2008), 'Stokeley Carmichael (1941–1998): Speech at University of California, Berkeley: October 29, 1966', *Say It Plain: A Century of Great African-American Speeches,* http://americanradioworks.publicradio.org/features/sayitplain/scarmichael.html, accessed 31 March 2008.

Carmichael, S. and Hamilton, C. V. (1969 [1967]). *Black Power: The Politics of Liberation in America,* Harmondsworth, Victoria: Pelican.

Du Bois, W.E.B. (1994 [1903]), *The Souls of Black Folk,* New York: Dover Publications.

Ebony, (1968), December, 24 (2): 124, 155, 160–1, 166, 182.

Ebony. (1969), 'Changing of the Guard: Blacks Watch, Wonder as the Nixon Era Begins', March, 24 (5): 29–42.

Edwards, H. (1969), *The Revolt of the Black Athlete,* New York: Free Press; London: Collier-Macmillan.

Hollis, R. (1997), *Graphic Design: A Concise History,* London: Thames and Hudson.

Jacobs, C. (2003), 'Fashioning the Past', *Y Magazine* (February/March): 57–60.

James, C.L.R. ([2008]), 'Black Power', *Marxist Internet Archive,* http://www.marx.org/archive/james-clr/works/1967/black-power.htm, accessed 8 April 2008.

Journal of the House, State of Indiana. (2001), 112th General Assembly 27 February, http://www.in.gov/legislative/reports/2001/HJOURNAL/J1227027.PDF, accessed 8 April 2008.

Kaiser, S. (2008), Personal communication, University of California, Davis, 7 May.

Kelley, R. (1997), 'Nap Time: Historicizing the Afro', *Fashion Theory: The Journal of Dress, Body and Culture,* 1 (1) December: 339–52.

Kirkham Simbao, R. (2007), 'The Thirteenth Anniversary of the Soweto Uprisings: Reading the Shadow of Sam Nzima's Iconic Photograph of Hector Pieterson', *African Arts,* 40 (Summer): 2.

Livingston, A. and Livingston, I. (1998). *Dictionary of Graphic Design and Designers,* London: Thames and Hudson.

Mercer, K. (1995), 'Black Hair/Style Politics', in R. Ferguson, M. Gever, T. T. Minh-ha and C. West (eds.), *Out There: Marginalization and Contemporary Cultures,* Cambridge and London: MIT Press.

Morrow, W. L. (1973), *Curly Hair: A Specialized Text on Styling the Natural Afro and Straight Hair,* San Diego: Black Publishers of San Diego.

Poinsett, A. (1968), 'Inawapasa Watu Weusi Kusema Kiswahili? Should Black Men Speak Swahili? Is Question Confronting Afro-Americans', *Ebony,* 24 (2) (December): 163–68.

Seuren, P. (1989), 'Hair and Combs', in M.-J. Vanden Haut (ed), *Kammen: An Art Collection of Combs,* Amsterdam: Marzee/Kammen.

Shelton, S. (2008), Personal communication, Graphicsi, London, 6 April.

Smith, T. and Steele, D. (2007), *Silent Gesture: The Autobiography of Tommie Smith,* Philadelphia: Temple University Press.

Stewart, S. (1993), *On Longing: Narratives of the Miniature, the Gigantic, the Souvenir, the Collection,* Durham, NC, and London: Duke University Press.

Triggs, E. (1995), 'Visual Rhetoric and Semiotics', in T. Triggs (ed), *Communicating Design: Essays in Visual Communication,* London: B. T. Batsford.

Tulloch, C. (1999), 'That Little Magic Touch: The Headtie', in A. de la Haye and E. Wilston (eds.), *Defining Dress: Dress as Object, Meaning and Identity,* Manchester: Manchester University Press.

Unger, M. (1989), 'A Collection of Combs', in M.-J. Vanden Haut (ed), *Kammen: An Art Collection of Combs,* Amsterdam: Marzee/Kammen.

Verney, K. (2000), *Black Civil Rights in America,* London and New York: Routledge.

Vischer, R., Mallgrave, H. F. and Ikonomou, E. (1994), *Empathy, Form and Space: Problems in German Aesthetics 1873–1893,* Santa Monica, CA: Getty Center for the History of Art and the Humanities.

White, S. and White, G. (1998), *Stylin': African-American Expressive Culture from Its Beginnings to the Zoot Suit,* Ithaca and London: Cornell University Press.

Wolseley, R. E. (1990), *The Black Press, U.S.A.,* Ames: Iowa State University Press.

11 CONCERNING BLONDENESS
GENDER, ETHNICITY, SPECTACLE AND FOOTBALLERS' WAVES

PAMELA CHURCH GIBSON

Surely you see my lady
Out in the garden there
Dazzling the glittering sunshine
With the glory of golden hair?

(Anon., possibly seventeenth century—arranged for music
by Sir Arthur Somervell nineteenth century)

This anthology, which seeks to examine the historical and socio-cultural significance of hair, needs some discussion, however brief and discursive, of the continuing popularity of blonde hair. In these days of obsessive celebrity culture, when the new raft of celebrity-centred publications (*Closer, More, Reveal* and their ilk) rival and outstrip the sales of conventional fashion magazines, we are frequently forced to confront and even to re-evaluate the potency of 'blondeness'. The covers and the pages of these publications are dominated by images of ultra-slim, white girls, with shoulder-length blonde hair (and silicone enhancements). This is not perhaps surprising, since Marina Warner has carefully chronicled the way in which blondeness and beauty are synonymous in Western myth and fairy tale (1994). Snow White is the only exception, although her black hair is more than compensated for by its striking contrast with her unusually pale skin. And modern celebrity culture is, of course, a bizarre mixing of myth and fairy tale with elements of melodrama and, increasingly, the medieval morality tale.

In 1980, a remarkably silly book *Blonde, Beautiful Blonde* was published. It was in fact discreetly sponsored by Clairol, the hair colour company whose promotional slogans famously include 'Blondes have more fun' and 'If I only have one life, let me live it as a blonde'. The book, written by one Liz Wyse, is noteworthy chiefly for its subtitle 'How to look, live, work and *think* blonde' (my italics). This suggests that there is in fact a blonde mode of thought—or as Wyse would have it, a 'blonde state of mind' (Wyse 1980: 7)—an assertion less than scientifically corroborated with the observation from an unreferenced muse: 'The trouble is that the blonde image is too horizontal for most vertical thinkers' (Barbaralee Diamonstein cited in Wyse 1980: 7). This concept, supported by the extraordinary quote, is the most interesting aspect of what is in fact a manual of blondeness; pages on diet, dress, exercise, make-up tips and decorating hints accompany the choosing and creating not just of blonde hair, but the correct colour and type of blonde hair. The would-be blonde can choose from the five best 'blonde looks' (Wyse 1980: 34–5): 'Newport', 'Palm Beach', 'California', 'Scandinavia' and 'New York', to effectively eliminate one's roots, presumably both hairy and geographical ('New Malden' as aspirational blonde look presumably does not have the same allure).

Some three years later another 'elective' blonde, television presenter and rock-star wife Paula Yates, followed this opus with a further set of blonde musings. Her own book, equally lightweight and lavishly illustrated, purported to be a historical survey; it certainly does seem to have subsumed and internalized Wyse's concept of 'blonde thinking'. The book is a very confused canter through history and mythology, blending the two seamlessly, refusing to acknowledge the source of any information presented, hopping backwards and forwards chronologically, and once again weaving a strange geographical pattern. It is as if the notion of blonde 'dizziness' Yates adopted as her own personal style has dictated the very form of the book and its prose and zigzagging narrative. She begins with an assertion which sets the overall tone: 'Eve like all the blondes to follow her was simply getting her priorities right … Scent, security, poodles, adoration, clothes & the heady sense of power were all hers from now on' (Yates 1983: 9). We are also told that Nitocris, Egyptian Queen in 3066 BCE, set a fashion among her fellow Egyptians for the wearing of blonde wigs (Yates 1983: 11). Ancient Rome yields: 'No chaste woman should make her hair yellow' (Menander, cited in Yates 1983: 13); and that Roman prostitutes wore blonde wigs both as a sign of their calling and a legal requirement. Consequently, depraved emperor Caligula sported a dyed blonde beard, whilst the notorious Messalina wore a blonde wig for her sexual trysts (Yates 1983, 15).

The linking of blondeness with transgression as well as its deployment 'against nature' is interesting in relation to Yates herself. In the early 1980s Yates was blonde in a new kind of way that disrupted any easy assumptions to be made about a 'dizzy blonde' persona, for this she self-consciously exploited as a particular form of transgressive performance. Yates's text is not transgressive, however, and certainly not interested in any kind of analysis. It does, nevertheless, describe the Western tradition of courtly love and its poetic conventions, where hair is always 'golden wire'; the characteristics of beauty listed by the medieval troubadours—the blonde tresses, red lips, eyes like the sun, the snow-white bosom—were to remain a constant in poetry and would also dominate Western painting (Yates 1983: 20). She does not go on, as she might, to show that these conventions assumed such a complete stranglehold on the creative imagination that Shakespeare thought it necessary to parody them, four centuries later, in Sonnet CXXX where he describes the 'dun breasts' and 'black wires' of his own mistress, possibly the problematic Dark Lady who forms a background to the Sonnet Sequence.

Perhaps, sadly, Yates's main legacy for any consideration of contemporary 'blondeness' is not this 'literary suicide' but her tragic and more noteworthy posthumous inclusion in the pantheon of women christened, by callous journalists, *suicide blondes*. This unkind term has been deployed to describe a particular type of self-destructive young woman, from

Marilyn Monroe to Princess Diana, all of whom began life quietly enough with brown hair. They entered the celebrity arena and there became blondes, their hair ever lightening in response to the glare of the public eye or the flashlight until the moment of their untimely deaths—when few remembered or cared that their blondeness was self-created. Significantly, it is always assumed that such blondes are women. Yet, the singer Kurt Cobain, certainly a cult figure following his own suicide, has never been known by this soubriquet, and indeed the term *blonde* itself is usually assumed to connote the feminine. Rod Stewart, in 1978, dyed his hair and produced an album *Blondes Have More Fun*. Whilst this offered, on a superficial level, a challenge to such gender assumptions, the transgressive value of Stewart's change of hair colour is undermined by what is seen by some as the start of his musical decline from talented blues singer to bloated, badly dressed pop star. Significantly, if the blonde and the 'feminine' are intrinsically linked, then the relation of the rock star to the masculine is similarly realized in the cultural imagination. Stewart's apparent decline could be framed in terms of a double emasculation; Stewart moved to the musical 'middle of the road' and the feminized realm of 'pop' with a blonde look that seemingly only women pop divas can successfully subvert.

However, the image of the male 'blonde bombshell' is one that continues to fascinate—particularly in its more recent incarnation in the plethora of bottle blondes to be seen on the football pitches of the world. This arguably began with the World Cup finals of 1998 when the Romanian team all sported badly bleached hair, but is perhaps more closely linked in the public imagination with the emergence of megastar England footballer David Beckham (Figure 11.1). Born with brown hair, Beckham made blondeness desirable and glamorous, both on and off the pitch. The World Cup of 1998 was the start of his blonde life in the public eye when he was infamously sent off in the second round for a petulant foul on Diego Simeone of Argentina. Soon after this, he was snapped by the paparazzi with his then-fiancée, now wife, Spice Girl Victoria Adams, wearing his equally infamous sarong; the images were splashed across all the tabloids. On both these public occasions, the bleached blonde hair of this latter-day 'David' fell in a heavy curtain across his face. But on his return to England, Beckham proceeded to play with styles that acted as a visible form of penance; something akin to the wearing of a hair shirt reformulated in a monastic skinhead crop, subsequently, a Mohican, and the epitome of footballing humiliation, a mullet. As if to symbolize his re-entry to the sporting arena and a new, more mature reflective fighting spirit Beckham finally opted for a white-blonde mane adorned with two tiny ponytails like those worn by Sumo wrestlers, when his then-team, Manchester United, toured Japan in 2002.

Like David Beckham, Occidental blondes are often self-created, not born—a fact that Richard Dyer (1997) examines in his book *White*. As Dyer emphasizes, the three best-known 'blondes' of the cinema—Jean Harlow, Marilyn Monroe and Brigitte Bardot—were all born with dark hair and only achieved screen stardom when 'peroxided within an inch of their lives' (Dyer 1997: 78). He cites film scholar Ginette Vincendeau's 1992 account of Bardot's career, noting that the actress had made no less than twelve unmemorable films

Figure 11.1   British football star David Beckham adjusts his ponytails during
Real Madrid's morning practice session at Hongta sports center in the
southwestern city of Kunming, 29 July 2003.
LIU JIN/AFP/Getty Images.

before she changed the colour of her hair, starred in *Et Dieu Crée La Femme* (1956) and thus
created both her career and her endlessly emulated style. Even the Virgin Mary and Jesus
Christ are with very few exceptions, Dyer notes, visually created and recreated blonde in a
way that clearly belies their ethnic origins. It is worth noting that Chris Ofili's African Madonna upset so many American fundamentalists when the 'Sensations' exhibition of 1998
crossed the Atlantic that the gallery was picketed throughout the duration of the show.

Significantly, the seemingly universal craving to be blonde is bound up in the fact that
there are two genetic characteristics which are confined to the whitest of white people
alone—the possession of both blonde hair and blue eyes: 'This is most obviously carried
in the notion that two specific variants, blond hair and blue eyes, are uniquely white, to
the degree that a non-white person with such features is considered, usually literally, to be
remarkable' (Dyer 1997: 44). Studies of black subjectivities in relation to hair problema-
tize any simplistic understanding of hairstyling practices such as straightening, relaxing
or lightening as symptomatic of racial self-hatred or indicative of a lack of agency (Banks
2000). Black and Asian hair dyed blonde can be seen as a strategy for self-expression and
survival in white-dominated society and as an act of disjuncture in terms of racial identity,
provoking rather than mimicking. Kobena Mercer argues,

> when hair styling is critically evaluated as an aesthetic practice inscribed in everyday life,
> *all* black hairstyles are political in that they each articulate responses to the panoply of

historical forces which have invested this element of the ethnic signifier with both social and symbolic meaning and significance. (1994: 104)

We could infer that the myth of racial exclusivity prompted the subversive Anglo-American street style that emerged in the mid 1990s, when young black and Asian people—men as well as women—dyed their hair very blonde indeed. Actor Samuel L. Jackson, who has experimented with every known African-American hairstyle in his various screen roles, has chosen to sport an egg-yolk yellow crop in his latest film, *Jumper* (2008).

Parallels can be drawn with one particular trend that has emerged in contemporary Japan. Amongst the plethora of styles in hair, dress and make-up sported by the young in Tokyo, the most notable is perhaps the *ganguro* style. The *ganguro* girls are a subcultural group who can be found in the district of Shibuya, meeting place of the young, and fanning out from Hachiko Square. The girls wear very short skirts, dress in neon colours, knee socks or knee-high boots and balance on ten-inch platform soles. The look is finished off with coloured contact lenses, glittery false eyelashes and brightly coloured acrylic fingernails. As one writer puts it, they resemble 'drag queens, anime heroines, messed up Barbie dolls' (Klippensteen 2000: 5). They also look in some ways like a more exotic version of those English girls so unkindly nicknamed 'Essex girls'—blonde-haired and faked-tanned, part pastiche, part luminous Lolitas. In their play on 'otherness' the *ganguro* girls seem to be playing with notions of gender and ethnicity and parodying different racial and sexual stereotypes through artifice.

These *ganguro* girls, fascinating in themselves, are clearly relevant to a consideration of blondeness, ethnicity and subversion in a global context. They dye their black hair platinum blonde, silver or orange or wear wigs, and change the colour of their skin to a dark, bright brown by using an excess of fake tan. Their new skin colour is accentuated by the white circles they paint around their eyes—the characters for *ganguro* translate, literally, as 'blackface'. It is open to question if this style does deliberately reference the Anglo-American music-hall 'blackface' first adopted by white entertainers in the late-nineteenth century, but it nevertheless subverts and undermines any easy equation being made between colouring—real or artificial—and racial identity.

Beckham's symbolic hair stylization on and off the pitch seems to change to meet the needs of the mood or the match, or to reflect his growing global identity and a diverse range of cross-ethnic influences. Blonde-on-black style as a Western cultural phenomenon, certainly in the UK, has perhaps most predominated on the football field. African players increasingly marked their participation in English football, like Beckham, with vibrant tonsorial statements. When Liverpool won the European Cup in 2004, the hairstyles were eye-catching. Djibril Cisse had a bright white crop. In the same match the white Europeans, Milon Baros and Luis Garcia, perhaps more timid in their choice of hair ornamentation, nevertheless opted for plastic Alice bands to keep their hair off their faces, in contrast to the conventional sweatbands seen on most professional tennis players. Ex-Liverpool defender Abel Xavier, a black Portuguese player renowned for his eccentrically styled

Figure 11.2   Los Angeles Galaxy's Abel Xavier in action against Real Salt Lake during match at the Home Depot Center, Carson, California, 17 June 2007.
Photo by German Alegria/MLS. © copyright 1999–2008 Getty Images, Inc. All rights reserved.

white-blonde hair, now plays with Beckham at LA Galaxy in the United States, where he has even brought his beard into the equation (Figure 11.2).

In a book *Footballer's Haircuts* (Cris 2003), the 'awful' nature of most on-pitch hair-styles is stressed. I would argue, however, that things have changed, and that the perms of yesteryear are a bad memory. In the recently concluded African Cup of Nations the football strips of virulent hue were matched only by the varied hair of the players. Many may have had 'sober-side' cuts, but those with experience in the English Premiership were the most experimental with dyed hair or shaven heads and spectacular tattoos, like Junior Agogo of Ghana and Leicester City. But it was the blondes who really drew the eye, particularly those such as Matsueka of Guinea and Binya of Cameroon with their plump, apricot curls.

Figure 11.3 Bakari Sagna of Arsenal speaks to media after the 'Emirates Cup' match between Arsenal and Paris St Germain at the Emirates Stadium, London, 28 July 2007. Photo by Clive Mason/Getty Images. © copyright 1999–2008 Getty Images, Inc. All rights reserved.

One of David Beckham's most interesting innovations was his adoption of the traditional plaited 'cornrows' which originated in Africa and through the black diaspora have travelled widely across the globe. Bleached blonde, however, David Beckham's 'white cornrows' have a cross-ethnic impact that has sparked off new innovations in blonde-on-black style, both as gesture and as an arresting 'look', and refined and developed on both street and on football pitch. Weaves have long been a vital part of black hairdressing and styling; now, however, highly coloured blue, red and purple and very obviously synthetic Dynel extensions are woven into long plaits to be seen on many Afro-Caribbean girls in England and lately on the head of the rugby player Lesley Vainikolo, born in Tonga and now playing for the English national team. In an interesting variation, head hair, grown and then plaited, can be interspersed with shorter, more widely dispersed neon nylon fronds, a style favoured by the Arsenal football team player Bacary (sometimes spelled Bakari) Sagna, originally from Senegal (Figure 11.3). This mixture of the 'authentic' plaits of real black hair practice and the deliberately bright, artificial strands of nylon is perhaps the most interesting in its socio-cultural implications.

Bakhtin's historical analysis of the canivalesque provides a useful conceptual framework within which to situate such phenomena, in its analysis of the carnival's facility to endorse social stability by enabling social protest and change. Through his reading of the works of Francois Rabelais, Bakhtin (1981) argues that the folk tradition of the carnival was a way of undermining the proscriptive constraints of official culture, particularly religious forms of social domination. For the brief time that the carnival lasts, ordinary rules are suspended; the world of carnival and those who participate in it are allowed a freedom to subvert and often debase dominant culture through spectacular excess and laughter. Such freedom, however, is always understood as temporary so that, Bakhtin argues, the social hierarchy, its conventions and their subversion always exist in ambiguous proximity.

An implicit understanding of the transient status of human hair—transient for a variety of reasons, temporal, medical, fashionable—ensures that it similarly offers an ambiguous liminal space of both conformity and experimentation. In the spirit of Bakhtian misrule, footballers are cheerfully playing with their appearance as well as with the ball. Arguably the footballing arena in this sense—and its increasing intellectual elevation to the status of folk culture—has taken over from the artistic avant-garde Bohemian art in the twentieth century and their appropriation of the 'festive ambivalence and transgression which had once been the provenance of carnival' (Stallybrass and White 1986 quoted in Wilson, 2000: 241).

Blonde hair and blue eyes once functioned as the guarantee of racial purity; always 'less a descriptive term about hair pigmentation than a blazon in code, a piece of a value system' (Warner 2004: 364), blondeness was embedded in the popular imagination in moral and social terms as evidence of racial superiority. However, blonde-black male footballers now provide an interesting contemporary take on Friedrich Nietzsche's 1887 Aryan fantasy of a blonde master race: 'At the base of all these aristocratic races the predator is not to be mistaken, the splendorous blond beast, avidly rampant for plunder and victory.' (1998: 134). But the enduring belief in the potent qualities of such colour-coded success is also open to question—and even becoming a little tarnished, at least on the football field. In fact it seems that some black players think that this aspect of the game has gone quite far enough. The final of the African Cup of Nations featured Egypt versus Cameroon—but it was sensible short-back-and-sides all round. Only the substitute, Binya, provided a sole splash of colour—and his team were defeated by the well-shorn Egyptians. Perhaps misrule has its time and place ...

BIBLIOGRAPHY

Bakhtin, M. (1981), *The Dialogical Imagination,* trans. C. Emerson and M. Holquist, ed Michael Holquist, Austin: University of Texas Press.

Banks, I. (2000), *Hair Matters: Beauty, Power, and Black Women's Consciousness,* London and New York: New York University Press.

Cris, F. (2003), *Footballer's Haircuts: The Illustrated History,* London: Weidenfeld & Nicolson.

Dyer, R. (1997), *White,* London and New York: Routledge.

Klippensteen, K. (2000), *Ganguro Girls: The Japanese 'Black Face',* Cologne: Koenemann verlagsgesellschaft mbh.

Mercer, K. (1994), *Welcome to the Jungle: New Positions in Black Cultural Studies,* London and New York: Routledge.

Nietzsche, F., Clark, M. and Swenson, A. J. (1998), *On the Genealogy of Morality,* trans. M. Clark and A. J. Swenson, Indianapolis, IN: Hackett.

Stallybrass, P. and White, A. (1986), *The Poetics and Politics of Transgression,* London: Methuen.

Vincendeau, G. (1992), 'The Old and the New: Brigitte Bardot in 1950s' France', *Paragraph* 15, 73–9.

Warner, M. (1994), *From the Beast to the Blonde,* London: Chatto and Windus.

Wilson, E. (2000), *Bohemians: The Glamorous Outcasts,* London: IB Tauris.

Wyse, L. (1980), *Blonde, Beautiful Blonde: How to Look, Live, Work and Think Blonde,* New York: M. Evans and Co.

Yates, P. (1983), *Blonde: A History from Their Earliest Roots,* London: Michael Joseph.

EILUNED EDWARDS

INTRODUCTION

Purity and pollution are key concepts in the orthodox Hindu schema, and also in the history, myths, folklore and devotional practice that surround hair in India. These concepts are manifested at a symbolic level through stories and worship, and at the level of lived daily experience through popular customs and vernacular medicine. Notions of ritual purity and pollution are also exemplified in the social and religious hierarchy of caste which offers a unique insight into the function of barbers, many of whom are ritual specialists. However, ritual, custom and trade co-exist and indeed, overlap, in the multimillion rupee business of 'temple hair' at Tirumala in which 500 barbers organized into three shifts work around the clock in order to cope with the scale of the donations—the hair is used for extensions and wigs, and has become a significant commodity in the global fashion market. The growth of the market for 'black henna', a herbal hair dye made from indigo (*indigofera tinctoria*) and henna (*Lawsonia inermis*), has likewise achieved a global reach, suggesting that ancient devotional practice and local cultures of hair have become entwined with modern technologies of hair care and grooming through the impetus of globalization.

HAIR MYTHS, HISTORIES AND TABOOS

Hair is a rich source of myth in India where each state and region has its own pool of stories. Customs to do with hair are assiduously observed and reflect local influences, although certain pan-Indian practices can be seen, for example, the popularity of uncut hair for women, and the prevalence of the moustache among men. Although the specifics of styling and maintenance may vary, groomed hair is a means of indicating social conformity, and is 'the hallmark of people with publicly recognized roles within society' (Hallpike cited in Olivelle 1998: 15).

Hair also plays a role in Hindu mythology. In a pivotal episode of the epic, *Mahabharata* (Narayan 2001), the rivalry between the Pandavas and the Kauravas is enacted in a game of dice. Prince Yudhistira stakes and loses his kingdoms, his brothers and finally their shared wife, Draupadi, to Duryodhana, head of the Kauravas.[1] Duryodhana commands an attendant to summon Draupadi to the court, who finds her clad in a single piece of cloth with her hair loose after bathing, and also because she was menstruating. Draupadi refuses twice to go to the court, which infuriates Duryodhana. He then commands his brother to drag her to the assembly hall by force, which he does, 'using his strength and holding her down, by her deep black locks' (van Buitenen 1975: 142). Duryodhana compounds the outrage by having Draupadi stripped naked. Lord Krishna protects Draupadi with a never-ending sari, and the sound of a jackal's cry—an ill omen—halts the assault, but her humiliation propels the rivalry of the two clans to outright war, and Draupadi damns her assailants and predicts their wives will suffer: 'Their bodies smeared with blood of their relatives, their hair loosened and themselves in their courses, the women shall offer up the water to their dead . . .' (van Buitenen 1975: 165–6).

The myth powerfully encapsulates Hindu notions of purity and pollution and uses the medium of hair to convey violation, grief and behaviour that breaks taboos. The hair of an auspicious Hindu woman—idealized as a wife and a mother (Fuller 1992: 22)—which traditionally is kept uncut, should conform to accepted local conventions and be restrained in a plait, or a bun, covered by a veilcloth, or the *pallu* of a sari (Hiltebeitel 1998: 144) (Figure 12.1). Unbound and dishevelled hair is the sign of a widow (if her hair has not been shorn), the insane, of unrestrained sexuality and of menstruating women who, in high-caste Hindu society, traditionally leave their hair unwashed, undressed and unbound for four days (Fuller 1992: 188). As the story of Draupadi shows, a woman's unleashed hair indicates that she is in her 'unclean state', i.e. menstruating, but as menstruation reveals her fertility, it is also related to the female power, *shakti,* which is threatening and must be brought under control, usually through marriage, sometimes through renunciation. In many parts of India, a woman goes into partial seclusion for the duration of her period. Similarly unkempt hair is also used to signal bereavement and mourning which again may call for temporary seclusion.

Unleashed, a woman's hair is a visual metaphor to indicate that she is outside accepted societal norms, be it temporarily or permanently (Olivelle 1998: 16–17), likewise the shaven head of a man in mourning and the dreadlocks of a renouncer. According to some versions of the Draupadi myth, Draupadi vowed that she would leave her hair unkempt until the Kauravas were defeated and she could dress it with Duryodhana's blood, using a comb made from his rib bone and a hair ribbon of his entrails (Hiltebeitel cited in Olivelle 1998: 17). Draupadi's wild hair, the result of her humiliation at the hands of the Kauravas, and her own subsequent pledge, placed her outside of societal norms.

But the symbolism of unkempt hair is nuanced; certainly it may have negative aspects but it offers a range of interpretations. Kali, the 'most exemplary goddess of dishevelled hair' (Hiltebeitel cited in Fuller 1992: 188), is a terrifying manifestation of the female energy, *shakti,* and is customarily shown with wild hair. Nonetheless, she is a popular form of the great goddess, worshipped especially in West Bengal. By contrast, the matted locks of ascetics, worn by male and female *sadhus* (renouncers), are a sign of their renunciation. Although unkempt hair still symbolizes a person outside societal norms, the association is positive and the perceived holiness of their withdrawal from worldly matters is a highly regarded practice among Hindus.

The ultimate ascetic, of course, is Lord Shiva, from whose matted hair (*jata*) the waters of the sacred Ganga are said to flow (Iyer 2001: 51). Popular images of Shiva show him to

Figure 12.1   Women wearing their hair plaited, oiled with *ghi* and dressed
with purifying flowers, Tirumala temple, south India.
Photo by Eiluned Edwards.

be a well-groomed renouncer, his dreadlocks—signalling his renunciation of the world—
are gorgeously styled coils of hair, and a delicate spurt of water issues from his topknot to
symbolize the source of the Ganga. These representations of Shiva show a stylized—one
might even say sanitized—version of asceticism (Figure 12.2). This accords with the status
of Shiva as the primary god of temple Hinduism (Davis 1997: 26–7), whose image
is abundant in India and the diaspora, printed on items as diverse as foodstuffs and fire-
works (Giannuzzi and Aldred 2000).

Figure 12.2   Shiva with his consort, Parvati. His *jata* (dreadlocks) are
elegantly styled, and the source of the Ganges issues from his topknot.
In the background are the Himalayas where Shiva performs his austerities.
Lid of storage box made from recycled cans. Collection of the author.
Photo by Eiluned Edwards.

PURITY AND POLLUTION: THE ROLE OF THE BARBER

There is a clear relationship between myth and social custom in India, as myths are often
instructive and determine forms of social behaviour. Many customs have evolved directly
from the round of myths and stories to be found in each state, and certain practices are

pan-Indian such as the shaving of the head when there is a death in the family (a custom adhered to by men rather than women, although not exclusively so). The roots of this practice lay in ancient India where the shaving of the head is recorded as a purificatory rite for mourners for whom exposure to the influence of death and ghosts was considered dangerous (Oldenberg cited in Kumar and Kumar 2003: 4139). Underpinning this custom is the belief that hair is ritually unclean; it potentially offers a route for evil spirits to enter a person causing pollution of the body (and soul). The associated belief that illness is caused by evil has established the removal of hair—be it full tonsuring or selective depilation—as a way to deflect or vanquish malign influences, in order to restore health and harmony. Hair removal as prevention or cure is prevalent in different forms throughout India. In most formal religious tonsuring ceremonies, the task is carried out by a barber who is versed in ritual practice, but in vernacular medicine, treatment may be self-administered by the afflicted person, or it may require the help of a specialist, often typified as a shaman.

Apart from its role in the control of malign spirits and ghosts, and in vernacular medicine, hair plays a critical role in rites of passage (*samskara*) and in signifying a change of status. A child's first haircut is marked by a ceremony that is customarily performed by a barber (*ajam*), who is a ritual specialist, when the child is about three years old. In the Rabari community of Gujarat, parents who have had difficulty conceiving do not name their child until after this ceremony; in the meantime the child is dressed in second-hand clothes and given abusive names such as *Bhiku* (beggar), or *Punjo* (refuse), and his or her hair is left uncut and uncombed, all strategies believed to avert evil eye and ensure the child's survival (Rabari 1997). Ideally the ceremony should take place at the shrine of Amba Mata at Mount Abu, Rajasthan, 'where Krishna's hair was clipped for the first time' (Kumar and Kumar 2003: 848). The Brahman ceremony to mark a boy's passage to adulthood, after which he is entitled to wear the sacred thread, requires a boy to undergo ritual tonsuring when his head is ceremonially shaved and then smeared with purifying sandal paste. Among Tamil Brahmans, the ceremonial renewal of the sacred thread, known as *avani avittam,* is marked by the symbolic removal of a length of hair three fingers deep from the forehead (Sivasubramaniam 2006). Traditionally, a shaven head, white sari, and the absence of any ornaments and decoration, mark the inauspicious state of a widow. Although the custom is rare now, a woman's head would be ritually shaved after the death of her husband, as described in this passage from Suguna Iyer's novel, *The Evening Gone:*

> At a signal from the priest, she was taken outside where the barber who had been summoned, waited. She sat very still and dry-eyed as the barber cut off the first lock.—He came close up to her, bent over her, and started clipping the short tufts, and then the razor was on her scalp. Meenakshi screamed and screamed at that, and wept loudly, and it was all very proper because she was mourning her husband, now dead and gone. (Iyer 2001: 70)

It is clear that shaving occurs at significant life stages, and yet the barbers who perform at such ceremonies are classified as so-called 'untouchables', defiled in the eyes of other

Hindus. The professional practice of a barber in India encompasses a surprisingly wide range of services apart from grooming for a mainly male clientele, especially as women have traditionally left their hair uncut, with grooming and styling an essentially domestic affair. Barbers carry out routine cutting and styling of men's hair, usually in small booths in the villages, towns and cities. In rural areas, barbers may also be itinerant, and it is not unusual to see an improvised salon at the side of the road, where the barber wields his scissors and razor—the cut-throat razor is still the favoured tool of the trade—his client seated on an upturned crate. However, as we have seen, many barbers are ritual specialists as well, who play a key role at religious functions and rites of passage (Figure 12.3). They offer massage and also pre-wedding preparation for Hindu bridegrooms, a practice known as *pithi* in rural Gujarat, which is carried out over several days when the groom undergoes daily massage with *ghi* (clarified butter) and turmeric to polish his skin to the desired golden sheen. Beyond burnishing the groom, the barber is effecting his purification, as *ghi* is one of the main purifying agents available for ritual cleansing (Dumont 1980: 51). It should be noted, too, that turmeric is used in *ayurvedic*[2] medicine as an anti-bacterial agent (Anjaria et al. 1997: 16). On the day of the wedding, the barber will spend several hours administering a final massage, cutting and oiling the groom's hair, shaving him, dusting him with talcum powder to lighten his skin and finally, applying pomade (Figure 12.4).

Figure 12.3   Barber shaving the head of a recently bereaved man near the Burning Ghats, Varanasi.
Photo by Eiluned Edwards.

Figure 12.4 Rabari groom undergoing *pithi* (massage and grooming) in the hands of a village barber in Kachchh district, Gujarat. Photo by Eiluned Edwards.

In spite of their ritual duties, the status of barbers in the caste hierarchy is low, and they belong to the former 'untouchable' classes. Caste is a hierarchical system that divides Hindu society into four classes: *Brahmans* (priests), *Kshatriya* (warriors), *Vaishyas* (merchants) and *Shudras* (servants). It represents an ideal religious model of Hindu society in which each class is a necessary and interdependent part of the whole. An underlying principle of caste is a ritual notion of purity and pollution, which is allied to a system of hereditary occupation. Brahmans are the purest caste, and Shudras the most polluted, but below even the Shudras come the 'Untouchables' who are outside the fourfold system of caste, and are now known as *Harijan* ('Children of God') or *Dalit* ('Oppressed'). The 'Untouchables' work has traditionally been 'barbering, laundering and removing nightsoil, so that the purity of the Brahmans and high caste people is preserved by others who perform polluting tasks for them' (Fuller 1992: 15).

Despite caste having been outlawed since independence in 1947, it is still a defining principle in the daily lives of many Indians, especially in the rural areas of the subcontinent. According to Hindu belief, 'virtually all bodily emissions and waste matter are sources of pollution (saliva, semen, menstrual blood, feces, urine, hair, and nail clippings in particular)' (Fuller 1992: 15). The interpretation of purity and pollution in the context of caste in India (and the diaspora) has little to do with hygiene and dirt. As anthropologist Mary Douglas suggests, if we define dirt as 'matter out of place—it implies two conditions: a set of ordered relations and contravention of that order.—This idea of dirt takes us straight into the field of symbolism and promises to link-up with more obviously symbolic systems of purity' (2002: 44). Viewed in this light, the idea of cleansing a house by sprinkling it with cow's urine and using cow dung as a floor surface, both common practices on the subcontinent, which may be repugnant to Western sensibilities, is entirely in accord with Hindu notions of cleansing which rely on the use of purifying agents, such as the five products of the sacred cow (urine, dung, milk, *ghi* and curd), ritual bathing and the removal of pollution by specialists.

Hair, as a body emission, is impure and left untreated, or uncontrolled, defiles the individual. Using Douglas's symbolism of 'dirt' as a challenge to the social order, and hair as dirt or defilement, the individual body can be interpreted as representing the social body. The analogy is apt as the four classes are said to have sprung from different parts of the original man created by the gods: '[From] his mouth came the Brahmin; his arms were made into the Warrior, his thighs the People, and from his feet the Servants were born' (O'Flaherty 1981: 29–32). The tension between the corporeal body and the idea of the social body is evident in the way a by-product of the individual body, such as hair, expresses taboos. Barbers operate in this conceptual framework: on the one hand, they provide a useful grooming service and on the other, they are ritual specialists, their function comparable in some respects with the priestly role of Brahmans. However, as they handle hair on a daily basis rather than sacred texts, a body emission that is impure, they absorb pollution either by direct contact or simply by proximity to defiling matter, all of which accounts for their lowly caste status (see Hiltebeitel 1998, Fuller 1992, Dumont 1980). Traditionally their role in daily and ritual life is essential to relieve higher castes of pollution and, if one accepts the orthodox Hindu purview of caste, to sustain the social order (see Miller 1998).

It is not coincidental that in several parts of India, barbers have traditionally been matchmakers. In rural Tamil Nadu, barbers have acted as intermediaries between families seeking a suitable match for their son or daughter, who should ideally be in a state of the utmost purity. The mobility of barbers, many of whom work from village to village, and their professional intimacy with their clients, puts them in a unique position to act as matchmakers. While the families in question will vet one another's reputation and economic status, and scrutinize the future prospects, health and marital potential of the candidates, it is the barber who relays early expressions of interest (Murugan 2006). This role implies trust, perhaps engendered by his function as a ritual specialist. Hair is an aspect of a person's appearance that can be scrutinized and interpreted as a sign that exceeds the physical boundaries of the individual body, and that reveals a person as part of, or apart from, the greater social body. In this context, hair becomes one of the media through which a man's potential as a husband and father is assessed. Evidence of ill health, a dissolute character and a lack of the desired signs of masculinity may be discerned by his barber, either through the condition of his hair and physique, or because of the nature of their regular contact. Thus, apart from acting as go-between, a barber may also be called upon to comment on the outward signs of a prospective groom's health. In Asian and Islamic cultures, a virile man should, ideally, have a full head of glossy black hair and an abundant moustache—'grey hair is not much appreciated and—facial hair is a significant symbol of masculinity' (Balfour-Paul 1998: 226). Who better to assess this than his barber?

PIETY AND PROFIT: THE TRADE IN HAIR AT TIRUMALA

Barbers may perform a range of crucial and highly personal services within in the social networks of local communities, but at Tirumala, in the state of Andhra Pradesh, a legion of barbers carry out their work on a gargantuan scale, with far-reaching, global consequences. Hair plays a key role in devotional practice in most of India's recognized religions. For Muslims, completion of the Haj, the pilgrimage to Mecca that should be made at least once in a lifetime by every able-bodied Muslim who can afford it, is marked by the removal of hair; men shave their heads and women cut an inch or so from the length of their hair. Devout Jains pluck the hair from their own heads, and the naked pate of both men and women is a mark of particular piety. In contrast to these practices, for Sikhs it is uncut hair that signifies purity (*khalsa*), piety and adherence to the tenets of the faith. For Hindus, the ritual removal of hair is seen as an act of purification and, at a metaphysical level, represents the abandonment of ego (*ahamkara*), the extinction of individuality, which is a prerequisite of achieving the soul's release, *nirvana,* or 'perfect bliss'.

Ritual tonsuring is thus carried out at religious sites throughout India, but it has reached an industrial scale at the temple of Lord Venkateshwara at Tirumala. Thousands of Hindu devotees make the pilgrimage to Tirumala each day and have their heads shaved as an offering to the temple (Figures 12.5 and 12.6). Although hair is polluted matter, the donations of hair earn devotees a blessing. The hair is handled in the first instance by specialist

Figure 12.5 Shaven-headed devotees emerging from the tonsuring sheds at the Temple of Lord Venkateshwara, Tirumala, Andhra Pradesh. Their heads are smeared with purifying sandalwood paste.
Photo by Eiluned Edwards.

Figure 12.6   Queue for the *kalyana katta* (tonsuring sheds) at Tirumala.
Photo by Eiluned Edwards.

barbers, and generates a significant source of revenue for the temple (and also for the state coffers). Income from the sale of donated hair has made Tirumala the wealthiest temple in India; in the financial year 2005–2006, the business of 'temple hair' earned the temple authority, the Tirumala-Tirupati Devasthanams (TTD), and associated exporters, an estimated US$300 million (McDougall 2006: 30).

The roots of the practice, which is centuries old, are to be found in a myth about Lord Vishnu, who at this temple site is known as Lord Venkateshwara:[3]

> At the time when Lord Vishnu resided in an anthill, Lord Brahma would visit him in the form of a cow to offer milk everyday. Angered by this, the cowherd aimed to strike the cow, but the Lord saved the cow and took the blow upon himself, which resulted in a deep wound on his head. On account of this, the Lord lost a lot of blood and hair. Being witness to this, Neeladri, a devotee of the Lord offered her hair to the Lord. Pleased by her generosity, the Lord proclaimed that devotees who offered their hair in Tirumala would be blessed (Reddy and Yajnik 2005: 156).

Today, tonsuring takes place at the *kalyana katta* (tonsuring sheds), and the scale of the donations is such that the TTD has introduced a computerized system for devotees who are issued with a token for tonsuring which is done free of charge by the temple barbers. Tonsuring takes place around the clock, and around 500 barbers are organized into three shifts, in order to meet the demand. At present, only male barbers are sanctioned to cut hair at Tirumala. However, the TTD is reported to have started to recruit women in the past year for the benefit of female devotees; they are subject to a 'talent test' and have to meet certain educational standards in order to work for the temple. *The Hindu* reported that a woman barber, Radha Devi, had launched a fast-unto-death in front of the TTD's administrative buildings, alleging 'irregularities in the recruitment of women' (Hindu 2006: np).

Apart from the main tonsuring shed at the Tirumala complex, a further sixteen mini *kalyana katta* have been established around Tirumala-Tirupati, which are open from 6.00 a.m., to 6.00 p.m., in order to serve pilgrims staying at guesthouses outside the temple site. Devotees are charged ten rupees to be tonsured at these sites. Donated hair is collected, washed, de-loused and graded by length, quality and colour at processing factories in Chennai in the neighbouring state of Tamil Nadu, where it is then auctioned. Much of the 'temple hair' is exported to Europe where it is transformed into extensions for the wealthy of Europe and the United States, notably the stars of the fashion, music and film industries. Italy is a centre for the manufacture of hair extensions and a recent article in the newspaper, *Corriere della Sera,* reported that 'Great Lengths', one of the leading companies producing hair extensions, based in Nepi, Viterbo Province, supplied 'temple hair' to fifty countries around the world, named many Hollywood luminaries on its client list, and had an annual turnover of US$10 million (Fubini 2006: 7–8).

The use of extensions in Western countries has escalated since the early 1990s and has generated such a demand for hair that in south India, many entrepreneurs have established themselves as independent agents, not affiliated to any of the temples. They tour the villages of Andhra Pradesh and Tamil Nadu, reportedly offering women one thousand rupees per foot of hair (*Chennai Chronicle* 2006: 1). However, this has led to women being mugged for their hair, or coerced by family members into selling it.[4] In 2006, E.V.K.S. Elangovan, the Minister of State for Textiles and Commerce in Tamil Nadu, stated that only twenty per cent of premium hair sold abroad came from temples, the remainder was from unknown sources, and that as 'there are no specific restrictions on the import and export of human hair … [it] can be done freely. This is obviously an environment that breeds illegality' (McDougall 2006: 30).

It is the globalization of the market that has led to a situation where demand is so great that unscrupulous traders will pillage hair in order to supply the commodity. Viewed from a postcolonial perspective, this aspect of the globalization of the hair trade is an uncomfortable echo of the colonial period when one of the foundations on which the British Empire rested was the exploitation of Indian resources and labour (Chandra 1989: 94).[5] But India has now been a sovereign state for sixty years, exercises control of its own economy, and since the economic reforms of the early 1990s, has actively sought to encourage international trade through the relaxation of import controls, the lifting of restrictions on multinational corporations and foreign investment and linking the exchange rate to the market. As state agencies seek to regulate this intrinsically Indian business, the authorized trade in temple hair is a lucrative by-product of devotional practice. It is well-monitored by the TTD, garners a huge income for the temple which is used for good works and also represents a substantial contribution to the state revenue of Andhra Pradesh.

Furthermore, hair as a commodity is a long-established fact in India and there is another old and much more low-key tradition of hair collecting and selling that not only co-exists with the temple hair industry, but that also undercuts the assumption that the hair trade can only be understood with reference to Western interventions and global economies. In the villages of south India, hair collectors, traditionally from the Koothadinayakan[6] wig-making community (Koothis) of Theni district in Tamil Nadu make regular visits (Murugan 2006). After daily combing, village women collect the hair they shed and store it on the roofs of their houses, ready for the monthly visit of the Koothis who barter small items such as toys, hairgrips and slides, in exchange for the wisps of hair. Their clients include touring theatrical troupes, the film industry in Chennai and Mumbai, nurses who are obliged to keep their hair short in the interests of hygiene but use hair pieces for festivals and weddings, brides requiring elaborate coiffure and those with medical conditions such as alopecia. What distinguishes this Indian wig-making from the so-called temple hair market is its focus on the local rather than the global; however, a different negotiation between Western and Indian influences can be seen in the Indian market for hair products.

'SOFT AS FLOWERS'—TRADITIONAL AND CONTEMPORARY HAIR PRODUCTS FOR INDIA AND THE DIASPORA

The poem, *Cilappatikaram,* or *The Epic of the Anklet* (c. fifth century CE),[7] reveals the luxury and sophistication of a courtesan's hair dressing, and gives an indication of the variety of products traditionally used for cleansing, conditioning and dressing hair on the subcontinent: 'To please him—she bathed her fragrant black hair, soft as flowers, till it shone, in the perfumed oil prepared by mixing up ten kinds of astringents, five spices, and thirty-two herbs soaked in water; she dried it in fuming incense and perfumed the different plaits with a thick paste of the musk deer' (Ramachandra Dikshitar 1978: 139–40).

At one level, cleansing is simply about removing dirt, but practical considerations overlap the concept of ritual cleansing. But how does this infuse the contemporary use of hair products in India? The range available is diverse—although the subcontinent is still a significant source of ingredients for natural hair products, which are viewed as *ayurvedic* treatments and remain popular, the arrival of multinational companies such as Garnier, L'Oréal, and Silvikrin on the Indian domestic market since the liberalization of the Indian economy in 1991 has been marked by an onslaught of so-called synthetic products. In some respects, Indian consumers are spoiled for choice but what influences the choices they make? Previously untapped by multinationals, the Indian market presents huge potential for consumer growth, not least because of the size of the population—India is predicted to overtake China as the world's most populous nation by 2045—but also because of its burgeoning middle class. In order to access this vast reservoir of consumers, superstars of the Hindi film industry, notably former Miss Worlds, Aishwarya Rai (1994) and Diana Hayden (1997), and former Miss Universe (1994), Sushmita Sen, have been recruited by Garnier et al. to endorse internationally known shampoos, conditioners, glosses, sprays and dyes (Figure 12.7). Their colossal popularity guarantees the appeal of these products to their fan base and, cannily, products for the Indian market have been somewhat modified to include locally recognized ingredients such as sandalwood and coconut oil. But the cost of these commercial products is prohibitive for many—a 200ml bottle of Pantene shampoo, which currently retails at seventy-five rupees, represents more than a day's labour in many parts of the country. Thus their popularity tends to be confined to the towns and cities at the heart of India's present economic boom, whilst elsewhere they are bought only for special occasions such as betrothal and marriage.

Figure 12.7   Advert for L'Oréal hair colour featuring Bollywood actress and former Miss World 1997 Diana Hayden.
Femina Magazine, 15 September 2001, 5.

Home or locally made hair treatments from plant extracts, dried leaves and oils from plants and fruits are still widely used: *shikakai* leaves and *aritha,* or soap nuts, are used for cleansing hair; coconut oil and the purifying *ghi* are rubbed into clean hair as conditioners to protect against the drying effects of the sun; sandalwood in powder or paste form, which is also used in Hindu devotional practice, is used to purify and fragrance hair; and henna powder, and henna mixed with indigo leaves, which is known as 'black henna', are used as herbal hair dyes (Figure 12.8). The properties of 'black henna' as a colourant, which gives hair a blue-black lustre, are matched by its perceived *ayurvedic* qualities: henna is believed to possess cooling properties and a 'cool head' is desirable, and indigo is used as an anti-bacterial agent (see Gittinger 1982; Balfour-Paul 1997, 1998). Its popularity has seen it travel beyond the geographical boundaries of the sub-continent, indeed, it has followed the South Asian diaspora across the globe and is also favoured by other Asian communities, so that dried indigo leaves are now an important agricultural export for a small but specialist group of farmers who cultivate indigo in Tindivanam, Tamil Nadu and in Vallur district, Andhra Pradesh (Figure 12.9). These farmers have traditionally made much of their

Figure 12.8   Packet of *kali mehendi* (black henna) made by Godrej, India.

income from supplying indigo, processed into cake form, to craftsmen throughout South Asia who dye, print and paint textiles. But they are now starting to shift the emphasis of their production from the national market for cakes to the international market for dried indigo leaves. The farmer who currently has the largest acreage devoted to indigo in India has 300 acres dedicated to leaves for 'black henna' and 700 acres devoted to indigo to be extracted for cakes; in 2007–2008 he plans to increase the acreage for leaves to 600

Figure 12.9   Indigo leaves being harvested near Tindivanam, Tamil Nadu.
Photo by Eiluned Edwards.

and reduce that for cakes to 400 acres (Anbalagan 2006). The reasons for the change are simple: he can make more money exporting dried indigo leaves and the process for producing them is far less labour-intensive than the extraction process required for indigo cakes. As environmental and ecological concerns become increasingly mainstream, the future for natural products such as 'black henna' looks bright and the indigo farmers of south India are hoping for an export boom to match that of 'temple hair'.

CONCLUSION

According to the Hindu belief, hair, like all emissions of the body, is polluted. Douglas makes the comparison between defilement, *dirt* to use her chosen term, and disruptions of the accepted social order. Thus coiffured hair, hair kept in order and pollution-controlled, signals compliance with the prevailing social order; conversely, unkempt hair, hair in disarray, indicates the suspension or rejection of societal norms, be it through violation as in the Draupadi myth, mourning, madness or renunciation. This symbolic system can be discovered in India today in myths, folklore, vernacular medicine and devotional practice. The role of barbers in this framework of purity and pollution makes explicit how these conjoined ideas are enacted through the orthodox Hindu system of caste. The conceptual underpinning of caste reconciles the apparent contradiction of a barber as a trusted ritual specialist whose religious service is an essential part of ceremonies that mark key life stages and being classified as 'untouchable'.

At the temple of Lord Venkateshwara at Tirumala, where the pious undergo tonsuring and donate their hair to Lord Vishnu, the industrial scale of the 'temple hair' business has a global reach, as does the business of hair itself to the business of hair products. Whilst the diversification of the hair care market in India in the past decade and a half has affected consumer choice in prestige, price and purity, it is the latter that has sustained the popularity of a home-grown product, 'black henna', and an emerging niche in the global market for the world's oldest dyestuff, indigo. The tension of ritual purity and pollution in India is manifested through local cultures of hair; however, the persistence of ancient systems of belief and social practice in a rapidly industrializing society are also revealed. Likewise, local, age-old practices of hair treatment co-exist with hi-tech products that are backed by multinational corporations and endorsed by the luminaries of Bollywood, the Hindi film industry based at Mumbai: different époques and technologies overlap. Similarly, ancient devotional practice exemplified by the donations of hair at Tirumala has segued into the global fashion business through the demand for 'temple hair'. A recent campaign to promote India as an emerging global power featured the slogan 'India Rising'; the medium of hair makes it apparent that in the twenty-first century, India's ascendant god is Mammon.

ACKNOWLEDGEMENTS

I would like to thank the following people for their generous help in the production of this chapter: Paba Rabari, Ismail Khatri, Saroop Dhruv, Dr M. D. Muthukumaraswamy,

T. R. Sivasubramaniam, Murugan, Prof. N. Bhakthavathsala Reddy, Prof. Anna Dallapiccola, Ritu Sethi, Anbalagan, Kannan, Diana Hayden, Dinesh Dayal and L'Oreal India. My thanks also to the British Academy, the Nehru Trust, the Luigi and Laura Dallapiccola Foundation and London College of Fashion for financial support for research in India.

NOTES

1. Draupadi marries the five Pandava brothers—Yudhistira, Bhima, Arjuna, Nakula and Sahadeva—at the behest of their mother, Kunti. Kunti advises her sons to share all that they have, or acquire, between them. Thus, Arjuna, who wins Draupadi's hand in marriage, shares her with his brothers. The union is also attributed to Draupadi's devotion to Lord Shiva whom she asked to grant her a husband with five desirable qualities. Shiva complies but the difficulty of finding these attributes in a single man results in her marrying the five brothers, each of whom represents a particular quality.

2. *Ayurveda* is the traditional Hindu system of medicine, based on the idea of balance in bodily systems that emphasizes diet, herbal treatment and yogic breathing. The term is from the Sanskrit 'science of life'.

3. Lord Venkateshwara is widely venerated in south India, and is a form of the deity, Vishnu, who is commonly referred to as 'the preserver'. 'Venkateshwara at Tirupati' is 'Vishnu on Venkata hill' (Fuller 1992: 37).

4. A comparable situation was recorded in Myanmar by *The Indian Express* (*Indian Express* 2007).

5. The British Empire ruled India between 1858–1947 but large parts of India had been under the dominion of the British East India Company since the late-eighteenth century when Robert Clive defeated the Nawab of Bengal and the British took control of Bihar, Orissa and Bengal in 1757.

6. Koothadinayakan is a colloquial name for a sub-division of the Korava caste of Theni district, seminomadic pig-breeders for whom wig-making is a secondary occupation. For further details on the Korava caste, see Thurston and Rangachari 1993: 438–504.

7. *The Epic of the Anklet* is a classic of Sangam literature, the classical literature of Tamil Nadu, which deals with different love themes. The poems devote a great deal of attention to the physical attractions of lovers, and the preparations made by them in anticipation of a tryst; consequently they are a rich source of information on details of grooming and dress.

BIBLIOGRAPHY

Anbalangan. (2006), Personal communication with indigo farmer, 13 September.
Anjaria, J., Parabia, M., Bhatt, G. and Khamar, R. (1997), *Nature Heals. A Glossary of Selected Indigenous Medicinal Plants of India,* Ahmedabad: Sristi.
Balfour-Paul, J. (1997), *Indigo in the Arab World,* Richmond: Curzon Press.
Balfour-Paul, J. (1998), *Indigo,* London: British Museum Press.
Chandra, B., Mukherjee, M., Mukherjee, A., Panikkar, K. N. and Mahajan, S. (1989 [1988]), *India's Struggle for Independence,* New Delhi: Penguin Books India.
Chennai Chronicle (2006), 'Hair Raising Tale of Profit 'n' Sale', *Chennai Chronicle,* 20 (September): 1.
Davis, R. H. (1997), *Lives of Indian Images,* Princeton, NJ: Princeton University Press.

Douglas, M. (2002 [1966]), *Purity and Danger,* Oxford and New York: Routledge.

Dumont, L. (1980 [1966]), *Homo Hierarchicus: The Caste System and Its Implications,* Chicago and London: University of Chicago Press.

Fubini, F. (2006), 'Nel Tempio delle extensions dove il sacrificio diventa affare', *Corriere della Sera,* 6 July, 7–8.

Fuller, C. J. (1992), *The Camphor Flame: Popular Hinduism and Society in India,* Oxford: Oxford University Press.

Giannuzzi, L. and Aldred, G. (2000), *Cock: Indian Firework Art,* London: Westzone.

Gittinger, M. (1982), *Master Dyers to the World,* Washington, DC: Textile Museum.

Hiltebeitel, A. (1998), 'Hair Like Snakes and Mustached Brides: Crossed Gender in an Indian Folk Cult', in A. Hiltebeitel and B. D. Miller (eds.), *Hair. Its Power and Meaning in Asian Cultures,* Albany: State University of New York.

Hindu (2006), 'Woman Barber on Fast-unto-Death', *The Hindu,* 28 September, 11.

Indian Express (2007), 'Hair Thieves Strike in Myanmar', *The Indian Express,* 14 May, 5.

Iyer, S. (2001), *The Evening Gone,* New Delhi: Penguin Books India.

Kumar, S. and Kumar, N. (eds.) (2003), *Encyclopedia of Folklore and Folktales of South Asia,* Vol. 4, New Delhi: Anmol.

McDougall, D. (2006), 'Trade in Hair Forces India's Children to Pay the Price', *The Observer,* 25 June, 30.

Miller, B. D. (1998), 'The Disappearance of the Oiled Braid: Indian Adolescent Female Hairstyles in North America', in A. Hiltebeitel and B. D. Miller (eds.), *Hair. Its Power and Meaning in Asian Cultures,* Albany: State University of New York.

Murugan. (2006). Personal communication, National Folklore Support Centre, Chennai, 6 September.

Narayan, R. K. (2001 [1978]), *The Mahabharata,* London: Penguin Books.

O'Flaherty, W. D. (1981), *The Rig Veda: An Anthology,* Harmondsworth: Penguin Books.

Olivelle, P. (1998), 'Hair and Society: Social Significance of Hair in South Asian Traditions', in A. Hiltebeitel and B. D. Miller (eds.), *Hair. Its Power and Meaning in Asian Cultures,* Albany: State University of New York.

Rabari, P. R. (1997), Personal communication, 15 August.

Ramachandra Dikshitar, V. R. (trans.) (1978 [1907]), *The Cilappatikaram,* Madras: South India Saiva Siddhanta Works Publishing Society.

Reddy, T. S. and Yajnik, B. R. (2005), *Tirumala-Tirupati: The Legends and Beyond,* Hyderbad: Visual Quest India.

Sivasubramaniam, T. R. (2006), Personal communication, 6 September.

Thurston, E. and Rangachari, K. (eds.) (1993), *Castes and Tribes of Southern India, Vol. III,* New Delhi and Madras: Asian Educational Services.

van Buitenen, J.A.B. (trans. and ed) (1975), *The Mahabharata,* Vol. 2, Chicago and London: University of Chicago Press.

PART 3
HAIR IN REPRESENTATION:
FILM, ART, FASHION, LITERATURE
AND PERFORMANCE

13 HAIRPIECES
HAIR, IDENTITY AND MEMORY IN THE WORK OF MONA HATOUM

LEILA MCKELLAR

The powerful role that hair can play in social rituals, and in personal life experiences, renders it an extremely potent material for artists to use. Since the mid 1990s, Mona Hatoum has produced a number of artworks using long hair from the head, pubic hair and body hair in order to explore ideas around the body, identity and memory. Hatoum is a Palestinian artist, who was born in Beirut and has lived and worked in Britain since 1975, when war broke out in Lebanon while she was visiting London. Her work is often discussed in terms of her status as an exile (Said 2000: 17). Although Hatoum has always resisted criticism that interprets her work in terms of her own experience, it is certainly the case that her artworks often explore notions of home and reflect the emphasis on cultural identity that has characterized much art produced since the 1970s. Hatoum's work is diverse in form, moving from performances dealing primarily with issues around the body in the 1970s and 1980s, towards installations and sculptures with an aesthetic that recalls work of the minimalist and Arte Povera movements.

Hatoum is one of a number of women artists since the early 1990s who have used hair as an artistic material in order to express powerful ideas about gender and identity. In *Loving Care* (1992), Janine Antoni soaked her hair with dye and mopped the gallery floor with it. In *Loop My Loop* (1991), Helen Chadwick entwined Barbie-blonde hair with glistening, pink pig's intestines, in order to explore notions of desire, disgust and the feminine body. The Colombian sculptor Doris Salcedo frequently uses hair in conjunction with simple wooden and metal furniture. She often wraps it around the pieces in order to explore the experiences of those affected by the Colombian civil war, as the hair suggests a process of holding together or the suturing of wounds.

These artists have used hair in very different ways and for different reasons. However, the use of hair in their work has occurred over a period in which women artists have interrogated ideas about the representation of the female body, which, as feminist critics have argued, has conventionally been an object of the masculine gaze (Mulvey 1975; Nead 1992). In the light of these debates, hair is notable for its ability to act as a metonym that stands in for the female body, while avoiding representing that body directly.

Hatoum has repeatedly used hair in her work. As a student at the Slade School of Art in London, she began to collect her own nail clippings, pubic hair and pieces of skin, and mixed them with pulp and bodily fluids to make paper, as a reaction against what she has described as the disembodied intellectualism of the art academy (Antoni 1998). Later in her career, Hatoum went on to use hair in a number of installations and photographs, often using hair that she had collected over the intervening years. This work explores a range of issues, however a constant and overarching theme has been one of identity, exploiting the connections between hair, female subjectivity and social taboos.

CROSSING BOUNDARIES

In 1995, Hatoum produced a piece entitled *Pull* (Figure 13.1), which was shown in Munich over three days. It consisted of a plait of hair hanging in a box, above which the artist's face appeared on a video monitor. At first glance it was unclear whether the piece was a performance or a video work. Viewers were invited to pull the hair, in response to which the face on the screen appeared to register sensations of pain. Gradually, viewers realized that the hair and the face were connected, that Hatoum was present behind the wall, with her hair hanging down, extended by an extra length. The realization that viewers were physically connecting with another human being, indeed causing her genuine discomfort, made for an unsettling experience. The fact that they were doing this by touching and pulling at her hair added an unusual degree of intimacy to the performance.

We would usually only touch the hair of close family members, lovers or children. To touch the hair is not a neutral act like the shaking of a hand. Rather, touching the hair of another person is an intimate act, suggestive of other forms of contact and substances that cross the borders of the body such as saliva, tears or sweat. The marginal status of

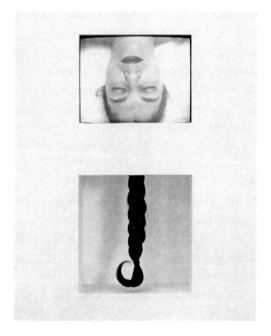

Figure 13.1   Mona Hatoum, *Pull* (1995)
(live video performance, dimensions variable).
© the artist. Courtesy White Cube/Jay Jopling.

hair, neither inside nor outside the body, but continually growing through its boundary, relates to notions of the clean and unclean which revolve around boundaries. In *Purity and Danger*, the anthropologist Mary Douglas famously explored these ideas, arguing that any matter that crosses the boundaries of the body, such as blood, milk, urine, faeces or skin, nail or hair clippings, possesses the potential to contaminate as a result of its marginal status (Douglas 1966: 150).

The hank of hair in *Pull* crossed boundaries on a number of levels. Hair traverses the border between the natural and the cultural. It is an involuntary product of human physiology that has nevertheless been made to signify as differences in cut, colour and arrangement convey cultural messages (Cox 2005). As they observed and handled the length of hair, viewers of *Pull* may, consciously or unconsciously, have read into it a variety of signals about its owner. The texture and colour of the hair communicate information about ethnicity, while long hair arranged in a plait is culturally coded as feminine.

In addition to existing at the threshold between the natural and the cultural, *Pull*'s plait literally crossed the boundary between representation and the real. As it emerges from the video screen, the hair mediates between the viewed image and the sensing body. The viewer of a conventional artwork is often in a position of control, as the distance required for apprehension allows the power relations of the gaze to operate. Hatoum's rope of hair crossed this space, meaning that the body of the viewer not only touched, but was touched by the viewed object. The staging of an interaction between the viewing body and hair that has emerged from the body of an other was repeated in later works by Hatoum, including the installation *Recollection,* in which viewers were brought into contact with strands and balls of the artist's hair.

PERSONAL RITUALS

In 1989, while staying with a friend in Cardiff, Hatoum noticed the hair that had collected in the plughole after having a bath. Not wanting to leave it there, she absent-mindedly rolled it into a ball and kept it. She found it aesthetically attractive, saying 'It was a perfect ball, very cocoon-like. It was beautiful' (Hatoum 1997: 19). This was the beginning of a six-year habit, during which time she compulsively collected hair from her hairbrush and plughole, keeping the resulting hair balls in shoeboxes under her bed.

In 1995 Hatoum was commissioned by the Belgian Kanaal Art Foundation to produce an installation for the *Inside the Visible* exhibition series curated by Catherine de Zegher. It was at this point that the compulsively formed hair balls found a home. Hatoum created a piece entitled *Recollection* (Figure 13.2), which was installed in the main meeting hall of the Beguinage Saint-Elizabeth in Kortrijk, Belgium. The *beguinage* is a collection of buildings inhabited by a lay sisterhood of the Roman Catholic Church, in which only a single last beguine and two aged companions now live; it is a space occupied solely by women throughout its history. *Recollection* consisted of hair balls scattered across windowsills and bare, polished floorboards, single strands of hair knotted together and hung from ceiling beams at 15 cm intervals and a small, handmade loom on a table, holding a fabric made

Figure 13.2   Mona Hatoum, *Recollection* (1995) (hair balls, strands of hair hung from ceiling, wooden loom with woven hair, table, dimensions variable). © the artist. Photo: Fotostudio Eshof. Courtesy Jay Jopling/White Cube (London).

from woven hair. In addition, a bar of smooth, white soap, sprouting curly, black pubic hairs lay on a windowsill.

The use of hair in *Recollection* relates directly to the space of the installation. Hatoum stated that 'When I saw the space in Kortrijk I felt that this was the time to use the hair balls, partly because the space had been occupied by women. I visualised the hair balls as dust balls that gather in the corners of rooms' (Hatoum 1997: 19). These 'dust balls' suggest the presence of women whose activity in the room has left bodily traces which may be repeatedly formed and swept away in the routines of everyday life.

MATTER OUT OF PLACE

The loom that Hatoum created in *Recollection*, with its woven strands of hair held taut with tape, may be read as representing an attempt to bring this unruly material back into a form of order. In 2001 Hatoum revisited this process in *Untitled (hair grid with knots)* and *Untitled (grey hair grid with knots),* producing small grids of hair, knotted and loosely woven on a loom. The process by which curly hair is pulled taught and woven in these pieces suggests the instruments of control that are routinely used by women to make hair conform to particular ideals of Western femininity. In fact, the strands that form the hair grids have been fixed into position using hairspray in order to stop them reverting to chaos.

The knotted strands of hair hanging from the beams in *Recollection* border on invisibility. Visitors entering the installation space of *Recollection* might well have felt the hanging hair strands before noticing them visibly. While in *Pull,* to touch the hair required a positive choice on the part of the viewer, the touch of hair in *Recollection* was unsolicited. This element of spontaneous contact was perhaps the most disturbing aspect of the piece for viewers, who felt the hanging strands brush their faces and the drifting hair balls touch their feet as they walked through the room. The strands also have the potential to catch in the viewer's mouth, eliciting bodily sensations of disgust (de Zegher 1997: 92).

Although hair may be seductively beautiful on the head, it also possesses the ability to evoke disgust when viewed as bodily waste, in the mouth or on a bar of soap. The meaning of hair thus depends on whether it is 'in place' or 'out of place.' Unlike the hair in *Pull,* the hair in *Recollection* has been detached from its natural place on its owner's body. This aspect of the work relates to the theories of cleanliness proposed by Douglas, who wrote of the notion of dirt as only understandable in relation to a system of boundaries and classification. According to Douglas, dirt is any element that does not occupy its rightful place in the system. It is 'matter out of place' (Douglas 1966: 50).

Systems of dirt and cleanliness relate to the theories of abjection proposed by the philosopher Julia Kristeva in *Powers of Horror* (1982). For Kristeva, the abject is literally that which has been thrown out, thrown beyond a border. It is threatening as it disturbs boundaries. *Recollection* performs this aspect of abjection beyond its formal use of hair, as the installation explores abjection in social and religious, as well as material and spatial terms.

Douglas suggested a correspondence between the physical body and the wider social corpus. Just as treatment of the body and its excrescences acts either to challenge or to consolidate societal norms, so the social body enacts the maintenance of its borders through movements of incorporation and expulsion (Douglas 1973: 93). This is evident in the case of Roman Catholic beguinages, communities of laywomen, active in the Low Countries from the early-thirteenth century, who devoted their lives to mystical piety. The beguines evade classification. They were described by the Franciscan Gilbert of Tournai in 1254 as 'women whom we have no idea what to call, ordinary women or nuns, because they live neither in the world nor out of it' (cited in Neel, 1989: 323). The beguines lived outside the (masculine) authority of both the church and the secular institutions of marriage and the family.[1]

The status of the beguines thus reflects Kristeva's description of the abject as 'The in-between, the ambiguous, the composite' (Kristeva 1982: 4). That which resists classification cannot be tolerated within the boundaries of the social body. It is perhaps for this reason that beguinages were often located at the edges of cities, or even outside their walls, performing the specialist task of caring for the dying, watching over dead bodies and performing wakes (Simons 2003: 61, 78). By placing such an evocative, yet abject material as hair in the space of the beguinage, which bears traces of a specific, gendered history of exclusion, *Recollection* maps the relationships between spiritual, spatial and bodily abjection.

BODILY MATERIALS

The system of classification which distinguishes the pure from the impure is most obvious in *Recollection* in the bar of soap embedded with pubic hairs. Here clean and unclean combine as a harmless household object becomes potentially hazardous. A disembodied strand of hair is doubly abjected as it has been discarded from the body and has become waste material that should literally be thrown out. A discarded pubic hair is most abject of all as it has also been placed beyond the boundary of what may acceptably be shown and seen.

Recollection was not the first artwork in which Hatoum had used pubic hair. In 1993 she produced *Jardin Public* (Figure 13.3), a wrought-iron garden chair with a neat triangle of pubic hair protruding through the seat. Like the bar of soap with its pubic hairs, *Jardin Public* resembles the surrealist objects of the 1920s and 1930s, which often took everyday objects and made them strange through paradoxical juxtapositions or references to a repertoire of the sexualized symbols of the unconscious. In this, the work contains echoes of pieces such as Meret Oppenheim's *Breakfast in Fur*, a teacup and saucer made from animal pelt, and Leonor Fini's 1939 *Corset Chair*, with stays of mother of pearl and black ribbons of wrought iron.

Figure 13.3   Mona Hatoum, *Jardin Public* (1993) (painted wrought iron, wax and pubic hair, 8.5 × 39.5 × 49 cm).
© the artist. Photo: Edward Woodman. Courtesy Jay Jopling/White Cube (London).

While hair on the head has been fetishized as a signifier of femininity, body hair has been almost entirely absent from representations of the female body until the twentieth century (Endres 2004). Body hair, especially pubic hair, has been considered particularly unfeminine as it interrupts what has conventionally been considered the aesthetically pleasing line of the female body. Diderot argued that 'the path of this infinitely agreeable line would have its course cut through by an interposed hair-tuft' (Diderot cited in Endres 2004: 20). Here, pubic hair is not only abject, placed beyond the limits of society, but is obscene in the literal sense: placed beyond the limits of visibility.

The framing of this argument presupposes a divide between nature and art, between humans as animals and humans as civilized creators of cultural artefacts. This binary is challenged in Hatoum's 1995 *Van Gogh's Back* (Figure 13.4), a photograph of a man's back, on which the hair has been lathered and coaxed into the painterly swirls characteristic of Van Gogh's work. The image humourously conflates representations of these two extreme visions

Figure 13.4   Mona Hatoum, *Van Gogh's Back* (1995) (C-print, 50 × 38 cm).
© the artist. Courtesy White Cube/Jay Jopling.

of human nature: here the body hair that attests to humans' animal origins and the instantly recognizable swirls that signify artistic genius are not opposed, but are brought together in a single piece of corporeal art.

Van Gogh's Back also finds a place in debates about the use of paint by women artists. In the 1970s and 1980s many artists rejected painting as a medium aligned with artistic practices which objectified female subjects and marginalized women artists (Deepwell 1987: 10). Painting was considered to be a politically retrograde practice, and was positioned in opposition to the supposed theoretical awareness of less historically loaded media such as performance, body art or the scripto-visual. *Van Gogh's Back* acts as a humorous counterpoint to this debate. Hatoum has replaced the female nude that has been the painter's subject par excellence with a male nude. Not only has the male body become the subject of the artwork here, but it has also become the canvas. At the same time, the paint, whose brushstrokes act as indexical traces of the body, has been replaced with hair that is part of the body. The piece challenges the distinction between painting and body art, suggesting that body art can be a form of painting, just as painting, like any art form, involves corporeal input and responses.

Similarly, *Jardin Public* literally interweaves two apparently opposed, yet foundationally linked concepts. Hatoum stated that the idea for the work grew out of the discovery that the words *public* and *pubic* come from the same etymological source (Hatoum 1997: 25). By displaying publicly what usually remains private, while the same time adding an erotically charged element to a mundane object, *Jardin Public* and the soap in *Recollection* may act to rehabilitate the pubic hair that has been excised from art history.

THE WORK OF MEMORY

Like the displaced pubic hair of *Jardin Public,* the discarded strands and balls deployed in *Recollection* disturbed the classificatory system in which hair's rightful place is attached to the body. In this, the remaindered strand of hair hints at the fragmentary nature of the subject, whose boundaries are literally liable to fall apart. Here the work's title, *Recollection,* suggests an attempt to reconstitute the subject by gathering together its scattered fragments. The process of re-collecting the lost object that is the work of mourning is also played out in *Recollection,* where the loom of woven hair recalls the way hair has been woven into bands and worn in memory of the dead. As well as being woven into intricate bracelets and necklaces, bodily relics such as locks of hair and even teeth have been enclosed in jewellery to be worn as a memento of a lost loved one. Such mourning jewellery became popular after the Reformation and reached the height of its popularity in the Victorian era (Pointon, 1999).

This theme reappeared in another of Hatoum's works, *Hair Necklace* (1995). Hatoum used some of the hair balls that she had collected to make a delicate string of bead-like spheres, which were displayed in the window of the Cartier boutique in Bordeaux as part of an exhibition entitled *Shopping.* Like the locks of hair worn in mourning jewellery, the hair beads of *Hair Necklace* that are displayed so openly possess private meanings, as they relate to an absent body whose identity remains obscure. In the case of *Hair Necklace,* however, the hair's owner is still alive. While a lock of hair as a relic of the dead seems to hold its subject in suspension between life and death, its pristine state allowing a disavowal of the body's death and decomposition, a relic of the living places its originator in the uncanny position of being memorialized while still alive. At the same time, the corporeal traces that will outlive the body prefigure that body's death.

Hair Necklace rehabilitates the abjected matter of the hair balls in a number of ways. Instead of detritus to be thrown out, the piece reframes the balls as precious material to be formed into jewellery and displayed in a prestigious setting. However, the piece does not simply work to invert oppositions, exchanging high and low, garbage and gold, but leaving hierarchies of materials essentially intact. It also acts to return the hair to the body, whence it emerged. While mourning jewellery places the relic of the lost loved one in bodily contact with the mourner, conducting the touch of the absent other, *Hair Necklace* holds out the possibility of placing abjected matter back into contact with the body that has expelled it.

HAIR, CULTURE AND IDENTITY

Seen as mourning jewellery, *Hair Necklace* blurs the boundaries between public and private through the display of bodily relics as a public sign of personal, sentimental meaning. Ideas of display and concealment reappear in *Keffieh* (1993–1999) (Figure 13.5), a work made using the type of scarf traditionally worn by Palestinian men. Hatoum had the very characteristic pattern of an Arab scarf embroidered with long strands of human hair on a "blank" scarf. These curl out from the scarf's edges, as if still growing. The piece plays with notions of the seen and the unseen as the strands of hair are alternately revealed and concealed as they are worked into and emerge

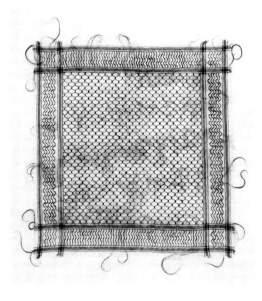

Figure 13.5 Mona Hatoum, *Keffieh* (1993–1999) (human hair on cotton fabric, 120 × 120 cm). © the artist. Photo: Hugo Glendinning. Courtesy Jay Jopling/White Cube (London).

from the scarf. The piece suggests that these concepts have a gendered aspect. Discussing the work Hatoum has stated: 'in Muslim countries many women … cover their hair with a scarf, because hair is associated with sexuality. In the case of my "Keffieh" the hair has broken the barrier, growing through' (Steiner and Herzog, 2004: 33). Here, covering and covered are woven into one, just as masculine scarf and feminine hair have become impossible to disentangle.

Keffieh clearly has powerful political and cultural meanings, however, these are not simple to pin down, but rather depend on the personal resonances that viewers bring to the piece. *Keffieh* asks the viewer to imagine what it would be like to wear a scarf like this; to be tickled by its wayward wisps; to smell another person's hair wrapped close to the face; perhaps to feel it catch in the mouth or brush the cheek. Like all of Hatoum's work, the piece is not just about the juxtaposition of opposing ideas, or the dismantling of absolutes. In its interweaving of hair and cloth into a palimpsest that is impossible to read clearly, *Keffieh* suggests multiple layers of meaning and sensation.

The intersection between gender and cultural identity is addressed once again in *Traffic* (2002) (Figure 13.6), in which Hatoum uses hair to explore notions of migration. The

Figure 13.6   Mona Hatoum, *Traffic* (2002) (compressed card, leather, metal, human hair and beeswax, 48 × 65 × 68 cm).
© the artist. Photo: Arturo González de Alba. Courtesy Laboratorio Arte Alameda, Mexico City, Mexico.

work consists of two battered suitcases which suggest untold stories of journeys made with the minimum necessary for survival, or the maximum that can be carried. The cases do not contain any ordinary luggage, however. They are connected by a swathe of human hair that appears to spill out of them, disturbingly alluding to the issue of people trafficking that is suggested by the piece's title. Here the human body and its parts are positioned as commodities that may be packed up, imported and exported. Long hair is in fact a valuable commodity that finds a place at the intersection of postcolonial, economic and gender power-relations, as hair is routinely imported from India to make hair extensions for Western women (McDougall 2006), to offer a disturbing version of commodity fetishism.

Traffic is uncanny in the sense that it makes familiar objects strange. This must be one of Hatoum's most disturbing works, as the hair makes the previously innocuous cases, unremarkable in terms of colour, size and shape, seem sinister in intent. The viewer must ask whether these inanimate objects in fact possess a life of their own, as they appear to be growing hair, or whether they are spilling open to reveal a secret; Freud's definition of the uncanny is that which 'ought to have remained secret and hidden but has come to light' (Freud, 1955: 224). The hair may suggest that what remains hidden here is the rest of a body, and reminds viewers of the widely held belief that the hair and fingernails continue to grow after death.

The piece is also uncanny in the sense of the *unheimlich* or 'unhomely'. The suitcases in *Traffic* point to a liminal space of transit between one place and another, inviting readings in terms of migration, homelessness and the crossing of borders. For the exile home may no longer be homely, but may be made *unheimlich* by experiences of displacement. As is the case with *Keffieh,* it is tempting to relate *Traffic* to the artist's own multinational identity. Hatoum's use of abject material such as hair has in the past been connected to her status as a Palestinian exile, as the exile is also 'matter out of place' (de Zegher 1997: 93). Hatoum has spoken, however, of her discomfort at criticism 'that wants to explain or validate my work specifically in relation to my background' (Hatoum 1997: 30).

Although her work deals consistently with notions of home and displacement, for Hatoum the experience they interrogate is not specified. She has stated of her work: 'It could be related to a number of people who are exiled, who are displaced, who suffer a kind of cultural or political oppression of . . . any kind' (Tusa, 2005). In *Traffic,* it is impossible to tell in which direction the hair is flowing as it crosses the space between the cases. Rather than a unidirectional movement of abjection, as the migrant body is 'thrown out' or displaced, the piece suggests a continuous movement of repeated passage and absorption. In this, the dynamics of *Traffic* recall the experience of migrants who are not only expelled beyond borders, but may cross and recross boundaries between nations, cultures and identities.

HAIRPIECES

Since the mid 1990s hair has proved to be an artistic material rich in allusions for Hatoum, providing a unique means of exploring a nexus of ideas around bodies, sensation and memory. Hair's unique material qualities have enabled it to be used for 'drawing', 'painting', jewellery and installation. In recent work, *Hair Drawing* (2003), and *Skin, Nail and Hair* (2003), Hatoum has returned to ideas first used in her student work, making paper out of hair, nail clippings and skin.

The use of hair has enabled Hatoum to create unsettling and paradoxical objects through the juxtaposition of incongruous elements and the making strange of familiar items. In Hatoum's work, hair is often abjected, literally thrown out: of the physical body, of the social body, even of representation, when hair moves beyond the abject to the obscene. Thus Hatoum's use of hair enables an interrogation of the margins and limits of aspects of subjectivity, including gender, religious, cultural and ethnic identity. Hatoum's work does not only perform simple acts of paradox or abjection, however, as memory, sensory experience, returns and repetitions always complicate the dynamics of her work. In making connections between hair, femininity and the body, Hatoum's use of hair has enabled a unique exploration of female subjectivity within society and within representation.

ACKNOWLEDGEMENT

Special thanks to the Leverhume Trust for funding my research.

NOTES

1. It has been argued that this ambiguous position eventually led to the beguines' condemnation on suspicion of heresy in 1312, after which the communities dwindled almost to extinction (Neel 1989: 324).

BIBLIOGRAPHY

Antoni, J. (1998), 'Mona Hatoum', *Bomb* (63), http://www.bombsite.com/issues/63/articles/2130, accessed 8 February 2008.

Cox, C. (2005), *Hair and Fashion,* London: V&A.

de Zegher, C. (1997), 'Hatoum's *Recollection:* About Losing and Being Lost', in M. Archer, G. Brett and C. de Zegher et al. (eds.), *Mona Hatoum,* London: Phaidon.

Deepwell, K. (1987), 'In Defence of the Indefensible: Feminism, Painting and Post-Modernism', *Feminist Art News,* 2 (4): 9–12.

Douglas, M. (1966), *Purity and Danger: An Analysis of Concepts of Pollution and Taboo,* London: Routledge.

Douglas, M. (1973), *Natural Symbols,* London: Pelican.

Endres, J. (2004), 'Diderot, Hogarth, and the Aesthetics of Depilation', *Eighteenth-Century Studies,* 38 (1): 17–38.

Freud, S. (1955), 'The Uncanny', *The Standard Edition of the Complete Psychological Works of Sigmund Freud,* Vol. 17, ed and trans. J. Strachey, London: Vintage.

Hatoum, M. (1997), 'Michael Archer in Conversation with Mona Hatoum', in M. Archer, G. Brett and C. de Zegher et al. (eds.), *Mona Hatoum,* London: Phaidon.

Kristeva, J. (1982), *Powers of Horror: An Essay on Abjection,* trans. L. S. Roudiez, New York: Columbia University Press.

McDougall, D. (2006), 'Trade in Hair Forces India's Children to Pay the Price', *The Observer,* 25 June, http://www.guardian.co.uk/world/2006/jun/25/india.theobserver, accessed 8 February 2008.

Mulvey, L. (1975), 'Visual Pleasure and Narrative Cinema,' *Screen,* 16 (3) (Autumn): 6–18.

Nead, L. (1992), *The Female Nude,* London: Routledge.

Neel, C. (1989), 'The Origins of the Beguines', *Signs,* 14 (2): 321–41.

Pointon, M. (1999), 'Materialising Mourning', in M. Kwint, C. Breward and J. Aynsley (eds.), *Material Memories,* Oxford: Berg.

Said, E. (2000), 'The Art of Displacement: Mona Hatoum's Logic of Irreconcilables', in M. Hatoum, *The Entire World as a Foreign Land,* London: Tate.

Simons, W. (2003), *Cities of Ladies: Beguine Communities in the Medieval Low Countries, 1200–1565,* Philadelphia: University of Pennsylvania Press.

Steiner, U. and Herzog, S. (2004), 'The Idea Is What Matters!', *Neue Zurcher,* 30 December, trans. I. Cole, http://www.qantara.de/webcom/show_article.php/_c_310_nr_144/i.html, accessed 8 February 2008.

Tusa, J. (2005), 'The John Tusa Interview: Mona Hatoum', *Radio, 3,* 4 September.

14 HAIR WITHOUT A HEAD
DISEMBODIMENT AND THE UNCANNY

JANICE MILLER

Claire: Did you use that conditioner I brought you?
Catherine: No. Shit. I forgot.
Claire: Well, it's my favorite. You'll love it, Katie. I want you to try it.
Catherine: I'll try it next time.
Claire: You'll like it. It has jojoba.
Catherine: What is jojoba?
Claire: It's something they put in for healthy hair.
Catherine: Hair is dead.

Proof (2005) Directed by John Madden,
Buena Vista Home Entertainment. 99 mins (DVD)

HAIR IS DEAD ...

The most contradictory fact about hair is that whilst many styling products are sold on the premise that they can create hair that has life, vitality and strength, hair is dead matter. Herein lies its complexity as symbol and as object. Hair is dead and yet in most dealings with it, it is its life-force which defines it. That hair should be 'lively' is a *familiar* concept, particularly for women; that it is dead is an *unfamiliar* one, repressed by the kinds of advertising that promise ecstatic experiences via the use of shampoo. This chapter is concerned with disembodied hair, cut from the body, dead and yet somehow alive. It will make connections between hair's place in memorial, ritual and magic, to emphasize its ambiguous and in some cases troubled relationship to the rest of the human body and in particular to notions of life and death, and the liminal space between the two. An analysis of this relationship using Freud's theory of the uncanny as a conceptual tool allows an exploration of the primal and fearful reaction that disembodied hair can cause, helping to explain why it has been an enduring device for the communication of disquieting emotions in a range of texts and narratives across a variety of cultures.

For Sigmund Freud, an inherent, intellectual uncertainty about death and all that pertains to it helps to explain many experiences of the uncanny: 'Biology has so far been unable to decide whether death is a necessary fate of every living creature or simply a regular, but perhaps avoidable, contingency within life itself. It is true that in textbooks on logic the statement that "all men must die" passes for an exemplary general proposition, but it is obvious to no-one' (2003: 148). Hair is dead and always has been, yet once it is removed from the body it seems to have an eerie ability to survive beyond us, sinister, because the dead nature of hair is masked by so many cultural representations of it. It is on many occasions a ghostly reminder of the absent body from which it originates. Thus disembodied hair becomes an uncanny and enduring motif in a variety of representations of the spectral and the supernatural discussed in this chapter, because fear and uncertainty lie in the questions it raises about the nature of the body, life and death itself.

HAIR ON AND OFF THE BODY

The natural place for human hair is the human body, and as such attitudes to it are shaped by a tacit understanding of that body as both a personal and social entity, central to a process of communication within a particular cultural context. Like many other customs concerned with the manipulation and fashioning of the human body, hairstyling and management is part of a range of culturally sanctioned practices and meanings associated with the communication of facets of social identity, including status, taste, sexuality and gender. The frequency with which hair is cut, shaped and cleaned, and the decisions that surround these seemingly everyday occurrences, are part of a range of bodily practices of self-management and discipline. Theoretical analyses of fashion and its associated customs have, using the work of the French philosopher Michel Foucault (Entwistle 2000), suggested that the shaping of the social body is subject to constant surveillance from a media and society which establishes a sense of normality (though what constitutes this may shift over time). Society then monitors its inhabitants in relation to this normality, subjecting transgressions, and those committing them, to ridicule and to its margins. Thus, there is pressure to fulfil ideals of bodily presentation as functioning and aware members of that society. Hair is an integral part of this social and cultural body.

As a result, hair is only rarely singled out for individual attention, but considered instead as a part of the embodied amalgam of the fashioned self (see Hollander 1994; Barnard 1996; Wilson 2005), or as historical, fashionable and shifting signifier with little explicit consideration of cultural meaning (see e.g. Keyes 1967; Corson 2000). As Alf Hiltebeitel notes, '[Hair] never seems to be explained the same way; rather, it always seems to be used differently to explain something else' (1998: 1). Yet it deserves more attention, because long, short, curled or straight, powdered, dyed or natural (and in the case of this chapter, cut away from the body), hair itself is clearly loaded with meanings that are both part of and contribute to our understanding of the social body, and the culture in which it is formed. But, at the same time, disembodied, hair has a shadowy and complex relationship to this body and implicit within this is an unspoken understanding of hair's potential unruliness.

Further, when examining disembodied hair, what is also revealed is the metaphorical way in which it comes to represent the body in a variety of encounters. Key to this are the activities that transform its status, contributing to its meanings as part of the body, as separate from it and as representative of it. Hair cutting is a moment of both physical and symbolic alteration, becoming a temporal marker of a particular moment which 'embodies materialized time' (Holm 2004: 140). In the 2006 film *When a Stranger Calls* the character of Jill Johnston is being harassed via phone whilst babysitting in an isolated house. As the attacker chases her and she escapes behind a heavy door, he manages to pull out a clump of her hair before she can close it. In the 1997 teen horror film *I Know What You Did Last Summer,* the character Helen wakens to find that during the night her hair has been cut off and on her mirror are written the words *soon.* In these narratives the removal of hair marks a moment in time: the early stages of a body under attack that promises to be the first of many violent incidents. As such, hair comes to symbolize the women's bodies. This is a moment of transformation, a warning of potential bodily and mortal danger. This disembodied hair seems to inhabit a hinterland between attacker and victim: at the same time, both familiar and unfamiliar.

THE FREUDIAN UNCANNY

Freud's discussion of the uncanny centres on notions of familiar and unfamiliar and the tension created by a transformation from one to the other, or perhaps more accurately from the space between the two, since the uncanny inhabits elements of both. The uncanny is constituted in Freud's terms by the revelation of something that 'should have remained hidden' (2003: 148). Freud uses the terms *das Heimliche* (directly translated as 'the homely', but sometimes better understood with the term 'familiar') and *das Unheimliche* (the 'unhomely' or 'unfamiliar') to reveal the nature of the uncanny which 'is actually nothing new or strange, but something that was long familiar to the psyche and was estranged from it only through being repressed' (2003: 148). Thus, when hair traverses the boundaries of the body by leaving it, by being cut or pulled out, as in these films, its nature, its meaning and symbolism and any cultural understanding of it undergoes an unsteadying shift. On the body, hair is controlled, familiar and homely: it is part of us. Off the body, it transforms itself into something at the same time alien, unfamiliar and unhomely.

HAIR IN THE MARGINS

To leave the body, to be cut off, to fall out, to be separate is for hair to reveal its marginality; to become alienated from its 'natural' bodily context and hence to become menacing. In the work of the Canadian artist Myfanwy MacLeod we find an example of hair at arguably its most threatening. In her work *Bound* (2006), a deep pile, white carpet—an expanse of purity and cleanliness—is interrupted by a lock of dark hair (Figure 14.1). In reviews and narratives supporting the work, the hair is variously described as ghostly and disturbing, left like a forensic trace element at a crime scene (Campbell 2006; MacLeod 2006). Clearly, the installation creates an unsettling sense of wrong-doing and discomfort. Here, hair is neither in its original bodily context, nor in a transformed one; it is hair in flux, inhabiting the margins between familiar and the unfamiliar. If we adopt Mary Douglas's maxim that 'dirt [is] created by the differentiating activity of the mind' (2002: 150) then this anonymous lock of hair constitutes dirt. We know nothing of the origins of the hair, who it belonged

Figure 14.1   Myfanwy MacLeod, *Bound,* 2006. Deep pile bound carpet, 108" × 144".
Courtesy Catriona Jeffries Gallery, Vancouver.

to, the person's presence or lack of hygiene, how it came to be there; what causes a reaction is that the clean, white angular carpet represents an orderliness that the hair disrupts. As Douglas argues, the flotsam and jetsam of societies are perceived as dangerous potential pollutants when 'their half-identity still clings to them and the clarity of the scene in which they obtrude is impaired by their presence' (Douglas 2002: 197). MacLeod's work creates responses that begin to demonstrate the instability of hair as matter and meaning, creating fearful reactions, primarily because this disembodied piece of hair is a troubling reminder of the absence of the body from which it originates. It has thus become this absent body's symbolic presence—its ghost—a reminder of the transient nature of the human body, and an emphatic assertion of hair's ability to both represent and exceed it.

HAIR AND RITUAL AND RELIC

As both elements and symbols of the body, hair and nail clippings have been central to a range of superstitions, fears and religious customs within a variety of cultural contexts (Frazer 1993). In a body of work concerned with comparative religion and its attendant folklore, James Frazer has traced the use of these types of physical matter in both positive healing rituals and negative vengeful magic. At the core of many of these has been the belief that bewitchment of some kind would be the result of any separation of an element of the body from its somatic whole. 'The general idea on which the superstition rests is that of the sympathetic connexion supposed to exist between a person and everything that has once been part of his body or in any way closely related to him' (Frazer 1993: 12). What Frazer's material reveals are the ways in which trace elements of the body become symbols of ephemeral corporeality in a variety of contexts, based on the conviction that affecting some vestigial fragment or remnant of the body would cause the living bodily whole to suffer the same fate (1993: 43). 'A Maori sorcerer intent on bewitching somebody sought to get a tress of his victim's hair, the parings of his nails, some of his spittle, or a shred of his garment. Having obtained the object, whatever it was, he chanted certain spells and curses over it in a falsetto voice and buried it in the ground. As the thing decayed, the person to whom it had belonged was supposed to waste away' (Frazer 1993: 268).

The notion that a part of the self and the soul might reside or be maintained in any part of the body separated from it is suggested not only by folklore, but also by some of the mourning practices in which lost loved ones were memorialized by the wearing of pieces of jewellery. Particularly in the eighteenth and nineteenth centuries, hair taken from the corpse was incorporated into the construction of objects such as bracelets, brooches and rings (Figure 14.2). That which was once dead finds new life and a transformation that allows meaning beyond

Figure 14.2 Gold-framed pendant containing a lock of hair, c.1850. Kodak Collection/NMeM/Science & Society Picture Library.

its original bodily context (Kwint 1999). In considering hair as substance and as object, studies of mourning jewellery reveal the metaphorical and symbiotic relationship between hair and the corporeal, highlighting the part that it plays in the sustenance of the social body lost in death, but hard won in life, and its symbolic representation as a focus for private grief in the Victorian period. As Christiane Holm notes, 'Mourning jewels are exhibited secrets' (2004: 140), which sustain a presence of the individual in the absence of the body itself.

Thus it would seem that objects and substances that have had close contact with, or which are remnants of, the body, here as cadaver, are the most potent tools for magic and memory, underpinned by the belief that retained within them lay trace elements of the power of the body and soul with which they shared an association. 'There is a position-ing of the corpse as a boundary "being"—it is possessed of a residue of "life" yet is also perceived as a physical marker of death' (Hallam and Hockey 2001: 109). In relation to this and by extension, anything taken from or associated with the corpse shares these kinds of meanings. Hair is dead matter and as such persists beyond the life-span of the human body, allowing a range of meanings, both public and private, to be interwoven into these intricate objects (Pointon 1999; Luthi 1998). As studies of memory and material culture note (Kwint 1999; Hallam and Hockey 2001; Pointon 1999), it is the marginal vestiges of the human body possessing their own material endurance (teeth, hair and bones) which come to be employed in the production of personal and holy relics.

The tradition of marking events, particularly grief and loss, by the wearing of pieces of symbolic jewellery traces its history from as early as the Middle Ages. Such practices are at times argued to be part of a symbolic transformation of the body of the deceased (Hallam and Hockey 2001) where its abject realities and the ultimate, and horrifying fate of the corpse, are hidden by its re-imagining into a sanctified object via the retention of remnants and the production of artefacts. Putrefaction and invisibility is replaced by resilience and visibility in the creation of objects that construct a representation of the absent body, pro-duced from its own elemental matter, repressing the realities of death, and culminating with a 'passage into otherness' (Hallam and Hockey 2001: 103). Beyond their personal function as catalysts for memory, they also, collectively, remain reminiscent of the kinds of transformative, primitive rituals traced by Frazer. Marius Kwint (1999: 9) establishes that the peripheral, enduring substances of the human body possess almost necromantic qualities because of the body's ephemeral nature. In the realm of the personal, such objects seek to lay ghosts to rest, yet the retention of the materiality of the corpse, through the use of hair in this way, means that in fact they remain as a shadowy influence, haunting these ob-jects. Hair here is supernatural and 'to many people the acme of the uncanny is represented by anything to do with death, dead bodies, revenants, spirits and ghosts' (Freud 2003: 148). Here, hair is both revenant and representation of the dead.

HAIR AND HAUNTING

The supernatural remnants of individual and identity that disembodied hair is believed to hold are illustrated by its use as an uncanny narrative device in a range of texts and examples which suggest that hair itself can haunt and be haunted. In the mid-nineteenth-century American novel *Uncle Tom's Cabin* by Harriet Beecher Stowe (1999), the young, pious character of Eva cuts off a lock of her hair when dying, for each of her father's slaves, encouraging them to embrace Christianity. The story is structured around a battle between Christian morals and immorality in relation to slavery, and the unstable meaning of the particular lock of hair is illustrative of this tension. Here the hair signifies her virtuousness, her morality, her purity and the maintenance of these qualities within the strands, beyond the life of her body. Later, the same lock of hair is encountered by the immoral plantation owner Legree, who mistakenly believes it to belong, not to Eva, but to his mother, who attempted to enforce upon him a Christian rectitude, and whom he cursed as a result. As he holds the hair it seems of its own volition to curl around his finger, and as a consequence, he lives in fear within his home, believing that by having this relic inside it, his mother's ghost must reside there too. Hair here is uncanny—a 'lifeless object' become 'animate' (Freud 2003: 135). The origin of the hair is unimportant, and Legree's experience has little to do with the realities of whom it belonged to or whether he imagined this movement of the hair. Hair may curl around a finger because of its material nature, but to conclude from this that it possesses life, or is the site of a ghostly presence is an example of the 'uncanny effect (that) often arises when the boundary between fantasy and reality is blurred, when we are faced with the reality of something that we have until now considered imaginary, when a symbol takes on the full function and significance of what it symbolizes' (Freud 2003: 150).

The idea that hair can be haunted is a common premise in Japanese folkloric tales, superstitions and sayings, many of which have a basis in the premedieval period, but whose influence can be traced far beyond into contemporary texts around the supernatural. Disembodied hair again suggests a sympathetic connection with its previous host, and a supernatural power lying within its own compounds. Hair was part of ritual and sacrifice, being offered in return for the protection of the self or loved ones, or interwoven into ropes contained within temples, demonstrating the often held and yet ambivalent association of hair and the sacred (Ebersole 1998; Douglas 2002). In Japanese culture, hair was also seen as possessing and relating to the life force of the individual, alongside its other supernatural symbolisms. Women's hair was seen to be a site of attraction for otherwordly spirits, both good and bad. For example, 'the long hair of young women was believed to have the power to attract *kami* or divinities, who would descend into it and temporarily reside there' (Ebersole 1998: 85). At the same time, 'The hair of women had the power to attract back the spirits or souls (*tama*) of absent lovers, as well as the *tama* of the dead' (Ebersole 1998: 86). Superstitions about such possession are situated both within ritual and outside it, whilst uncontrolled hair 'is a sign of psychic or spiritual turmoil' (Ebersole 1998: 95). As a result, unmanaged, dishevelled and out-of-place hair has become a signifier of the ghost in many Japanese cultural productions.

The archetype of the female vengeful ghost, and the central role privileged to hair in relation to it, finds reference in the traditions of kabuki theatre and in particular the story Yotsuya Kaidan (Ortolani 1995; Cavaye, Griffith and Senda 2005). Here we can trace the significance of disembodied hair to such narratives. The character of Oiwa is killed by the betrayal of her husband Iemon, who tries to poison her in order to free himself to make a better marriage. Before her death, the act of poisoning itself has failed to kill her and leaves her disfigured instead, with a drooping eye and most significant here, a loss of hair that leaves her partially bald. In theatrical scenes the magnitude of her hair loss is emphasized visually when, as she combs it in front of a mirror, it forms a vast mass of disembodied hair, representing the degradation of her feminine identity, sexuality and life force. After other acts of evil, Iemon flees to a mountain cabin where the notion of Oiwa as vengeful ghost and the haunting of her murderous husband is symbolized when the smoke from a fire outside of the cabin transforms itself into her hair. The absent body of Oiwa, and her ghostly replicant, is re-imagined and re-presented by her hair, abstracted and disembodied, and as such we encounter hair as uncanny and a revelation of 'everything that was intended to remain secret, hidden away, and has come into the open' (Freud 2003: 132) Here hair and smoke symbolize both Oiwa's murder and her return.

Hair and its symbolism in Asian culture and religion carries into the original and Hollywood remakes of Japanese horror films such as *The Grudge* (2004), *The Ring* (2003) and their sequels. Disembodied hair is used as a narrative device that repels, frightens and threatens, and in all of these films, hair is often the first signifier of the presence of a malevolent female ghost. In *The Grudge*, a clump of hair is pulled from a bath full of water and is both suggestive of an act of violence and a future act of revenge or, at least, the presence of a ghost with such an intention. In *The Ring*, the character Rachel coughs up matted strands of black hair interwoven with the wires and electrodes used on the spectral character of Samara in life. In *The Grudge 2* (2006), hair fills a room, covering and engulfing the ceiling like smoke as a manifestation of the ghost. In all, hair is abstracted from the body and takes on a new significance as the signifier of the absent body and the presence of the malevolent spirit. Thus hair is the catalyst for an uncanny return of some kind in all of these narratives, relating to death and all that we associate and *dis*associate with it. In Freudian terms, the uncanny nature of disembodied hair finds its referent in the notion that 'Severed limbs, a severed head, a hand detached from the arm ..., feet that dance by themselves ... —all of these have something highly uncanny about them, especially when they are credited, as in the last instance with independent activity' (Freud 2003: 150).

CONCLUSION

Disembodied hair is liminal, existing somewhere between body and other, and inhabiting this no man's land contentedly. To consider the significance of *disembodied* hair is to identify a range of eerie and uncanny meanings relating to the dichotomy of life and death surrounding it, but also, equally it is to reveal the uncanny nature of *embodied* hair too. The only living and sensory link between hair and the body is at its root and as such its nature as living or dead is contested ground. In the ways in which hair most commonly leaves the body—falling out or being cut—no pain is felt: it is sensorially distant from us.

We seem to distrust hair and believe it to possess and exercise agency in deceitful ways: it easily becomes other. This ambiguity may explain the rich superstitions and narratives that exist around it, across cultures. In this, we return to what Freud terms 'the old *animistic* view of the world', a belief in supernatural forces, magic and the 'omnipotence of thoughts' (Freud 2003: 147). It is the marginal nature of hair, the perceptible gap between and yet intertwining of it and the body, its *familiarity* and concurrent *unfamiliarity*, that is the basis of uncanny hair. It can both haunt and be haunted, it is us and it is other, and most important, it is dead yet seems alive.

BIBLIOGRAPHY

Barnard, M. (1996), *Fashion as Communication*, Oxford: Routledge.

Campbell, D. (2006), 'Pop Pastoral', *Vancouver Review*, http://www.vancouverreview.com/past_articles/poppastoral.htm, accessed 7 February 2008.

Cavaye, R., Griffith, P. and Senda, A. (2005), *A Guide to the Japanese Stage: From Traditional to Cutting Edge*, Tokyo: Kodansha International.

Corson, R. (2000), *Fashions in Hair: The First Five Thousand Years*, London: Owen.

Douglas, M. (2002), *Purity and Danger*, London: Routledge.

Ebersole, G. L. (1998), 'Long Black Hair Like a Seat Cushion: Hair Symbolism in Japanese Popular Religion', in A. Hiltebeitel and B. D. Miller (eds.), *Hair: Its Power and Meaning in Asian Cultures*, Albany: State University of New York Press.

Entwistle, J. (2000), *The Fashioned Body: Fashion, Dress and Modern Social Theory*, Cambridge: Polity Press.

Frazer, J. G. (1993), *The Golden Bough: A Study in Magic and Religion*, London: Wordsworth.

Freud, S. (2003), *The Uncanny*, London: Penguin.

Hallam, E. and Hockey, J. (2001), *Death, Memory and Material Culture*, Oxford: Berg.

Hiltebeitel, A. (1998), 'Introduction: Hair Tropes', in A. Hiltebeitel and B. D. Miller (eds.), *Hair: Its Power and Meaning in Asian Cultures*, Albany: State University of New York Press.

Hollander, A. (1994), *Sex and Suits*, New York: Random House.

Holm, C. (2004), 'Sentimental Cuts: Eighteenth-Century Mourning Jewelry with Hair', *Eighteenth Century Studies*, 38 (1): 139–43.

Keyes, J. (1967), *A History of Women's Hairstyles 1500–1965*, London: Meuthen.

Kwint, M. (1999), 'Introduction: The Physical Past', in M. Kwint, C. Breward and J. Aynsley (eds.), *Material Memories: Design and Evocation*, Oxford: Berg.

Luthi, A. L. (1998), *Sentimental Jewellery: Antique Jewels of Love and Sorrow*, Princes Risborough: Shire Publications.

MacLeod, M. (2006), 'Where I Have Lived and What I Have Lived For', www.contemporaryartgallery.ca/media/education/MacLeod_Teachers_Guide.pdf, accessed 14 June 2007.

Ortolani, B. (1995), *The Japanese Theatre*, Princeton, NJ: Princeton University Press.

Pointon, M. (1999), 'Materializing Mourning: Hair, Jewellery and the Body', in M. Kwint, C. Breward and J. Aynsley (eds.), *Material Memories: Design and Evocation*, Oxford: Berg.

Stowe, H. B. (1999), *Uncle Tom's Cabin*, London: Wordsworth.

Wilson, E. (2005), *Adorned in Dreams: Fashion and Modernity*, London: IB Tauris.

FILMOGRAPHY

The Grudge (2004), Directed by Takashi Shimizu, Universal Home Entertainment, 92 mins (DVD)

The Grudge 2 (2006), Directed by Takashi Shimizu, Universal Home Entertainment, 98 mins (DVD)

I Know What You Did Last Summer (1997), Directed by Jim Gillespie, Entertainment/Mandaley, 100 mins (DVD)

Proof (2005), Directed by John Madden, Buena Vista Home Entertainment, 99 mins (DVD)

The Ring (2003), Directed by Gore Verbinski, Universal Home Entertainment, 110 mins (DVD)

When a Stranger Calls (2006), Director Simon West, Screen Gems, 87 mins (DVD)

15 HAIR AND FASHIONED FEMININITY IN TWO NINETEENTH-CENTURY NOVELS

ROYCE MAHAWATTE

HAIR: A SIGNIFYING BODILY PHENOMENON

Women's hair has a particular resonance when it is considered as a part of the body. Joanne Entwistle's idea that fashion operates as a 'situated bodily practice' applies, with some adjustment, to hair as well: 'our experience of the body' she writes, 'is not as an inert object but the envelope of our being, the site for our articulation of self' (Entwistle 2001: 45–6). Arguably, this articulation of self is even more suggestive in hair than it is in dress. Its meaning is affected by the way it is styled, shaped and altered, and these meanings are crucial to understanding the way that gender and identity is enacted (Synnott 1993). There is an unspoken assumption that hair is a part of the body, and so somehow less changeable than fashioned apparel, but hair is a bodily language: it is personal, social and highly contingent (Hallpike 1978). Thus, the history of women's hairstyles can be read as a history of the perception of femininity, and a part of this history lies in the way that hair is represented.

The readerly qualities of women's hair feature extensively in literature but, particularly, in nineteenth-century fiction and poetry. Elisabeth Gitter asserts that the sentimental figure of 'the angel of the parlour' was most likely to be imagined blonde; the seductress, or fallen woman, as dark-haired, or at least with hair flowing freely (Gitter 1984). The sign systems around nineteenth-century hair are numerous: loose, bound and styled hair, as well as hairpieces— perukes, 'false fronts' and braids—all feature in fiction and have meanings that alter the way femininity is both considered and understood. As a bodily practice, women's hair does not simply connote abstract and timeless values, but connects with the economic and social world around it. 'The body is pivotal to representations of emotions and physical activity, of sex, sexuality, of eroticism, as supposedly natural facets of human experience ... social practices and the beauty and fitness industries. All these discursive structures often hinge on *unwritten laws and naturalised assumptions*' [my italics] (Cavallaro and Warwick 1998: 8).

Women's hair functions as a 'signifying bodily phenomenon' both in and out of fiction. Hair in fiction, as in life, is dressed so that styles and meanings become virtually the same thing. A women's hair is often seen as an indicator of her morality, her social position and her allure. Fiction of the nineteenth century makes this code strikingly clear as the meaning of hair is often used to advance narrative; the hair of fictional women enhances character and provides a commentary on how a woman's sexual power engages with the wider world. Of course, the use of hair as a literary device is very much in keeping with the tendency of nineteenth-century fiction and in particular, the melodramatic varieties, to use the surface of the body as a vehicle for meaning (Booth 1965: 13–15; Howells 1978: 20; Spooner 2004: 4). Bodies, movements and clothes are all employed to convey character, social position and, most important, emotion and morality.

Hair is therefore widely represented in nineteenth-century fiction, but surprisingly little has been written on the subject. Elisabeth G. Gitter (1984) looks at the role of women's hair in Victorian fiction and poetry and provides a catalogue of examples of the ambiguous ways in which hair is used as a mythology. Nina Auerbach (1975, 1982) and Susan Gilbert and Sandra Gubar (1979), in their important work, link together the conflicting symbolisms, archetypal and sexual, found in the writing of hair and link them to the complex rebellions that women writers engaged in. Their work, however, can be advanced by drawing on cultural studies' approaches that help to place the writing of hair within a system of contemporary fashioned ephemera. This chapter, therefore, examines two key texts that span the latter half of the nineteenth century, and in which the hair of the female characters plays a significant role within the narrative: *The Mill on the Floss* (George Eliot, 1860) and *The Woodlanders* (Thomas Hardy, 1887). In both these works, hair comes to represent polarities of character, of morality, of social status and culture. George Eliot and Thomas Hardy engage with the ambiguities offered by the representation of hair and exploit its symbolic potential: goodness versus badness; the rural versus the urban; the natural versus the artificial; and the controlled against the uncontrollable. How do these supposed binaries relate to a contemporary fashion culture through concepts of beauty, both natural and enhanced, and the economic relations that exist between individual and social bodies?

DARK, HEAVY LOCKS AND FALSE FRONTS: SYMBOL AND RITUAL IN *THE MILL ON THE FLOSS*

The Mill on the Floss is a novel about an unorthodox young woman who is defeated by both a lack of opportunities and her own self-repression. Intelligent, impulsive and precocious, Maggie Tulliver is considered a misfit, unable to assimilate into her immediate social environment. Her hair, and the emotional journey figured through the representation of her hair—especially in the early sequences of the novel when she is a child—embodies Maggie's wayward characteristics. When she is first introduced into the novel through a conversation between her parents, Maggie is pictured plaiting her hair and singing like 'a Bedlam creature' (Eliot 1980: 13) so that her unconventional behaviour is immediately connected to her hair and conceptualized in relation to both control and containment. The Royal Bethlehem Hospital, or Bedlam as it was popularly known, was the most notorious psychiatric institution in England of the day, and opened its wards for public display. The image of Maggie, therefore, absorbed in singing and plaiting her hair, is introduced to the reader, not as an image of child-like innocence and beauty, but as a morbid spectacle, as if she were an inmate of such a place. The Victorian mythology of wayward hair is alive as the references to Maggie's hair continue: it will not be styled and her dark and unruly tresses are contrasted with the compliant blonde curls of her young cousin, Lucy Dean. Like the phrenologists who could determine temperament and personality from the shape of the skull, the reader can determine that the meaning inferred from Maggie's childhood hair will not bear well on her adulthood.

The novel is set prior to 1832 and Eliot is careful to place the Tullivers within an emergent social class amidst the early waves of industrialization in England, and an increasing affluence that finds expression in the hair fashions of the period. Maggie grows up in a world where the wearing of hair is a complex social ritual, which the novel's introduction of her Aunt Glegg and her hairpieces make very clear:

> Mrs Glegg had doubtless the glossiest and crispest brown curls in her drawers, as well as curls in various degrees of fuzzy laxness; but to look out on the weekday world from under a crisp and glossy front, would be to introduce a most dreamlike and unpleasant confusion between the sacred and the secular. (Eliot 1980: 53)

During the course of the nineteenth century, the styling of a woman's hair involved less cutting and usually more dressing, particularly with the addition of extra pieces of 'false' hair (Cox 1999: 17). For example, the 'false front' favoured by Aunt Glegg was a weft, secured at the crown and curled and draped down to the chin or even the shoulders to frame the face (Figure 15.1). The woman's naturally growing hair would be drawn to the back of the head to give the impression that the hair was thick and abundant on all sides. This practice had its origins in the Napoleonic and Regency wigs that covered the whole head, and Aunt Glegg's sense of fashionable and social aspiration clearly relates to this period. Her best false front is only to be worn in church, yet it was 'doubtless' that there was always another one in her drawer for other occasions. What is important here is that whether lustrous or frizzled, on a number of levels, Aunt Glegg's hairpieces function as a sign of conspicuous consumption. The hair would have come from the head of a poor working-class girl, or from Asia, via Marseilles (Cox 1999: 7, 24), but its dressing would equally have been a difficult task without the services of a maid to attach the weft discreetly to the crown.

As a sign of abundance on all levels, therefore, the pun 'false front' is clearly intended, and the tone Eliot uses here emphasizes the relationship between fashion and snobbery. Mrs Tulliver, Maggie's mother, described as 'weak', we are told 'had hurt her sister's feelings greatly by wearing her own hair' (Eliot 1980: 43–4). The implication here is that Mrs Tulliver's avoidance of fake hair is not simply a fashion faux pas. The wearing of fake hair can be understood as part of public dress and an allied range of social codes whose eschewal signals a lack on the part of Mrs Tulliver of both individual effort and of social aspiration. Of course, Maggie's transgressions exceed those of her mother. When the Aunts come to visit, along with Cousin Lucy, Maggie's hair is criticized for not conforming to the contemporary standards of beauty. Much hurt by the comments and stung into action, impulsively Maggie cuts her hair off and then enrols her brother to help:

> The black locks were so thick—nothing could be more tempting to a lad who had already tasted the forbidden pleasures of cutting the pony's mane. I speak to those who

know the satisfaction making a pair of shears meet through a duly resisting mass of hair. One delicious grinding snip, and then another and another, the hinder-locks fell heavily on the floor, and Maggie stood cropped in a jagged, uneven manner, but with a sense of clearness and freedom, as if she had emerged from a wood into the open plain. (Eliot 1980: 64)

This vividly described physical and emotional release plays on the sensual qualities of haircutting and provides a strong contrast with the measured and sarcastic prose associated with Aunt Glegg and her hairpieces. The reference to the 'pony's mane' develops an idea, referenced earlier in the novel, when Maggie is described as having the 'air of a small Shetland pony' (13) reinforcing an understanding of her as close to nature, perhaps too close for her family or society to readily accept. The impromptu haircut is simultaneously an act of self-mutilation—of Maggie's 'natural' femininity—and an expression of her natural temperament. The literally headstrong girl is reacting to the negative reception of her hair and she takes her family's comments to their logical extension. Aunt Glegg's response to this new style is, however, telling: 'Little gells as cut their own hair should be whipped and fed on bread-and-water—not come and sit down with their aunts and uncles' (Eliot 1980: 68). The problem here lies in the tensions that come into play through the characterization of Maggie's hair within the clash between these competing forces of the natural and the social. In following the inclination of the one, Maggie disregards the conventions of the other.

As Maggie grows up, she rails against the strictures of contemporary beauty conventions— or rather those emphasized in the literature she reads, where the dark-haired heroine is always seemingly doomed to suffer disappointment. On reading Walter Scott's *The Pirate* and Madame de Stael's *Corinne,* Maggie rejects such novels and jokes that she wants to avenge them. ' "I am determined to read no more books where the blond-haired women carry away all the happiness" ' (Eliot 1980: 332). Ironically, Maggie does get a type of revenge, but it is a hollow one: it is she who inadvertently steals the heart of Stephen Guest, her Cousin Lucy's fiancé. Guest falls in love with Maggie's spirit, transfixed by her bewitching gaze and her 'jet-black coronet of hair' (Eliot 1980: 376). Maggie's hair once more acts as the emotional conduit for the transgressive energies that so worried her family when she was a child—and which now looms large in the narrative's trajectory from transgression to tragedy.

'THE LADY THAT WANTS IT WANTS IT BADLY': THE VALUE OF HAIR IN *THE WOODLANDERS*

The literary anxieties and moral contradictions associated with beauty and artifice equally find expression in Thomas Hardy's *The Woodlanders,* a sexual melodrama that explores the impact of modernity on rural England. The main story tells of Grace Melbury, a simple country girl educated out of her station, and who rejects the love of her childhood sweetheart, Giles Winterbourne, in favour of the philandering Doctor Fitzpiers. When the subject of hair is considered, the subplot once again articulates the problematic relationship between nature and beauty that had achieved almost a mythological status by the late-nineteenth century. The fashionable socialite-widow, Felice Charmond, comes to the woodland village of Little Hintock and decides to take the doctor as her lover. Felice seizes on the idea that the auburn hair of Marty South, an unrefined local girl, and its transformation into a fashionable hairpiece, will make her romantic designs all the more effective.

The novel sets up a sexual competition and a circle of desire around and between these three women and their different fashioned states. Felice Charmond is urban, competitive and fully aware of the fashion cycle; Grace Melbury is educated, and although appreciative of fashion culture, is rather naïve; Marty South, sadly, becomes aware of fashion, not as a consumer, but as its living raw material: it is she, or at least her hair, which is consumed. By the 1880s, the image of the girl forced into selling her hair had become a stock tale in contemporary culture. The notions of conspicuous consumption alluded to in a novel like *The Mill on the Floss* were a prominent feature of sexual melodrama and are now used by Hardy to explore not just Felice Charmond's self-serving character, but also Marty South's selflessness. Hair and its fashioned embodiment conflate different values and conflicting forms of capital and social exchange as Marty's innocence and her naturally beautiful and abundant hair are both sacrificed to ornament Felice's contrived fashionable artifice. The commercial and cultural worth of such a valuable commodity elevates Marty South's status by association with Felice Charmond's social position and connections. This allows her to—at least superficially—exploit her natural beauty for her own ends. However, within Hardy's narrative, short-term gain only effectively serves as a symbol for

WATER WAVED
FRINGES.

No. 1, Price 4/6.

No. 2, Price 6/-

No. 3, Price 8/-

No. 4, Price 8/-

The above goods are extremely light, durable and natural, and are made upon the new transparent ventilated Patent Hair Foundation. WAVED Fringes are the present fashion in Paris and New York.

Figure 15.1 'Water Waved Fringes', *Hairdressers' Weekly Journal*, 3 November 1883: 727. From *Hairdressers' Journal*, www.HJi.co.uk.

a rural body—Marty's and England itself—that cannot compete with either fashionable modernity or its inexhaustible resources.

The early events of the novel are predicated around this concept of the commercial exchange of Marty's hair, and also the inequitable and sometimes exploitative relationship between rich and poor, country life and urban society. The work opens in Hardy's characteristic style, with the reader brought into the Wessex countryside by a stranger, who turns out to be Barber Percomb, the gentleman barber who attends the coiffure of fashionable society. Like a true villain, while toying with the glinting bows of his scissors, Percomb tries to get Marty to part with her hair. ' "The lady that wants it wants it badly. And, between you and me, you'd better let her have it. 'Twill be bad for you if you don't" ' (Hardy 1998: 13). At this stage in the novel, Marty refuses, but when her family faces financial ruin, the hair is sold. In a highly charged melodramatic scene, Marty cuts her hair and prepares it for the barber: 'Upon the pale scrubbed deal of the coffin-stool table they [the locks of hair] stretched like waving and ropy weeds over the washed white bed of a stream' (Hardy 1998: 20). The cutting is therefore figured as a kind of sexual death for Marty, the reference to the coffin-stool table reinforcing this potent symbolism.

These locks are sexual symbols, but the power relations are necessarily economic. *The Hairdressers' Weekly Journal* was a contemporary trade magazine that advertised hair products and appointments alongside fashion plates illustrating hairstyles and innovations. Any issue therefore includes a number of adverts for braids, perukes and false fringes and fronts like those so valorized by Aunt Glegg in *The Mill on the Floss,* and coveted here by Felice Charmond, as well as the latest examples of their dressing (Figure 15.2). In the European circles that Felice frequented, Marty's chestnut hair would have turned heads and caused comment. Naturally blonde, red and white hair could fetch a competitive price on the open market, and was seen as especially desirable when taken from rural girls such as Marty, who were considered untainted by the adulterated foods found in city diets (Woodforde 1971: 104) (Figures 15.3 and 15.4). Such themes are reflected in the novel but these are, however by no means restricted to the abstract and symbolic (Gitter 1984: 945). Rather, Hardy explores the conflicting interests of fashionable femininity on the one hand, and the price to be paid for it on the other—an issue which was of widespread contemporary concern. There was clearly a flourishing trade in false hair at the end of the nineteenth century but features within magazines and trade journals entitled, for example, 'Ten Pounds for a Single Hair' (*Hairdressers' Weekly Journal,* 1884: 568) and 'The Value of Hair' (*Hairdressers' Weekly Journal,* 1886: 367), increasingly brought the social and cultural effects of false hair and its exploitation to the popular reader's attention.

In *The Woodlanders,* when Felice Charmond is first seen with her new hair by Grace and Marty, the reception is significant:

> Mrs Charmond did not see them, but there was sufficient light for them to discern her outline between the carriage windows. A noticeable feature in her tournure was a magnificent mass of braided locks.

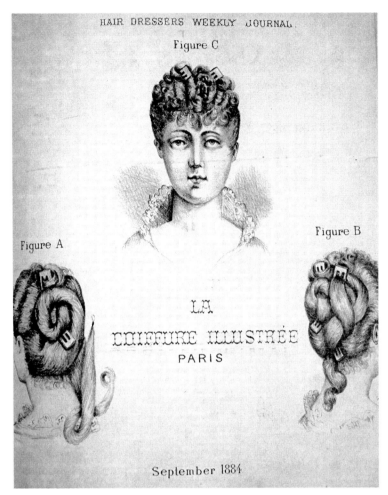

Figure 15.2   Supplement to Fashion Plate, *Hair Dressers Weekly Journal* [sic], September 1884: iii, *Hairdressers' Weekly Journal,* 13 September 1884: 576. From *Hairdressers Journal,* www.HJi.co.uk

'How well she looks this morning!' said Grace, forgetting Mrs Charmond's slight in her generous admiration. 'Her hair so becomes her worn that way. I have never seen any more beautiful!'

'Nor have I, miss,' said Marty drily, and unconsciously stroking her crown. (Hardy 1998: 97)

Grace, for all her cultivation, is still innocent in the ways of fashion and quite literally does not see the fakery. Nor does she remember how Felice Charmond slighted her appearance earlier in the novel. Such innocence marks her out as essentially a heroine. Marty, of course, waxes sarcastic. Grace's unawareness is contrasted with Marty's knowledge about the process and, most painfully, the price of Felice's beauty. She knows and is implicated in the deception.

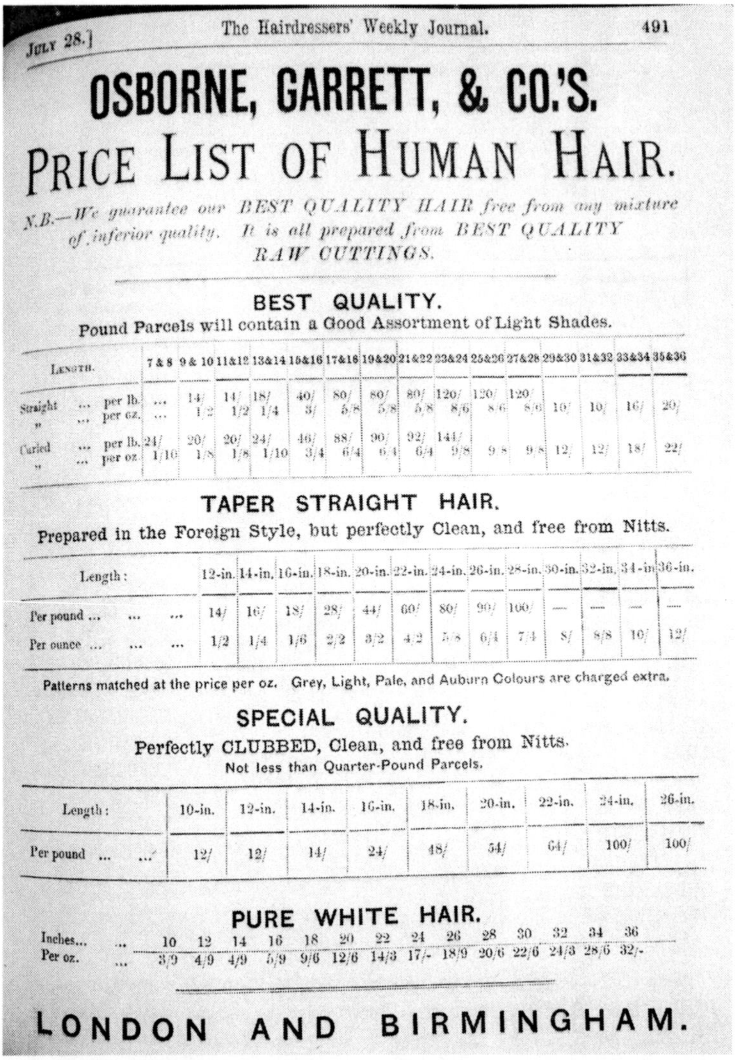

Figure 15.3 Advertisement for 'Sale of Human Hair', *Hairdressers' Weekly Journal*, 28 July 1883: 491.
From *Hairdressers' Journal*, www.HJi.co.uk.

This sequence has the bleak humor that is often found in Hardy's work, but when viewing this text as a discourse around hair, the tone is revealing. An appreciation of beauty, Grace's view, is met with a resentful resignation to the construction and economics of beauty. Fake beauty invariably leads to satire. The bleak humor is increased when Marty, later in the novel, tries to break up the relationship between Grace's husband and Felice. She writes a letter to the doctor, exposing the origins of Felice Charmond's hair. Of course, this reveals her naïvety, as by now the hairpiece has served its purpose. Hair in *The Woodlanders* operates as a cipher for the exchanges of power between women, and between labour and capital. Marty's letter naïvely tries to destroy the sexual allure of Felice

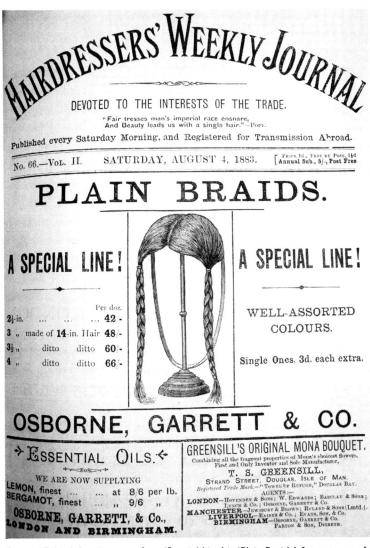

Figure 15.4 Advertisement for a 'Special Line' in 'Plain Braids', front cover of *Hairdressers' Weekly Journal*, 4 August 1883.
From *Hairdressers' Journal*, www.HJi.co.uk.

and her hairpiece, but its arrival after the event only confirms that the power exchange ultimately lay within the cutting and procurement of the hair and surprisingly less with the wearing of it.

HAIR AS COMMODITY: SYMBOLISM AND SATIRE

The stories of Marty South's and Maggie Tulliver's hair can both be placed within a much wider commercial and cultural context than is suggested in their respective narratives. Women's individual hair and hairstyles in Eliot's narrative function as part of a wider social body, almost as public property. Maggie's uncontrollable dark hair is symbolic of an earthy natural and wild femininity, but its wanton destruction equally places Maggie beyond the reach of polite society. Maggie cuts her hair but in doing so is herself cut off and treated as an outcast. Yet, at the same time, in *The Mill on the Floss*, fashionable hair practices are not portrayed as any kind of corrective, but rather only work to oppress Maggie further—even more than the natural waywardness of the hair they seek to contain and control. Rather than being a fixed text, therefore, hair works in nineteenth-century fiction as a debate about the nature and authenticity of idealized beauty and the gender assumptions that go along with it.

Women who take pride in their appearance, whether it is their hair or their clothes, occupy a problematic place in nineteenth-century fiction. Female protagonists are rarely ugly but are often praised for their plainness. However, a female character overly preoccupied with her physical appearance is only in the rarest of cases allowed to become a heroine by the end of the novel. The problems posed by fashion and fashionable hair for nineteenth-century fiction writers stem from the very fundamentals of what makes a female character work in English fiction. Traditionally, the nineteenth-century heroine finds her virtue in the everyday rather than the embellished because any adherence to fashionable life and the attractions of ornament would make her appear both vain and worldly (Brownstein 1982: 153).

For a writer like Eliot, a puritan upbringing ensured that Maggie Tulliver—and also, for example, Dorothea Casaubon in *Middlemarch* (1876)—would reject finery and all of its worrying associations in favour of a more morally certain plainness that denied any heroine wearing a false front. But the rapidly expanding hairstyle and product industries of the nineteenth century equally present a contradiction for writers, particularly for those interested in verisimilitude like Hardy. As Caroline Cox (1999: 24) points out, the hair industry itself was morally problematic in that it promoted excess, both in style and in worldliness, but every thickly piled head of hair also told a story of the exploitation of a young girl forced to sell her hair as an alternative to begging or worse.

The symbolic meanings of hair provide an important and varying function in nineteenth-century literature. Rather than taking a purely representative role, hair in this fiction clearly engages with commodity culture of the time. This commodity culture is, however, questionable and frequently satirized as the status of a heroine often depends on her beauty being natural and her interests unworldly. Both Eliot and Hardy place their heroines away from the corrupting and exploitative excesses of beautification, yet at the same time are drawn to the drama of problematic hair and female misfits. As an ambiguous fetish, hair is natural, but not overly so. Imbued with human qualities, it is a site of both individual rebellion and of middle-class conformity.

In twentieth-century literature, hair ceased to have the same type of symbolic value. The advances in psychology and the publication of the works of Freud gave writers a way of accessing the inward aspects of female characters. In literary culture, a Modernist mode of writing assumed predominance within which the description of surfaces became less important as vehicles for meaning. The fashion for short hairstyles altered the symbolism and brought modernity and social mobility to hair. That is not to say that only long hair has signifying practices, but in the nineteenth century it was able to contain many of the problematic conflicts around femininity, status and economic power. Elizabeth Gitter (1984) rightly emphasizes the contradictions around the mythology of women's hair but these can be extended into the problems inherent in the hair and beauty industries. She argues, 'If a woman's hair is the text that explains her, clearly it makes hard reading' (Gitter 1984: 941). Maggie Tulliver's self-mutilation was an act of hot-tempered defiance, Marty South's was one of economic pragmatism: but the stakes are equally high.

BIBLIOGRAPHY

Auerbach, N. (1975), 'The Power of Hunger: Demonism and Maggie Tulliver', *Nineteenth-Century Fiction*, 30: 150–71.

Auerbach, N. (1982), *Woman and the Demon: The Life of a Victorian Myth*, Cambridge, MA: Harvard University Press.

Booth, M. (1965), *English Melodrama*, London: Herbert Jenkins.

Brownstein, R. M. (1982), *Becoming a Heroine*, Harmondsworth: Penguin Books.

Cavallaro, D. and Warwick, A. (1998), *Fashioning the Frame: Boundaries, Dress and Body*, Oxford: Berg.

Cox, C. (1999), *Good Hair Days, A History of British Hair*, London: Quartet Books.

Eliot, G. (1980), *The Mill on the Floss*, first published 1860, Oxford: Oxford University Press.

Eliot, G. (1986), *Middlemarch*, first published 1871–1872, Oxford: Clarendon Press.

Entwistle, J. (2001), 'The Dressed Body', in J. Entwistle and E. Wilson (eds.), *Body Dressing*, Oxford and New York: Berg: 33–59.

Gilbert, S. M. and Gubar, S. (1979), *The Madwoman in the Attic: The Woman Writer and the Nineteenth-Century Literary Imagination*, New Haven: Yale University Press.

Gitter, E. G. (1984), 'The Power of Women's Hair in the Victorian Imagination,' *PMLA: Journal of the Modern Language Association*, 99 (5): 936–54.

Hairdressers' Weekly Journal (1884), 'Ten Pounds for a Single Hair', Volume 3: 568.

Hairdressers' Weekly Journal (1886), 'The Value of Hair', Volume 3: 367.

Hallpike, C. R. (1978), 'Social Hair', in T. Polhemus (ed), *The Body Reader: Social Aspects of the Human Body*, New York: Pantheon Books: 134–46.

Hardy, T. (1998), *The Woodlanders*, first published 1887, Harmondsworth: Penguin Books.

Howells, C. A. (1978), *Love, Mystery and Misery: Feeling in the Gothic Novel*, London: Athlone Press.

Spooner, C. (2004), *Fashioning Gothic Bodies*, Manchester: Manchester University Press.

Synnott, A. (1993), *The Body Social: Symbolism, Self and Society*, London and New York: Routledge.

Woodforde, J. (1971), *The Strange Story of False Hair*, London: Routledge and Kegan Paul.

16 HAIR CONTROL
THE FEMININE 'DISCIPLINED HEAD'

THOM HECHT

This study of the 'disciplined head', in the form of buns, chignons, knots and pulled back 'up-dos', has its origins in the escalating interest in cultural approaches to the body (Turner 1996; Shilling 2003). Disciplined hair can be read as a symbolic code, loaded with cultural and historical significance that goes far beyond the simple control of locks. Examples discussed in this chapter are typical female figures of authority, their disciplined personae and their controlled hairstyles: the classical ballerina, the spinster, the schoolmistress and the dominatrix. It might be argued that these pervasive stereotypes of disciplined femininity control their hair to an almost obsessive extent in order to achieve, maintain and express an embodied discipline. These figures of feminine self-discipline can thus be evaluated in relation to French philosopher Michel Foucault's (1979) theories of the disciplined body, to explore how states of control and discipline are achieved through hair practices.

BALLERINA 'BUNHEAD' CULTURE: 'MY BUN IS STAPLED IN'

In *A Day in the Life of a Ballerina* (2002), British comedians Dawn French and Jennifer Saunders illustrate the great significance of the ballerina's bun. Here two ballerinas are looking at a scrapbook:

Saunders: This is me when I was four!
French: Don't you look different with your hair down?!
Saunders: Yeah, but I didn't 'go up' until I was six, which is really late ...
French: Really?
Saunders: Yes, it is called 'going up' when your bun is stapled in.
French: I would have gone up when I was three, but once you are gone up, it is for life.
Saunders: You can't take it down ...
French: ... otherwise your face falls off!

The stereotypical ballerina bun is indeed intimately bound to the classical dancer's head, so much so that the word *bunhead* has become a slang term in the ballet world for a zealously dedicated ballet student (Wulff 1998; Hecht 2006). Dance scholars agree that classical ballet is an art form that almost obsessively encapsulates the total control of the body (Royce 1984: 27; Banes 1998). From the nineteenth century onwards, female dancers were identified as playing a primary role and from this point onwards the ballerina rose to the tips of her toes and contributed to a new dance aesthetic (Hecht 2005: 43). This includes the ballerina's hair, which is firmly slicked back into a tight bun or pinned into a French *chignon*, so as not to distract from balletic lines, alignments and positions (Figure 16.1). It also guarantees the uniformity of the dancer's appearance on and off stage. Aesthetically pleasing through its enhancement of the long neckline of the ballet dancer, the controlled hairstyle also represents an almost compulsory health and safety device for the dancer. Securely pinned-up hair allows the dancer to perform multiple pirouettes *en pointe*, to jump gracefully and to be lifted in *pas-de-deux* work without restrictions. Classical ballet

Figure 16.1   Elena Louise Savva, ballet dancer.
Photo by Sarah Roesink.

repertoire often requires an intimate proximity to other dancers that leaves them no choice but to control their locks.

The bun of the classical ballerina is thus an extension of the straight back and body control, both of which signify the embodied discipline of the female dancer. Arguably, and rather provokingly, the ballerina's bun might appear as a phallic extension of the lifted body (Foster 1996: 1) (Figure 16.2). Even when the ballerina jumps, turns and gets lifted into the air, her controlled hairstyle never moves: securely pinned up, the ballerina's hair represents an example of discipline *per se.*

For centuries, ballet dancers have dedicated their lives to disciplining their bodies to conform to the stringent aesthetic required to succeed in the art of classical ballet. Clearly, these aesthetics require a subordination of female sexuality as loose hair is combed, gelled, sprayed and fixed invisibly with hairnets and bobby pins to create the stereotypical ballerina hairdo. Achieving a clean and well-groomed chignon requires artistic skills and tedious discipline. Disciplined hair is part of the social life of the ballet for female dancers, and learning to control the body in classical dance entails learning to control the hair. Silently, this is accepted by the ballerina-to-be, as 'learning [in ballet] is a process that takes place in a participation framework, not in an individual mind' (Lave and Wenger 1991: 15), where

Figure 16.2   Elena Louise Savva, ballet dancer.
Photo by Sarah Roesink.

the disciplined body is internalized as part of the dancer's value system (Hecht 2006: 194). Indeed, controlling the ballerina's hair represents the first step in the preparation for balletic exercises, mentally and physically. Although dancers use the body all the time when they work, hair in classical ballet does not move. Dancers agree that controlling the hair represents a preceding mental preparation for the physical and emotional demands of the daily classes, rehearsals and stage performances that make up the life of a dancer (Savva 2007). At any stage, the ballerina's embodied femininity is in total control.

The bun also makes an appearance in stories that revolve around the world of ballet, such as Noel Streatfield's *Ballet Shoes* (1936), Katharina Holabird's *Angelina Ballerina* series (1983) and more recently, Mattel's *Barbie of Swan Lake* (2003). Ballet finds a place within the normalization of femininity and the social training of girls, offering the opportunity to indulge in romantic fairy-tale storylines, physical elegance and frothy pink tutus. Ballet is seen as a 'normal' feminine activity with fixed dress *and* hair codes that include the controlling style of the bun.

SPINSTERS AND SCHOOLMISTRESSES: HAIR CONTROL AND SEXUAL REPRESSION

In Victorian times, controlling 'hairy' femininity included endless variations on the bun and the *chignon*. The 'letting down' of hair, as Caroline Cox (1999: 18) writes, 'was considered a very private activity, in part due to the traditional associations of cascading hair with sexual temptations.' Western traditions in the styling of women's hair can also be related to the shift from girl to woman. 'As the Victorian woman entered adulthood and thus a more public sexual maturity', Cox argues, 'her hair was safely upswept to show a distinction between the girl and the woman, and hair played an important symbolic role in this transitional period' (1999: 18). Thus, hair can be considered as an extension of the body, on the one hand representing a powerful tool in the expression of femininity, on the other requiring controlling measures to discipline the overly *sexual* nature of cascading hair, and thus the unruly body.

In the late-nineteenth and early-twentieth century, women's hair was disciplined with a variety of complicated buns, *chignons* and knots that visibly demonstrated the importance of controlling the female body and the embodiment of disciplined hair as part of 'repressed' sexuality. However, whilst the controlled hair (of controlled women) can be seen as part of the normalization of a submissive femininity, disciplined hair can also express a sense of self-control that is connected to the strength to triumph over the needs of the body.

The frumpy hairstyle of the stereotypical spinster—long hair neatly controlled in a low bun—presents us with the docile, submissive and desexualized image of the unwanted woman. Historically, a spinster was a woman who had passed marriageable age without finding a husband, and culturally the term carries with it a stigma of sexual frigidity. The long hair, symbolizing a perpetual girlhood, is removed from the realm of the erotic by its restraint within a bun that reads as a limitation of sexuality and emphasizes the de-eroticized status of the spinster's womanhood. In films, spinsters have been portrayed with pinned-up hair as a stigma of negative femininity. Bette Davis plays Charlotte Vale in *Now,*

Voyager (1942) as the mousy spinster who 'fits the classic stereotyped image of a spinster and we have compartmentalized her as such in our minds before she has a chance to speak her first line. Charlotte is dressed in a drab, ill-fitting dress; her hair is pulled back in a bun; and she wears old-fashioned, wire-framed spectacles' (Mustard 2000). Similarly, in *The African Queen* (1951), Katherine Hepburn as the character *Rosie* features the spinster look with 'her high-necked dress, long hair pinned up in a severe knot on top of her head' (Mustard 2000). The spinster's bun represents the romantic and sexual abstinence of a lifestyle marked by morality and transformed sexual desires.

The stereotypical hairstyle for the schoolmistress is disciplined and controlled hair in the form of a strict bun, demonstrating that disciplined hair also goes along with authority, trustworthiness and an educated mind (Figure 16.3). The disciplined hair of the schoolmistress signifies not only visibly disciplined *hair,* but also the unseen disciplined *mind* of an educated person, and the prioritizing of mind over matter, and thought before flesh. British children's writer Enid Blyton's adventures at fictional boarding schools such as St Clare's (1941–1945) and Malory Towers (1946–1950) highlight the importance of discipline in educational institutions. Blyton's boarding school stories also reflect a popular acceptance of a moralistic approach to a tidy and neat appearance in dress and hair in the 1940s and 1950s.

The school is a good example of the 'specialized' institutions that Foucault theorized as organizations of social discipline and correction (Foucault 1979), with the classroom providing a training ground in societal norms. In Blyton's fictional writings, the ultimate goal is to educate young girls, who are eager to accept responsibility for their lives, and this is reflected in the nature of the characters' behaviour, dress and ultimately their hairstyle. The disciplined bun plays a vital role, for example, in *First Term at Malory Towers* (1946), both

Figure 16.3   Marianne Hindle, make-up artist, styled as a stereotypical schoolmistress.
Photo by Sarah Roesink.

French Mistresses wear a bun: the hot-tempered Mam'zelle Dupont is described as a short, fat and round person who wears 'her hair in a little bun on the top' (Blyton 2006: 23), while the sour-minded Mam'zelle Rougier appears to be skinny, tall and bony with 'her hair done up in a little bun, but at the back instead of on top' (Blyton 2006: 27).

The preferred student hairstyle at Malory Towers is a simple ponytail or plaited hairstyle, which does not draw attention to the wearer. However, the spoilt first-term student Gwendoline has long, silky, golden hair that she frequently tosses back over her shoulder. While Gwendoline is obsessed with frantically brushing her golden locks a hundred times each night, her house mistress, Mrs Potts, insists on a neat hair-do and informs Gwendoline in an authoritarian manner that she is not allowed to go to class with undisciplined hair. Mrs Potts adds in a threatening tone: 'If you can't plait it and keep it tidy, perhaps your mother could have it cut short next holiday' (Blyton 2006: 31). Gwendonline is both tremendously irritated and very angry, 'as if her mother would dream of cutting off her beautiful fine sheet of hair', put it in a bun or insist on a domestic haircut. At *Malory Towers* then, the state of hair presents an essential criterion of respect towards the mistresses and an acceptance of authority. The growing maturity of the girls is expressed through disciplined hair in the form of tidy buns and neat plaits.

A FOUCAULDIAN PERSPECTIVE ON DISCIPLINED HAIR

Exploring Foucault's (1979) ideas about the disciplined body unpacks the forceful relationship between the body and discipline, where the body either creates power, or is created by power. Foucault's work on social institutions of discipline, such as the school and the prison, proposes that in modern societies, citizens docilely submit to the established power relations, and even take responsibility for their own discipline according to the state's wishes. Self-discipline is seen as a positive attribute, and this extends to an active management of the body in order to maintain social norms, such as cultural constructions of gender. As Rabinow (1991: 172) argues 'it is always the body that is at issue—the body and its forces, their utility and their docility, their distribution and their submission.'

Systems of 'biopower', as Foucault terms it, maintain femininity through the careful management of women's bodies by the women themselves. The wearing of high heels, the use of cosmetics and the existence of the exercise and diet industries have all been highlighted as examples of how women, through submitting their bodies to various forms of discomfort and manipulation, have engaged in a power relationship with men that continually underlined women's subordinate position in society through the use of bodies (O'Grady 2004; Allen 2004; Bordo 2003).

In the Foucauldian analysis of discipline, the gaze and notions of surveillance play a crucial role. An acute awareness of being watched at all times creates the social pressure to be 'normal'—to behave in ways that adhere to the dominant social norms. Thus, the body is constantly at the centre of attention, and needs to be maintained under the critical eye of society. This constant maintenance and improvement of the body equates to 'a mechanism of objectification so that one's presence in society is performed as a parade, an ostentatious form of examination' (Rabinow 1984: 199). Revisiting Foucault's approach to the question of bodies and power, the socially conspicuous nature of head hair makes it a versatile example of embodied power: disciplined hair is a powerful representation of controlling authority on and off the body.

The perception of disciplined hair as authoritarian plays directly into stereotypical notions of women in control or in need of control. Authoritarian schoolmistress knots do not merely reflect the hierarchical structure in educational institutions, but they also attest to appropriate hairstyles for women in education. From the mid- to late-nineteenth century in particular, the occupation of schoolmistress or governess was one of the few careers open to middle-class women in need of employment. At a time when the only respectable destiny for a young woman was marriage and motherhood, teachers and governesses were single, relatively impoverished, and with poor marriage prospects, doomed to lives of virginal spinsterhood. The repression of sexuality and the *nonsexual* identity of the schoolmistress underlies this discourse about the disciplined nature of educators' hair. In educational establishments, Foucault (1990: 27) comments, although 'one can have the impression that sex was hardly spoken of at all ... the question of sex was a constant preoccupation.'

In Jill Murphy's *The Worst Witch* (1974), Miss Hardbroom is an authoritarian character with highly disciplined hair. Hardbroom is described as a 'tall, terrifying lady with a sharp, bony face and black hair scragged back into such a tight knot that her forehead looked quite stretched' (Murphy 2001: 15). Miss Hardbroom's stringently disciplined hairstyle reflects her personality as an extremely strict educator who is feared by her pupils. The form mistress' pulled-back, black hair matches her piercing black eyes, and her entirely black wardrobe emphasizes her bony, skeletal frame. In fact, it might be argued that we understand intuitively that Miss Hardbroom's hairstyle plays a key role in the definition of her bitter, unpleasant character. Thus, the schoolmistress' bun can be interpreted as a powerful educational statement, representing significant tools of discipline and acting as a generational testimony of the value of controlling the body, sexuality and the locks. The severe hair-knot can be interpreted as the sign of an authoritarian persona who is perfectly in control, in the educational *and* the private sphere of bodily urges. The tightness and placement of the knot literally speaks for the educator; the tighter her bun, the stricter her teaching philosophy.

However, the transformative power of the pulled-back bun hairstyle is also revealed when Miss Hardbroom proudly shows off the length of her hair before a 'broom stick flying display':

> Miss Hardbroom looked particularly impressive, sitting bolt-up-right with her long black hair streaming behind her. The girls had never seen her hair loose before and were amazed how much of it she could possibly scrag into that tight knot every day. It came down to her waist.
>
> 'H.B. looks quite nice with her hair like that [...] she doesn't seem half as frightening'. (Murphy 2001: 65–66)

Enjoying her loose hair flying in the wind, Miss Hardbroom's look and persona are now very different. This does not necessarily indicate that her personality has suddenly changed from mean to nice; however, it uncovers another, almost uncontrolled (and usually repressed) aspect of her character. Miss Hardbroom, riding the phallic broomstick, reveals her hair in an almost sexual manner that takes away her authoritarian appearance.

In the figures of the spinster and the schoolmistress, the bun metaphorically contains their sexuality. In ballet, too, hair that is let down implies that mastery over the body has been relinquished in order to embrace sexuality. The predominantly female modern dance groups that emerged after World War I reformed and liberalized dance and its costume, and let down the tight bun of classical ballet (Hecht 2005: 339). Avant-garde choreographer Martha Graham's loose and wild hairstyle was symbolic of artistic rebellion, and whilst her costumes, hair and make-up took on a more unisex look (Hecht 2005: 339), Graham's approach to dance explicitly emphasized an overt sexuality. However, the liberated look of unfettered hair belies the inescapable role of body discipline even within modern dance, and also in the norms of social behaviour. As Graham stated: '[y]our goal is freedom, but freedom may only be achieved through discipline' (quoted in Preston-Dunlop 1995: 168). Thus there is room for ambiguity and paradox within the hair up/hair down, sexually repressed/sexually active, disciplined/undisciplined set of dichotomies. Turning to the realm of erotic fetishism, the controlled hairstyle of the dominatrix contributes to connotations of sensual restraint as a form of sexual pleasure.

CONTROVERSIAL DISCIPLINE: THE DOMINATRIX

A dominatrix controls and dominates a male or female *submissive* sexual partner. Thigh-length, high-heeled black boots and a rubber or leather corset characterize the image of the powerful dominatrix. Not surprisingly, perhaps, the stereotypical hairstyle of the dominatrix is a strictly pulled-back high ponytail. This hairdo is slicked back to guarantee the total control of every single hair, and yet is combined with the sexual charge of long, cascading locks of the ponytail (Figure 16.4).

As Foucault (1979) has argued, disciplinary punishment gives 'professionals' (psychologists, programme facilitators, parole officers, etc.) power over the prisoner. The prisoner's length of stay may depend on the professional's opinion that the prisoner possesses sufficient self-control not to re-offend. When we apply this thinking to the dominatrix, it becomes clear that her domineering appearance plays a part in rendering her partner a submissive being, in a clear and succinct power/control/discipline relation with the ultimate goal of training a passive, obedient persona. Indeed, it could be argued that, as with the schoolmistress and the ballerina, the dominatrix's controlled appearance is a visual representation of her profession; the 'art of correct training' starts with the control of her own appearance, which develops into a powerful tool of eroticized control and disciplinary punishment of others.

When considering the opposing characters of the dominatrix and the spinster, it could be argued, then, that both share common hair practices involving a (de)sexualized

Figure 16.4   Natalie Brazier and Kelly Chow, performers, styled as stereo-typical dominatrices.
Photo by Sarah Roesink.

control of femininity. The controlled hairstyle of both figures is implicitly associated with eroticism, but also paradoxically with the absence of tangible sexuality. Thus, a controlled hairdo can be interpreted as an indicator of two different kinds of controlled feminine sexuality. Where the spinster appears meek and submissive, trained by society into controlling her hair in order to avoid sexual attention, the dominatrix demonstrates her position of strength and authority through forms of hair and dress that discipline the body.

A central paradox emerges in which the disciplined self is both submitting to power *and* exercising power, so that controlled hair represents both weakness and strength at the same time. This paradox is inherent in Foucault's work, in the notion that modern subjects are 'caught up in a power situation of which they are themselves the bearers' (Foucault 1979: 201). The body becomes a location for a contest of power, and tidy hair is the sign of a woman who is in control and yet is being controlled by society. In this respect the 'disciplined heads' of apparently opposing personas share a common ground in sexuality, femininity and self-control.

ACKNOWLEDGEMENTS

I wish to record my gratitude in particular to Elena Louise Savva, Marianne Hindle, Kelly Chow and Natalie Brazier for modeling, to Rebecca Smith for styling and to Sarah Roesink for photography. I also wish to thank Solange Goumain for providing studio space at the Urdang Academy, and Cherry Klein as well as Katharine Stimson for their helpful comments.

BIBLIOGRAPHY

Allen, A. (2004), 'Foucault, Feminism, and the Self: The Politics of Personal Transformation', in D. Taylor and K. Vintges (eds.), *Feminism and the Final Foucault*, Urbana and Chicago: University of Illinois Press.

Banes, S. (1998), *Dancing Women: Female Bodies on Stage*, London and New York: Routledge.

Blyton, E. (2006), *First Term at Malory Towers*, London: Egmont UK.

Bordo, S. (2003), *Unbearable Weight: Feminism, Western Culture and the Body*, Berkeley: University of California Press.

Cox, C. (1999), *Good Hair Days: A History of British Hairstyling*, London: Quartet Books.

Foster, S. L. (1996), 'The Ballerina's Phallic Pointe', in S. L. Foster (ed), *Corporealities—Dancing Knowledge and Power*, London: Routledge.

Foucault, M. (1979), *Discipline and Punish*, New York: Pantheon.

Foucault, M. (1990), *The History of Sexuality* (R. Hurley, trans. Vol. I: An Introduction), New York: Vintage Books.

Hecht, T. (2005), 'Pointe Shoes', in V. Steele (ed), *Encyclopedia of Clothing and Fashion* (Vol. 3), New York: Charles Scribner's Sons.

Hecht, T. (2006), 'Teaching Silent Bodies—Historical and Contemporary Perspectives on Emotional Aspects in Ballet Education and Performing Art Pedagogy at Elite Dance Conservatoires', in M. Bischof, C. Feest and C. Rosiny (eds.), *E_motion*, Münster, Hamburg, London: LIT Verlag.

Lave, J. and Wenger, E. (1991), *Situated Learning: Legitimate Peripheral Participation*, Cambridge: Cambridge University Press.

Murphy, J. (2001), *The Worst Witch*, London: Puffin.

Mustard, D. J. (2000), 'Spinster: An Evolving Stereotype Revealed through Film', *Journal of Media Psychology* [online journal], 20 January, http://www.calstatela.edu/faculty/sfischo/spinster.html, accessed 2 August 2007.

O'Grady, H. (2004), 'An Ethics of the Self', in D. Taylor and K. Vintges (eds.), *Feminism and the Final Foucault*, Urbana and Chicago: University of Illinois Press.

Preston-Dunlop, V. (ed) (1995), *Dance Words*, Amsterdam: Harwood Academic.

Rabinow, P. (ed) (1984), *The Foucault Reader*, New York: Penguin Books.

Rabinow, P. (ed) (1991), *The Foucault Reader*, New York: Penguin Books.

Royce, A. P. (1984), *Movement and Meaning—Creativity and Interpretation in Ballet and Mime*, Bloomington: Indiana University Press.

Savva, E. L. (2007), Personal communication, London Studio Centre, 10 March.

Shilling, C. (2003), *The Body and Social Theory*, London: Sage Publications.

Turner, B. S. (1996), *The Body and Society: Explorations in Social Theory* (2d edn), London: Sage Publications.

Wulff, H. (1998), *Ballet across Borders—Career and Culture in the World of Dancers*, Oxford and New York: Berg.

17 HAIR-'DRESSING' IN *DESPERATE HOUSEWIVES*
NARRATION, CHARACTERIZATION AND THE PLEASURES OF READING HAIR

RACHEL VELODY

Desperate Housewives is a highly successful black comedy, produced by the American television corporation, ABC, that concerns the complicated lives of five women living in the same suburban street, four of whom will be considered here (analysis of the character of Edie Britt, played by Nicollete Sheridan, is not included because of her more peripheral narrative position in the series). The series' use of fast-paced, complex storylines, a mixture of melodrama and comedy, and close attention to the styling of the female leads, has all helped to establish its commercial and popular success. A key pleasure is the four honed central performances and their highly stylized characterization: widow Bree Van De Kamp (Marcia Cross) (Figure 17.1), spoiled ex-model Gabrielle—'Gaby'—Solis (Eva Longoria) (Figure 17.2), hard-working mother and marketing executive Lynette Scavo (Felicity Huffman) (Figure 17.3), and divorcee Susan Mayer (Teri Hatcher) (Figure 17.4).

This chapter uses close textual analysis to explore the ways in which hair in its dressing, styling and colouring characterizes these four women and narrativizes their lives. In order to look at these processes, a single storyline is examined: 'Listen to the Rain on the Roof' (TX 24.9.2006). The first part of the chapter considers hair grooming and styling as a method of developing viewer identification with Gaby and Susan, and with the actresses who play them. This initial exploration introduces Roland Barthes's concept of inter-textual address which stresses that texts—in a range of cultural forms including TV, advertising, film, and the body itself—invariably reference one another (Barthes 1974: 16). This inter-textual approach is further utilized in an analysis of advertisements for hair products endorsed by Teri Hatcher and Eva Longoria, the stars who play Susan and Gaby.

The second section explores hair as both a narrative framing device and as a generic approach to the reading of filmic characterization. These dual characteristics and their dynamic interaction help us to compare the visually distinct and narratively differentiated worlds of Lynette and Bree: Lynette's socially realistic and liberal milieu, and Bree's melodramatic and more conservative sphere. The chapter examines how hair and its styling strategies function to equally reinforce the links between the two women through storylines that illustrate the illusory nature of domestic power in the lives of both characters. First, however, I want to discuss the uses of textual analysis as a structuralist tool.

Figure 17.1 Marcia Cross at the *Desperate Housewives* press conference at the Four Seasons Hotel in Beverly Hills, California, on 28 September 2007.
Photo by Vera Anderson/WireImage. © copyright 1999–2008 Getty Images, Inc. All rights reserved.

Figure 17.2 Eva Longoria at the *Desperate Housewives* press conference at the Four Seasons Hotel in Beverly Hills, California, on 28 September 2007.
Photo by Vera Anderson/WireImage. © copyright 1999–2008 Getty Images, Inc. All rights reserved.

Figure 17.3   Felicity Huffman at the *Desperate Housewives* press conference at the Four Seasons Hotel in Beverly Hills, California, on 28 September 2007.

Figure 17.4   Teri Hatcher at the *Desperate Housewives* press conference at the Four Seasons Hotel in Beverly Hills, California, on 12 October 2007.

THE NATURE OF INTER-TEXTUAL ADDRESS

Structuralism considers the ways in which meaning can be found or 'fixed' within a text (Sarup 1993: 3), for example, how the underlying meanings of hair and hairstyling practices can be discovered by carefully 'unpacking' its cultural signs or 'connotations' (Barthes 1974). In the field of all popular cultural forms, however, we do not experience signs or textual meaning in isolation: 'the text is always mobilized, placed and articulated with other texts' (Morley 1996: 287). Allen, referencing Barthes, suggests that inter-textuality is 'something that can never be contained or constrained within the text itself' (Allen 2003: 86). Thus, the effectiveness of an episode such as 'Listen to the Rain on the Roof' exists, not just through its ability to engage audiences in terms of individual storylines, characters or as an individual episode, but also through its capacity to be read as part of a larger text or series of texts.

The inter-dependency of these cultural signs, i.e. the idea that there is a whole range of different but inter-related potential meanings, leads Fiske to assert that television texts are, in this sense, 'open', or 'polysemic', i.e. having many possible interpretations (Fiske 1987: 67). Further, he argues that the television viewer is an active agent in the process, through the act of interpreting (and sometimes differently interpreting) texts, so that cultural signs *and* their reading 'function as a crucial element in the production of cultural meaning' (Fiske 1987: 108). Stardom exemplifies this procedure, exploiting the connotations of the actresses not only through their iconographic status within a show like *Desperate Housewives*, but also through a star's spectacular relationship with other media texts and settings such as magazine interviews, red-carpet appearances and advertising campaigns.

This approach to textual openness reflects the work of Stuart Hall exemplified in his seminal paper on communication, 'Encoding/Decoding' (1996). Like Fiske, Hall suggests that the reader, or decoder, can interpret encoded messages from a number of perspectives, although he is anxious to emphasize that '"polysemy" must not, however, be confused with pluralism' (Hall 1996: 45). Whilst there are a (limited) number of positions from which readers, or 'encoders' can affirm, negotiate, oppose and reject the primacy of dominant—or 'hegemonic'—media messages, the actual systems of communication work to naturalize meanings, encouraging us to follow their dominant/preferred reading and decoding (Turner 1990: 90).

'MULTI-TONAL ...'

Desperate Housewives employs a repertoire of identifiable stereotypes which exploit a range of familiar physical tropes of idealized femininity including those relating to hair colour, style and length (see Cooper 1971: 65–83; Synnott 1993). These then draw on a pool of cultural meanings to provide the spectator with rapid access to both personalities and individual and plot motivations. Susan (Terri Hatcher), for example, reflects contemporary interpretations of 'laid-back' femininity and this easy athleticism is reflected in her hairstyling: shoulder length and either left free-flowing or simply tied back to link health and fitness with natural 'grown-up' sensuality. Gaby's character (Eva Longoria), in contrast, encapsulates the processes of excessive consumption, through a variety of constantly changing stylized coiffures that implicitly function to convey Gaby's social and economic status as a successful second-generation (Hispanic) American woman.

Lynette Scavo (Felicity Huffman), meanwhile, is styled in terms of social reality and the difficulties faced by many women juggling careers and family life. Lynette's hairstyling often directly reflects this in dull, lacklustre colouration and weak 'do-ups'. Equally such simplicity functions to symbolize spontaneity and authenticity to produce perhaps the most nuanced interpretations of feminine sexuality in the series, precisely because of its realisticness. Of the four women, Bree (Marcia Cross) is directly rendered as a 'desperate' figure. Bree is in a constant state of anxiety and conflict. This tension is underlined in a clinical fixation with grooming and flawless imitation, figured in immaculately styled but very red hair—the traditional marker of fiery feminine sexuality—which produces a powerful framing device in the episode analysed in this chapter, 'Listen to the Rain on the Roof'.

To briefly establish the context of the episode, Susan is looking after her boyfriend, Mike, who is comatose after a hit-and-run accident. Bree, attempting to rebuild an ordered family life after the death of her first husband, Rex, is obstructed by her manipulative children. Lynette, in addition to coping with the demands of her job, and a young family, is performing the role of stepmother to her husband's love child, Kayla; a situation made more difficult by the youngster's scheming mother, Nora. Following disastrous attempts to procure a child, including illegal adoption and baby snatching, the exploitative Solises, Gaby and Carlos, have engaged their resentful maid, Xiao Mei, as a surrogate mother to bear them a child. 'Listen to the Rain on the Roof' typifies the ways in which *Desperate Housewives* incorporates hairstyling into its dramatic and comedic mise-en-scene to allow access to the dominating narratives of the series: the relationship between consumption and desirable forms of femininity; and the struggle that many women face in balancing their roles as carers with their own needs and desires.

CHARACTERIZATION, GLAMOUR AND INTER-TEXTUAL ADDRESS: CONTRASTING GABY AND SUSAN

In the opening montage device of short visual snapshots that weekly bring the viewer up to date with various plot lines and the story so far, the camera tracks over Gaby Solis discussing her impending divorce settlement in the formal confines of the arbitrator's office. Wearing a bright, revealing top, and gesticulating wildly, Gaby's strident performance is reinforced by her hairstyling: a stunningly huge ponytail—voluminous, heavily curled, waist length, and tonally frenetic, shaded from brown to blonde. These combined features indicate that Gaby is indulging in the popular use of hair extensions, with all their connotations of stylistic indulgence and instant gratification. For the viewer, Gaby's vanity and socio-economic confidence combine to emphasize the excessiveness of her particular exploitation of this hairstyling practice by being privileged only the briefest glimpse of it, for just one moment, in the entire episode.

Recently, complex and/or central roles for Hispanic American actresses have been progressively developed within American TV drama, challenging their previous traditional marginalization. That this is a contemporary phenomenon is illustrated by the fact that there is little theorizing of these identities and characterizations. We must turn, largely, to authors who explore the representation of Afro-American subjectivities including hair styling and dressing practices. Mercer argues that with the exception of colour, hair is the strongest signifier of racial identity (Mercer 1994: 98), but its styling and dressing consistently operate within a discursive conflict between racial oppression and determined self-expression (Banks 2000; Weitz 2005). However, drawing on her practice, Rooks (1996) suggests that black women exploit a range of hair styling and dressing strategies both from and outside of their immediate cultural heritage, and use ostensibly 'white' hair products, as ways of moulding their own personalized image. This concept of negotiation is developed more positively by Banks, who argues that such hair dressing is less concerned with replicating white looks than with taking pleasure in crafting self-identity (Banks 2000: 11–12).

In one of the few articles on hair and the experience of Mexican American women, Weitz (2005) argues that Hispanic women seek out ways of constructing an identity that is true to their cultural heritage. Long hair is critical: 'to maintain their ethnic identity and to attract Mexican men ... they must keep their hair waist-length, heavily sprayed, full of volume, and styled into large curls' (Weitz 2005: 121). Yet they must somehow modify this form of hair dressing so that they can successfully navigate the white society within which they live and work. The character and stylization of Gaby Solis raises fundamental questions concerning the drive to homogenize her Hispanic American identity along the lines of white normative practice. Yet, her maverick streak and the pleasure she takes in stylistic performance constantly disrupts any simple reading of 'adopting' white-ness.

For example, later in the plot line Gaby meets her 'desperate' buddies for lunch at the local country club and her hair is once again transformed through a cacophony of flicks and skilful colouring techniques, almost in homage to the cult 'Farrah Fawcett look' of the late 1970s. This is not a clear-cut transference of 'white' looks. Rather, Gaby's version combines subtle, variegated tones to appropriate and modify an iconic look of white-ness to reinforce her character as an active agent in her own self-fashioning. This becomes more significant when we consider the setting of the sequence. Gaby's brash and ostentatious Hispanic American version of the 'beach babe look' is a direct challenge to the dominant ideology and formal dress codes of the country club. It pointedly disturbs a site emblematic of white-ness, middle-class conformity, institutionalized racism and patriarchal control.

Susan, by contrast, with her dark auburn colouring framing her pale face, effectively embodies normative ideas of white beauty in the highly 'organic' appearance of her hair, realized in this episode through its consistently simplicity of style. This look draws our attention to the framing of her face, which frequently produces Susan as the point-of-view character of the show. It directs us to her classical facial features, her high forehead, clear skin, and the contrast of white skin tone and teeth, against her large, brown eyes. Susan's seemingly natural beauty acts as a counterpoise to Gaby's constantly changing artifice, but also functions within the narrative to unify the disparate areas of comedy and glamour through two processes.

First, in relation to comedy, simple hairstyling maximizes access to Susan's exaggerated facial gestures; her open-mouthed, wide-eyed reactions replicate our own shock at the disasters she unwittingly causes and helps to further indent comedy in these mini-narratives of catastrophe. Furthermore, these garner sympathy, and her calamitous mishaps and consequent gestures depict her as a kind of 'innocent', a comedic 'fool'. Second, Susan's hair unifies an innate capacity for chaos with an idea of 'effortless' beauty emphasized through simplicity of both hair cut and colour. While the ends of the hair are thinner and unregulated, signifying disorder, the look is at the same time subtly glamorized. Expertly graduated cutting and blow-drying techniques give volume and increase the sense of movement and texture so that the hair appears 'naturally' glossy and sleek.

Gaby and Susan's contrasting presentations offer up an ideological conflict in the episode 'Listen to the Rain on the Roof', between the natural and naïve characteristics articulated in Susan's normative 'white' looks, and their interruption, through Gaby's vociferous, 'savvy' creative styling. These interpretations of Gaby and Susan extend to other settings, including their advertisements for hair products, and it is pertinent here to consider the place of stardom in the cultural circulation of meaning that surrounds viewer identification. Dyer (1991: 59; 1992: 38) suggests that the aura or charisma of the star correlates to her or his ability to condense a range of ideological contradictions, with which the spectator can identify. Further, theories of stardom highlight Hollywood's historical relationship with the fashion and cosmetics industries that encourages the spectator to identify with, and to imitate, the star (Eckert 1991: 35). Such concepts can be usefully applied to *Desperate Housewives,* in part because of its high production values, but also because of the position and effect of stardom within the text, and inter-textually across a range of media forms, including television advertising.

The viewer's relationship with Gaby extends beyond the show, because actress Eva Longoria, who plays her, performs as 'ambassadress' for cosmetic company L'Oreal, Paris. The inter-textual relationship between the show and L'Oreal's advertisements can be seen in the television commercial for its hair highlighting crème, Couleur Experte (L'Oreal, March 2007). Here, Eva stands in her apartment, looking directly at us. She snaps her fingers and a young, muscular, white male magically appears, with a tray of Couleur Experte. The notion of the male 'servicing' Eva is confirmed as she raises an eyebrow, joking: 'Talk about home delivery!' We then cut to Eva standing in front of a mirror, effortlessly applying the product, whilst explaining that Couleur Experte can deliver colour 'where you want it, how you want it'. Such statements encapsulate L'Oreal's brand image but equally operate at a level of inter-textual address to embody Gaby's on-screen character: that the merchandise is luxurious (it's a 'crème'), infinite in its range of colours (it's 'multi-tonal'), alive to the pleasures of play, and transient, a shade that fades quickly and safely, and can be replaced with another look at will.

Eva Longoria markets Couleur Experte—but in doing so she simultaneously markets and brands her own celebrity image, sealing two distinct personalities into a 'dyad', a single unit treated as one entity, Eva/Gaby, TV actress/TV character. The advertisement invites us to make connections between Longoria's high-profile star status and Gaby's self-confident repertoire of hair designs, styles and colours. The two come together in the L'Oreal's familiar address, 'Because you're worth it', voiced by Longoria, but embodied in Gaby.

The advertisement and its tag line implicitly acknowledge the struggle to reconcile vanity and artifice with the pleasure that we as viewers enjoy in the spectacle of glamour. Similarly, equally attempting to close the gap between the two is the rival hair-colouring company Clairol and its parallel campaign using Terri Hatcher, the actress who plays Susan Meyer. The ambivalence is perhaps further reinforced in the disparity between the sight of Hatcher's 'effortless' 'natural' beauty and the knowledge of the impossibility of its artificial achievement. However, Clairol, like L'Oreal, utilizes Hatcher's TV alter-ego to full effect. Susan's inherent 'klutziness', much in evidence throughout the show and in the episode under discussion, is pivotal to what might be termed the 'trip, tip and pick-up' commercial promoting Clairol's Colour Seal Gloss in which Hatcher stars.

In the ad, Teri enters a coffee shop, picks up her drink, turns, trips and tips the contents over a dashing young guy. At the point of the accident the camera cuts to a series of slow-motion close-ups of the actress. This allows us to gauge the star's faux-pas, specific to the commercial, and to link the incident to both the clumsy actions typical of Susan and her repertoire of facial expressions. The montage of shots focuses our gaze on Teri and her range of reactions to the 'dishy guy': shocked, smiling and apologetic. These images, in turn, give us the time to better appreciate her enviable appearance: the rich auburn hair, its movement, body and shine that all reference attendant discourses of health and youth. Teri's advertisement, merging innocence, ineptness and erotic display, mimics Susan's representation, reconciling us to both the possibility of life's disasters and its compensations. This strategy of narrative and aesthetic ambiguity provides a useful framework for further considering the crucial thematic role of hair and its styling in *Desperate Housewives*.

NARRATING CONTROL: THE CONTRASTING WORLDS OF LYNETTE AND BREE

In this second analysis of hair dressing, I contrast the realistic presentation of Lynette Scavo with the melodramatic staging that underpins the characterization of Bree Van De Kamp, linking the two women through the theme of control. At the same time, I want to explore the ways in which hair acts as a tool of narration: in relation to Lynette, for example, how the plot line in 'Listen to the Rain on the Roof' helps position her as the socially realistic figure of the show; for Bree, how the fragments of the episode taken together skilfully inscribe her in a melodramatic tale of desire and loss.

Lynette Scavo (played by Felicity Huffman) is consistently styled in the series to convey the endless battle many women face in attempting to contain and control the chaos of contemporary life. The difficulty that Lynette experiences in shifting between her various roles as business woman, mother and wife are often directly transmitted through the presentation of her hair and hairstyling. This is particularly demonstrated in the new plot point that ricochets into the Scavo household: the discovery that Tom has a love child, Kayla. The sequences in the episode narrativize Lynette's frustrated efforts to keep Kayla's predatory mother, Nora, away from her children and Tom, and the presentation of hair is once more used to illustrate Lynette's tenuous control over the highly volatile situation.

Early in the episode, Nora drops off Kayla at Lynette's house and we notice her youthful individuality; glossy, auburn-red hair reflects a bohemian, eccentric pose, accentuated through a semi-moulded chignon, making the style appear artless and relaxed. A pretty comb holds the hair up high whilst wisps fall around her face, adding an element of youthful exuberance. Red hair stereotypically implies unbridled sexuality, a point emphasized in Nora's aggressive flirtation with a bemused Tom. By contrast, Lynette's exhaustion is shown through a limp, tiny ponytail and clumps of hair lying across her face. Her blonde locks are poorly dyed and streaked, with dark roots showing through.

This re-inscription of stereotypical blondeness does three things. First, it acts as a foil to Nora's lively, sexy characterization. Second, it destabilizes the stereotypically sexual connotations of the blonde bombshell, undercutting any potential of eroticism for the harried Lynette. Finally, her poor grooming disrupts the routinized glamour of the show, asserting the codes of social realism instead. These three elements, signifying Lynette's failure in effective fashioning, generate audience sympathy through identification with, and recognition of, the impossibility of managing the various parts of her life. By creating this context of empathy in the initial sequences of the episode, we are positioned to identify with Lynette, when she is (covertly) threatened by Nora later in the storyline.

Our 'housewife' has set up a Christmas photo session with the extended family, begrudgingly including Nora. Lynette has clearly had her hair professionally dyed and cut for the event. Now uniformly blonde and waved, it sits rather stiffly on her shoulders. Her presentation connotes the formality of the 'sitting', and Lynette's determination to control the extended family, in particular Nora's erotic address, by drawing attention to her own artfully coiffed and managed appearance. Yet we are alerted to the risk of disturbance, in part because of the viewer's understanding of the inherent artifice of Lynette's presentation. As if to highlight this, Nora provocatively positions a red Santa hat atop her notably loose, long and flowing auburn locks. The length and position of her tousled hair draws attention to her cleavage, as she perches on the edge of the sofa where the children huddle together. Nora's sexual persona and sensuality offer a direct challenge and contrast to Lynette's more contrived, forced performance, and hints at what is to follow.

As the camera clicks, Nora deliberately crashes sideways across the sofa, her breasts falling out of her spaghetti-strap dress, tresses falling over her face and bust, Santa hat askew. We cut to an image of the extended family: Lynette frozen in horror. Despite her best attempts, she is unable to maintain the façade of idealized family life and the codes of female glamorization, particularly when confronted by a younger, feminine, highly sexualized rival. Yet it is these very moments of 'failed femininity', as mother, lover and breadwinner that draw us to Lynette.

The need to control—and its failure—also provides an explanatory framework by which to decode Bree, whose hair in this episode shifts between fastidious grooming and dishevelment, as she too struggles with the self-imposed constraints of appropriate femininity and what constitutes fitting suburban behaviour. The concept of suppression is a theme central to the aesthetic form and film genre known as melodrama (Doane 1987; Mulvey 1987). Marked by an emotional intensity, articulated visually, verbally and gesturally, it often circulates around female tragedy. Consequently, melodrama 'always has the ability to provoke strong emotions in audiences, from tears of sorrow and identification, to derisive laughter' (Mercer and Shingler 2004: 1). Bree's obsession with surface grooming and clinical precision parallels her intense and controlling relationships with husbands, lovers and children. Marcia Cross's red hair is exploited as a familiar metaphor of hot-tempered, fiery female sexuality, but functions to create a constant state of tension against Bree's contained and repressed characterization.

In 'Listen to the Rain on the Roof', Bree's hair plays a significant part in fusing character and storyline in an episode within which physical containment and emotional collapse are central tropes. Gledhill, analysing the development of melodrama within Western cinema, suggests that the genre's excessive tone is evident in the lush mise-en-scene; opulent set designs are matched by the glamorization of the female protagonist (1987). These elements contribute to the narrative, as excess or emotion gradually split the realist surface of the text, to expose the true feelings of the central character. Bree is romantically involved with the sinister figure of Orson Hodge, unaware—unlike the spectator—that the body of his first wife, Alma, is shortly to be unearthed in Wisteria Lane. This adds piquancy to the opening sequence. As a voice-over tells us that 'it hardly ever rains in the town of Fairview', amidst driving rain, we witness Bree and Orson passionately kissing. Bree's usually immaculately groomed hair is here dishevelled and sodden, and her characteristic brittle façade similarly abandoned to reveal a vulnerable, passionate woman. Hair functions as a vital part of melodramatic mise-en-scene to signify a kind of rapture in the expressive embodiment of Bree's release from sleek, gelled perfection to liquidity.

Yet, just as Nora's very visible presence fractures Lynette's attempts to manage her life, so we are sensitized to the potentially illusory nature of Bree's happiness as order is once more restored through her visual affectation. In the penultimate sequence of the episode, the engagement party, Bree and Orson reverse their original appearance. The façade of suburban success is played out through the couple's regimented looks, which notably mirror one another, their hair immaculately cut and gleaming. This dynamic of superficial control and imminent catastrophe gathers momentum with the uninvited arrival of Orson's neighbour, Carolyn Bigsby. Carolyn's appearance initially enhances a sense of the couple's social accomplishment, through her own miserable state. Caught in a rainstorm, she knocks on the door, soaked through. Her wet, short, mousey brown hair matches her bland, beige raincoat. A spindly fringe, plastered against pale skin, draws attention to dark under-eye circles and black mascara streaking down her heavily lined face. Carolyn's wretched appearance clearly alludes to, and contrasts with, Bree's earlier manifestation, drenched yet still beautiful in the act of physical and emotional liberation.

To reinforce the point, as she opens the door and greets Carolyn, Bree's vivid red hair is backlit, which gives it extra luminosity. Pulled up high into a smooth half-ponytail, tresses swept away from the face, its self-conscious classical styling operates as a sophisticated, if highly normative, illustration of suburban femininity. At this point in the plot line, Bree's visual presentation positions her as the more powerful of the two women. In melodrama, however, the suppression of emotional truth is always linked to illusory power and is punished. Carolyn barges past Bree and announces to the assembled guests that Orson has murdered Alma. The party stops. Dead.

At the close of the episode, and in the final part of this storyline, we have come full circle. The ruination of the evening and Bree's humiliation are highlighted in a reprise of the opening scene. It is dark and all the guests have left. Bree exits the house alone, still wearing her party dress and high heels. Trash bag in tow, she makes her way down the garden path, oblivious to the dark sky and lashing rain. Her hair is saturated once again, yet inverts its earlier eroticism. She now echoes her adversary, Carolyn, for she too is an interloper, teetering on the periphery of community and romance. If her wet hair once signalled hope and fulfilment, then here in the closing sequence it now signifies devastation.

CONCLUSION: THE (GUILTY) PLEASURES OF THE TEXT

'Listen to the Rain on the Roof' illustrates how hair operates at a number of levels as an important televisual device in *Desperate Housewives* in creating verisimilitude and establishing patterns of realism as an integral part of the series' mise-en-scene, characterization and narrative progression. In particular, hair and its coded signifying practices situate the show's female protagonists within wider social structures of gender, class and race, but also provide a way of addressing issues around the nature of contemporary femininity.

All the women, including Lynette, are glamorized through hairstyling, demonstrating the text's concern with aesthetic pleasure. This extends out from the show itself in a circular relationship of inter-textual address as the roles of Gaby/Eva and Susan/Teri illustrate. Framed around this pleasurable exchange, stardom generates a strong relationship between the reader and her or his experience of the characters. This process of polysemic address, i.e. actively combining meaning from different sources, does nevertheless suggest an adherence to dominant ideologies and hegemonic images of idealized femininity. This is perhaps most visibly underlined in the implicit but highly significant commercial presence of companies like L'Oreal and Clairol that act as part of the discourse surrounding the production and consumption of femininity through a range of texts that constitute, but equally commodify, its meaning.

The viewer of *Desperate Housewives* takes pleasure in recognizing the codes and conventions of hair dressing and styling in Western culture depicted in the show. They judge issues of verisimilitude, i.e. truthfulness and authenticity, in terms of the stars and their styles, through their placement within appropriate and identifiable cultural and generic settings. In this context of verisimilitude, the depiction of both socially realistic and glamorous forms of hair dressing within *Desperate Housewives* helps us to consider how hair functions as a site of ideological exchange. Yet, hair dressing in the show equally illustrates the interplay between the enjoyable processes of commodification, and the critiquing of those same practices in the act of reading and interpreting. The four *Desperate Housewives*, through their different characterization, discursively invite a shared understanding of differentiated regimes of female beauty. They spectacularly strive to negotiate the demands of culturally appropriate femininity, whilst experimenting with those very regimes. However, the consistently ambivalent nature of such an address and the constant conflict of their lives also offer the spectator the dynamic pleasurable fantasy of idealized femininity, and the opportunity for its critique.

BIBLIOGRAPHY

Allen, G. (2003), *Roland Barthes,* London: Routledge. (See particularly Chapter 6, 'Textuality': 79–94).

Banks, I. (2000), *Hair Matters: Beauty, Power and Black Women's Consciousness,* New York: New York University Press.

Barthes, R. (1974), *S/Z,* trans. R. Miller, Oxford: Basil Blackwell.

Cooper, W. (1971), *Hair: Sex, Society, Symbolism,* London: Aldus.

Doane, M. (1987), *The Desire to Desire: The Woman's Film of the 1940s,* Indianapolis: Indiana University Press.

Dyer, R. (1991), 'Charisma', in C. Gledhill (ed), *Stardom: Industry of Desire,* London: Routledge.

Dyer, R. (1992), *Stars,* London: BFI. (See particularly Chapter 7, 'Stars and "Character"': 100–19).

Eckert, C. (1991), 'The Carole Lombard in Macy's Window', in C. Gledhill (ed), *Stardom: Industry of Desire,* London: Routledge.

Fiske, J. (1987), *Television Culture,* London: Routledge. (See particularly Chapter 7, 'Intertextuality': 108–27).

Gledhill, C. (1987), 'The Melodramatic Field: An Investigation', in C. Gledhill (ed), *Home Is Where the Heart Is: Studies in Melodrama and the Woman's Film,* London: BFI.

Hall, S. (1996), 'Encoding/Decoding', in P. Marris and S. Thornham (eds.), *Media Studies: A Reader,* Edinburgh: Edinburgh University Press: 41–9.

Mercer, J. and Shingler, M. (eds.), (2004), *Melodrama: Genre, Style and Sensibility,* London: Wallflower Press.

Mercer, K. (1994), *Welcome to the Jungle: New Positions in Black Cultural Studies,* London: Routledge.

Morley, D. (1996), 'Populism, Revisionism and the "New Audience" Research', in J. Curran and V. Walkerdine (eds.), *Cultural Studies and Communications,* London: Edwin Arnold.

Mulvey, L. (1987), 'Notes on Sirk and Melodrama', in C. Gledhill (ed), *Home Is Where the Heart Is: Studies in Melodrama and the Woman's Film,* London: BFI.

Rooks, N. (1996), *Hair Raising: Beauty, Culture and African-American Women,* New Brunswick, NJ: Rutgers University Press.

Sarup, M. (1993), *An Introductory Guide to Post-Structuralism and Postmodernism,* London: Harvester Wheatsheaf.

Synnott, A. (1993), *The Body Social: Symbolism, Self and Society,* London and New York: Routledge.

Turner, G. (1990), *British Cultural Studies: An Introduction,* London: Unwin Hyman.

Weitz, R. (2005), *Rapunzel's Daughters: What Women's Hair Tells Us about Women's Lives,* New York: Farrar, Straus & Giroux.

18 HAIRSTYLING IN THE FASHION MAGAZINE
NOVA IN THE 1970S

ALICE BEARD

I love my fringe.
It suits all the clothes that I have and all the clothes that I have wanted.

(Nerrida Piggin, Fashion Consultant, 'Ahead of Hair', *Nova,* February 1974: 90)

In the late 1960s and early 1970s women's magazines offered the possibility of endless design choice and pages of competing fashionable looks. Responding to the rise of the West End hair salon and the increasing fashionability of the hairdresser in 'Swinging London', magazine fashion and beauty editorial covered trends in hair fashions. As a result, hair played an important role in the finished product on the fashion page. The contribution of the fashion editor with the task of 'styling' a model through clothing, and hair and make-up, was therefore crucial. Fashion became less about what was worn and more about *how* it was worn:

> Dressing up has never been so much fun. A girl can dress to express her personality, the mood she feels or like her envied idol ... The clothes are all there. And what better time than now to play the schizophrenic when there are so many opportunities for showing off, which is what dressing up is all about. (Baker 1970c: 64)

Make-up and hairstyling were presented to magazine readers as a means to achieve both a complete 'look', and as a way of adding that important mark of individuality.

Nova, the influential and innovative style magazine published in Britain from 1965–1975, aimed to be 'a new kind of magazine for the new kind of woman' and this in part involved a new take on beauty, appearance and the body. This chapter explores the language of hair in fashion photography and the different narratives that are constructed by editorial text in four fashion spreads from *Nova* in the early 1970s. In his study of the representation of fashion in French magazines, Roland Barthes offers an important structural analysis of the textual language of the garments featured. Barthes's work emphasizes how there is always an important link between words and image on the fashion page, and how it is these descriptions that render the image 'intelligible' (Barthes 1984: xii). This chapter analyses textual descriptions and visual images from *Nova*'s fashion spreads to reveal how hair operates as an intrinsic part of both achieving a particular 'look' *and* as a signifier of a new young reader and fashionable consumer.

Jennifer Craik argues that 'fashion images are consumed both compliantly and defiantly by readers who lust for the pleasures of the image as much as the clothes they depict' (Craik 1994: 114). On these pages, how the clothes and models are photographed is just as important as what is being photographed. This is particularly pertinent to *Nova*'s treatment of fashion and beauty editorial. Its focus on design and layout marks out both its specific appeal, and its difference to other women's magazines. *Nova*'s fashion pages encouraged an activity beyond that of just buying the clothing or accessories featured; images were more actively consumed—torn out of the magazine, cut up and pinned to walls. In the 1970s 'fashion was not in fashion' but rather became 'optional' (Steele 1997: 280). Instead, there was an emphasis on fashionability defined by individuality. *Nova*'s fashion pages demonstrate how at this time 'style ceases to be a matter of what you are wearing and becomes more the way you wear it' (Brooks 1989: 187), an attitude exemplified in a feature entitled 'Head for the Haberdashery':

> Fashions will go on changing endlessly ... There is no one definitive 'look' that can be said, with certainty, to be the 1970 look ... you can make yourself into Jean Harlow, ... and yet another day you can look as much like a man as you dare ... Today it is the accessory that gives you away ... that indicates fashionability, individuality. You need that very much as clothes become more mass produced. The way you wear your clothes ... has become the most important part of today's look. (Baker 1970a: 41)

FASHIONING THE NEW/RE-STYLING THE OLD

The latest 'new looks' promoted by beauty editorial were often in fact re-workings of classic styles; a case of the old being sold as the new. In 'Profile of a Profile' Penny Vincenzi illustrates the selling points of the 'new bob', and in doing so makes reference to both the business of hairdressing and the commodification of style and fashionability:

> The profile, classic or otherwise, is making a comeback. For a very long time now it has been obscured by fringes, layers, freakouts and just plain hair—and very plain a lot of it is, too ... Now we have the rebirth of the profile, along with the rebirth of the bob, and people have necks again, which is nice ... Hairdressers report a general rush to the scissors; Leonard's are doing 50 bobs a day and at Vidal Sasoon they are bobbing 250 heads a week ... The new bob is angled to the cheek, rather than carved straight into the jaw; it's more flattering and doesn't look like you never got round to growing out your 1960s' version. (Vincenzi 1972: 76)

Fashion photography in the 1970s often looked back to the past and took stars of the silver screen as direct inspiration with historical references to popular cultural icons made explicit in the accompanying text. As Borrelli points out, 'metaphor aids in the visualization of style by linking a look or a garment to a point of reference outside of the world of fashion' (Borrelli 1997: 255). For example, in 'Old-time Favourites' the editorial acknowledges the influence of Hollywood legends Greta Garbo and Marlene Dietrich; photographed by

Sarah Moon, black-and-white photos replicate the image of a 1930s starlet with 'fashion-ably wavy hair and the heavy contrast made-up face right down to black on eyes and lips' (Baker 1973b: 72). In a later issue, a fashion consultant interviewed about her latest haircut reveals she is 'fond of her Claudette Colbert style curly fringe' (Baker 1974: 63). Importantly, however, editorials and features stress the role of the old not in terms of reprise but as the reference point in the construction of the new in terms of hair, femininity and fashionable sexuality: The new cut may be 'Sleek and smooth like Valentino or cropped and brush-like à la Bowie' (Newberry 1973: 90); 'Maria Schneider, of *Last Tango* fame, put the big endorsement on the curly look and it threatens to take over, at last, from the long, blonde, Bardot hairdo that has until now been the sexy way to do hair' (Baker 1974: 63).

For example, in 'The Heavenly Suited' (1972), photographed by Terence Donovan, models are 'divinely dressed in winter's classics' but hairstyling transforms the picturesque. Shot with a hazy, grainy filter and very deliberately posed, the images resemble film stills. The shoot is retrospective in styling, copying the look of the 1940s but deliberately subverted by key details; dyed pink-and-orange hairpieces, an over-sized pearl necklace and fluorescent pink socks. As Baker's editorial points out, 'Altogether, winter's look is one of studied elegance, carried through to the well-coiffured hair, which is made more unusual by the use of coloured fringes, and crowned with a beautifully made-up face' (Baker 1972a: 61). Set against the seductive visual and textual imagery of these soft-focus fantasy worlds, the stock list details offer the reader a very real solution to achieving the look themselves, 'Hair, including coloured fringes (obtainable from Joseph, £3.50), by Paul Nix' (Baker 1972a: 68).

'ALL DRESSED AND MADE UP': WOMEN AS FASHION DOLLS

As well as ideas on what to look like, *Nova* offered advice on how to achieve the new, fashionable hairdos and encouraged an active participation in home styling through a constructive 'Do-It-Yourself' approach that promoted experimentation:

> To those of us who remember being knotted to bus rails, rung like a bell and released at weekends into a horizontal mass of crinkles, the news that plaits are back will come as a blow. But this time it'll be different … And to get the fashionable crinkly look, plait when wet and undo when dry. Look at these styles done for us by Celine at Leonard and then have a go yourself. (Baker 1975: 71)

Fashion was defined by the choice of styles and looks on offer. Promoting specific garments or haircuts, *Nova*'s fashion editorial similarly describes the fun to be had in 'playing' with fashion and promotes the creative activity of constructing different fashionable personas. Photographed by Harri Peccinotti, 'All Dressed and Made Up: The Biba Doll' (Figure 18.1) tells the story of a young girl playing a game of dressing up in her bedroom. At its most literal level, the fashion photograph functions to advertise clothing, accessories, hairstyles and make-up which can then be consumed by the reader. The editorial caption discloses this information: 'The Biba Doll … wears all the pinks. Her clothes, accessories and make-up are all available from her very own boutique, Biba in Kensington High Street, where she can furnish parts of her house at the same time' (Baker 1972b: 63). Fashion pages like these emphasize the fantasy of dressing up and the idea of playing with different styles.

The model appearing on these pages resembles a life-sized peg dolly, posed with stiff arms and legs and seated with her feet in a ballerina's 'first' position. Her face appears painted on, with round circles of pink blush adorning her cheeks and a pretty rosebud mouth. Her hair is not the glossy nylon of a plastic toy's, but more resembles a rag doll's

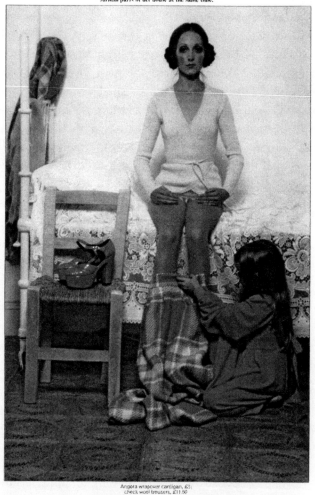

The Biba Doll
— wears all the pinks. Her clothes, accessories and make-up are all available from her very own boutique, Biba in Kensington High Street, where she can furnish parts of her house at the same time.

Angora wrapover cardigan, £5;
check wool trousers, £11.50

Figure 18.1   'All Dressed and Made Up: The Biba Doll', *Nova*, November 1972.
Photograph by Harri Peccinotti. © IPC+ Syndication.

soft wool, coiled plaits. There are a few loose strands tickling the back of the neck—as if the child had arranged it herself. It is the deliberate 'naturalness' of the hair that reveals that this model is not completely doll, but *doll like*. Despite her static poses and the rigidity of her posture, she is soft and yielding, compliant in the routine of being 'All Dressed and Made Up'.

Paradoxically, whilst *Nova's* fashion pages can be seen to encourage experimentation and promote creativity in the active production of a 'look', the Biba Doll, and the reader who is addressed, are rendered passive by the work of the stylists, designers and photographers who create the products and the image. The editorial text makes explicit reference to this process of transformation:

> For those who would rather be dressed than dress themselves—to save themselves thinking, searching, confusion and headaches—there are two girls, designers extraordinaire, who do it all for them: from the very first layer that goes on the skin to the final one that's painted on. They are Mary Quant and Barbara Hulaniki (better known as Biba). (Baker 1972b: 62)

As Paul Jobling outlines, such imagery 'beckons us into a world of unbridled fantasies by placing fashion and the body in any number of discursive contexts' (Jobling 1999: 2). The fashion image, as it appears on the page of the magazine, is itself 'All Dressed and Made Up'. This made-up-ness, then, can be read as both a fabrication and a construction. In a fashion spread, images are tied together by the thematic progression of an unfolding picture story, or by common formal concerns and motifs, like layout, colour or lighting. Within the narrative sequence of this spread, and framed by its wide expanse of white border, each image resembles a page in a children's picture book. The progressive element of clothes accumulating on the model's body as the little girl dresses her suggests the chronological passing of time (Scott 1999). The interlinking roles of title, caption and text are crucial in introducing the theme of the photo story and in establishing tone and pace. Desire for the image and the product is fashioned through the relationship between the words and pictures on a page. Hairstyling can be understood here not as mere dressing, but as a vital element in the visual grammar of a fashion statement.

'DRESSED TO KILL': FASHION AND ANTI-FASHION

Nova's fashion editor, Caroline Baker, was encouraged to explore alternative forms of fashion, and different ways of presenting it, in order to mark out the magazine from other women's titles like *Vogue* and *Queen*. Collaborating with art director and photographer Harri Peccinotti, the pair created fashion pages which 'were almost an insult to fashion' at times (Williams 1998: 106), and the result was often what appeared to be an 'anti-fashion' statement. Working on a limited budget, Baker clothed and styled the models as she would have chosen to dress herself and explored Portobello Market and the Kings Road. In the many second-hand shops and stalls to be found in these London streets, Baker sourced baggy, pinstripe zoot suits and ethnic jewellery. Army surplus stores like Lawrence

Corner and Badges and Equipment were filled with U.S. uniforms from Vietnam and these provided the raw materials for spreads like 'Dressed to Kill: The Army Surplus War Game' (Baker 1971b) (Figure 18.2). The inspiration for the photo story came from the film *M*A*S*H* (1970 directed by Robert Altman), and later television series, and to a contemporary new consumer these clothes looked very different, exciting and sexy. This was 'alternative fashion' then, not the Haute Couture versions of the surplus look produced

Figure 18.2   'Dressed to Kill: The Army Surplus War Game', *Nova*, September 1971.
Photograph by Harri Peccinotti. © IPC+ Syndication.

by designers like Katherine Hamnett some years later, but authentic drill uniforms, which were cheap, used and then customized, cut up and dyed for the shoot.

One of Baker's aims was to challenge established notions of ideal femininity, in particular the sort of conformist, pretty, girlish look that dominated the pages of other magazines at the time (Baker 2007). In 'Dressed to Kill' the styling of hair, make-up and accessories add feminine intrigue to the androgyny of work wear and inject army surplus clothing with a distinct sexual tension. The uniforms are soft, creased, worn and frayed but by folding up the sleeves and tying the oversized shirts tightly on the model's body, this masculine attire serves to emphasize feminine attributes rather than disguise them. As Stella Bruzzi argues, the practice of cross-dressing often draws attention to the wearer's gender and sexuality rather than undermines it (Bruzzi 1997: 148) and in this image the round swell of the model's belly is revealed by the tightness of her shorts and the worn-in softness of fabric against her skin. The model's hair is obviously and deliberately 'non-regulation', and the antithesis of the shaved, army crew cut. Its length, softness and looseness is accentuated by the light of a setting sun and the wind which lifts stray wisps and strands. This hairstyling and the details of drawn-on freckles and sun-kissed skin articulate the rhetoric of 'natural', youthful prettiness. The 'Army Surplus' girl's hairstyle is marked out by its length, looseness and volume, which McCracken suggests: 'the first thing it says is youth ... long hair is after all abundant hair' (McCracken 1997: 160).

'A LITTLE KNIT': CAMP HAIR

From the 1960s the shift in fashion photography away from the studio was symptomatic of developments in the technology of photography which allowed 'outside' fashion (Harrison 1991), and which constructed a new feminine ideal: the young woman who was 'on the move' (Radner 2000). During its decade of publication, *Nova* magazine offered a 'running portrait' of the 'new kind of woman' (Williams 1998: 105), and this often included a satirical take on the media stereotypes of femininity which circulated in contemporary visual culture. Christa Peter's photograph for 'A Little Knit Doesn't Go a Long Way' (Figure 18.3) plays on the notion of a *Playboy* magazine centre fold, with a special 'pull-out poster' featuring an almost life-sized image of a highly stylized model in a tight sweater suggestively sucking on a rocket-shaped lollypop.

The model here is very obviously 'made-up'. Her hair is again long, blonde and curly, but unlike the loose, natural waves of the 'Army Surplus' girl, it is styled and set, and looks as if it has just been taken from its rollers. She wears noticeably false, thick, spidery eyelashes and her lips are painted with thick, glossy colour. She is photographed in an interior space, and whilst her body extends off the page her frame appears contained within it. The editorial text is squashed into the curve between her waist and arm and emphasizes the shape of her figure which stretches out from the confines of the tight-cropped jumper. 'A little knit doesn't go a long way ...' the caption reads, '... It's not meant to. Sweaters now come in mini proportions, barely ending at the waist' (Baker 1971a: 27). The girl adopts the hairstyle, coded body posture and facial expression of 'the pin-up' to indicate sexual

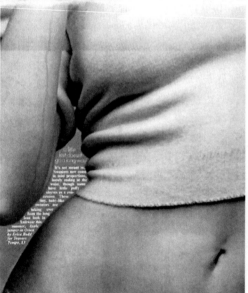

Figure 18.3   'A Little Knit Doesn't Go a Long
Way', *Nova*, February 1971.
Photograph by Christa Peters. © IPC+ Syndication.

arousal—self-consciously acting out, it seems, a characteristic repertoire of glamourized sexuality established in other forms of visual culture, from soft pornography to advertisements for chocolate (Goffman 1979).

Elizabeth Wilson (1985: 158) argues, 'Photography paradoxically enhanced both the mystery and the suggestiveness of fashion—and fashion magazines come on rather like pornography, they indulge the desire of the "reader" who looks at the pictures, to *be* each perfect being reflected in the pages, while simultaneously engaging erotically with a femininity ... that is constantly being redefined.' With her lips parted, eyes closed and head thrown back, it seems that the phallic lollypop in 'A Little Knit' is the source of her pleasure, and the juices trickling down her arm direct the viewer's eyes across her body. Like the artificiality of the lollypop and the brightly coloured styling of the page, she is totally contrived to fulfil Susan Sontag's concept of a camp stereotype (Sontag 1994). Derived from the French slang word *camper* meaning 'to pose in an exaggerated fashion', this aesthetic prioritizes gloss, surface and artifice over the rhetoric of naturalness. As McCracken points out, 'voluptuous hair has a sexual message ... The fullness and the curves of the hair are symbolically consonant with the fullness and curves of the body below ... increasingly voluptuous hair said "bimbo"' (McCracken 1997: 160–2). The model's obviously styled but 'just-got-out-of-bed' hair, tousled, curled and falling across her face, constructs the erotic, but it's a self-conscious 'come-on'—a typical 'saucy' performance designed for the knowing pleasure of the audience. The falsity of the pin-up girl's hairstyle contrasts clearly with that of the 'Army Surplus' girl's natural look and plays into another kind of *Nova* image which is defined here by the self-conscious performance of sexuality, glamour and consumerism.

'TIGHT IS RIGHT': HAIR AS A MANNERISM

The words and pictures of *Nova*'s fashion spreads sought to inform the reader not simply *what* to wear, but *how* to wear it: how to move, how to stand, how to style your hair and at what angle to tip your hat. As this editorial text describes:

> The only way to wear these clothes is to realise that they demand their own accessories ... You need to stand and move around exaggeratedly: smoke coloured cigarettes (rather wickedly), lean dramatically ... Wear your hair curly and your hat at just the right angle. Then you will love the feeling they evoke. (Baker 1970b: 50)

Hairstyling is crucial to the achievement of an overall 'look', but equally significant, as a way of dressing as a means to a *way of being*. In an article on the enduring feminine ideal of 'The Blonde', singer Linda Blazer described the creation of her own look:

> I knew there was no use in just plonking blonde hair on top of my head and leaving it at that—I thought the whole thing through and arranged my hair, quite deliberately, in a Forties style. Then I found one of my mother's old outfits: black pencil skirt, jacket nipped-in at the waist ... and it's just right for me. It adds up to not exactly a sexy look, more a kind of 'mannerism'. (Baikie 1975: 40)

We can see an example of how hair, clothing and attitude adds up to such 'mannerism' in 'Tight Is Right', photographed by Helmut Newton (Figure 18.4). This spread tells the story of girls getting drunk at a cocktail party and typical of Newton's repertoire, the image seems highly staged. The models have an extraordinary appearance; a statuesque beauty which is highly polished, and again visibly contrived and all 'made-up'. However, this time their hair, complementing the cut of the suits, makes explicit reference to styles from the

1940s; smoothed into a long, blonde, glossy bob, or carefully curled and folded under, or pinned-up under a veiled pillbox hat. Rosetta Brooks (1997) identifies the artificiality of models in Newton's fashion photography as posed so rigidly as to appear almost literally life-less. However, like 'The Biba Doll', it is the detail of styling that animates this stasis. Whilst the bodies in this example retain an impression of rigidity—as if the models are holding their poses—hair is caught in a moment of movement escaping beyond the boundaries of the picture frame and enlivening both the wearer and the image. The hair pictured here is extraordinary (how can it stand up on end in this way?). But unleashed, these long blonde tresses look natural, unadorned and in sharp contrast to the carefully constructed style of the girl who responds in shocked astonishment at the spectacle in front of her.

A defining feature of *Nova*'s treatment of fashion is visual humour and an element of fun in images that offer a frivolous pastiche of a visual genre. Editorial use of humour functions to indicate a certain kind of knowingness about contemporary concerns and issues, and the use of parody works to satirize stereotypes and popular images of gender and sexuality. Despite their haute couture attire and high end fashionable status, the models in 'Tight Is Right' demonstrate a playful and irreverent, self-conscious 'mannerism'. The fashions may be chic, sleek and sophisticated, but their behaviour is at odds with this glossy and

Figure 18.4   'Tight Is Right', *Nova*, April 1973.
Photographs by Helmut Newton. © IPC+ Syndication.

controlled appearance. These women are not overly concerned with looking elegant and composed but instead jump in the air, steal each other's food and, as the story progresses, throw glasses of wine around the room. They all look away from the viewer and photographer to appear much more interested in what's going on amongst them.

Whilst there are obvious differences in the scale of the two sets of women, the double-page spread format and the common acid green background invites us to consider the separate photographs as a whole event—indeed the model on the centre right appears to be distracted by the hair spectacle on the left. Meanwhile her companion takes advantage of this moment to cheekily steal a bite of her sausage. The text running along the far side of the page is cropped into a narrow column, echoing the 'tight fit' of the clothing with its nipped-in waists and long narrow pencil skirts. Accessories 'add ... the fun' to clothes which 'have gone back to black—strict classic: the little black dress, the two-piece skirt suit' (Baker 1973a: 53). However, it is the movement of the model's hair and the positioning of their bodies that transforms these 1940s–style dresses from picturesque, retro pastiche into a contemporary cutting-edge fashion image.

CONCLUSION: 'AHEAD OF HAIR'

In *Nova*'s fashion and beauty editorial, a clear and important relationship emerges between clothing and hair as parts of a fashionable ensemble. In an article from 1973 entitled 'Hair Today', designer Caroline Charles makes a direct link between clothing and hairstyling: 'I think you change your hair because with a new fashion it's the first thing that *feels* wrong' (Newberry 1973: 90). As fashion editor Caroline Baker points out, 'Hair styles change as often as fashions—with them, in fact, as each fashion brings in a new hairdo' (Baker 1974: 60). So how did the *Nova* reader stay 'Ahead of Hair'? It was about both looking *and* feeling up-to-date, even if, as we have seen, the stylistic influences were drawn from other eras or imagined places; 'If it feels right ... it looks right, right now' (Newberry 1973: 90).

Hairstyling is more than simple dressing. Whilst subject to constant shifts and changes in the pursuit of the new, it maintains its crucial dynamic in the transformative processes of fashioning desire and identity. Rather than just an accessory to pivotal moments and shifts in style and the iconography of style, hair is always part of the narrative drive of fashion's relentless and cyclical movement. In *Nova*'s fashion and beauty pages, hair is always more than just a superficial finishing touch; it is integral to the creation of a complete look and the embodiment of a feeling. The cut, texture, colour and movement of hair attaches subtle detail to the surreal dream worlds of the photo-story, adds feminine intrigue to the androgyny of army surplus clothing, injects pin-up posters with a distinct sexual tension and transforms models in 1940s–style dresses from picturesque pastiche into *Nova*'s own new kinds of contemporary women. These fashion pages capture not simply mere truths about the garments, styles or products featured but also serve to offer the reader, as Elizabeth Wilson describes, 'the mirage of a way of being' (Wilson 1985: 157).

BIBLIOGRAPHY

Baikie, P. (1975), 'Ladies Prefer Blondes', *Nova*, January: 40.

Baker, C. (1970a), 'Head for the Haberdashery', *Nova*, February: 41.

Baker, C. (1970b), 'Once Too Divine ... Now Groovy Baby', *Nova*, July: 50.

Baker, C. (1970c), 'Fancy Dressing', *Nova*, December: 64.

Baker, C. (1971a), 'A Little Knit Doesn't Go a Long Way', *Nova*, February: 27.

Baker, C. (1971b), 'Dressed to Kill: The Army Surplus War Game', *Nova*, September: 52–3.

Baker, C. (1972a), 'The Heavenly Suited', *Nova*, September: 61, 68.

Baker, C. (1972b), 'All Dressed and Made Up: The Biba Doll', *Nova*, November: 62–3.

Baker, C. (1973a), 'Tight Is Right', *Nova*, April: 53.

Baker, C. (1973b), 'Old-time Favourites', *Nova*, December: 72.

Baker, C. (1974), 'Ahead of Hair', *Nova*, February: 63

Baker, C. (1975), 'Pigtails Grow Up', *Nova*, April: 71.

Baker, C. (2007), Personal communication, 23 February 2007.

Barthes, R. (1984), *The Fashion System*, London: Jonathan Cape.

Borrelli, L. O. (1997), 'Dressing Up and Talking about It: Fashion Writing in *Vogue* from 1968–1993', *Fashion Theory: The Journal of Dress, Body and Culture*, 1 (3): 247–60.

Brooks, R. (1989), 'Sighs and Whispers in Bloomingdales: A Review of a Mail-Order Catalogue for Their Lingerie Department', in A. McRobbie (ed), *Zoot Suits and Second-Hand Dresses: An Anthology of Fashion and Music*, London: Macmillan.

Brooks, R. (1997), 'Fashion: Double-Page Spread', in J. Evans (ed), *The Camerawork Essays: Context and Meaning in Photography*, London: Rivers Oram Press.

Bruzzi, S. (1997), *Undressing Cinema: Clothing and Identity in the Movies*, London: Routledge.

Craik, J. (1994), *The Face of Fashion: Cultural Studies in Fashion*, London: Routledge.

Goffman, E. (1979), *Gender Advertisements*, New York: Harper.

Harrison, M. (1991), *Appearances: Fashion Photography since 1945*, London: Jonathan Cape.

Jobling, P. (1999), *Fashion Spreads: Word and Image in Fashion Photography since 1980*, Oxford: Berg.

McCracken, G. (1997), *Big Hair: A Journey into the Transformation of Self*, London: Indigo.

Newberry, P. (1973), 'Hair Today', *Nova*, September.

Radner, H. (2000), 'On the Move: Fashion Photography and the Single Girl in the 1960s', in S. Bruzzi and P. Church Gibson (eds.), *Fashion Cultures: Theories, Explorations and Analysis*, London: Routledge.

Scott, C. (1999), *The Spoken Image: Photography and Language*, London: Reaktion.

Sontag, S. (1994), *Against Interpretation*, London: Vintage.

Steele, V. (1997), 'Anti-Fashion: The 1970s', *Fashion Theory: The Journal of Dress, Body and Culture*, 1 (3): 279–96.

Vincenzi, P. (1972), 'Profile of a Profile', *Nova*, May.

Williams, V. (ed), (1998), *Look at Me: Fashion Photography in Britain 1960 to the Present*, London: British Council.

Wilson, E. (1985), *Adorned in Dreams: Fashion and Modernity*, London: Virago.

CONCLUSION

19 CONCLUSION
HAIR AND HUMAN IDENTITY

SARAH CHEANG AND GERALDINE BIDDLE-PERRY

Hair texture, colour and styling expresses a complex range of subject positions with respect to gender, ethnicity, race, class, nationality, religion, sexuality and age (Weitz 2004). These identities are both culturally and biologically constituted, and discursively and physically experienced (Merleau-Ponty 1962; Goffman 1971; Foucault 1977). The dressing of hair creates a division between the socially marked, culturally constructed body, and the frank nakedness of an undressed body. Important distinctions are therefore made between the symbolic meanings of dressed hair and of natural hair, ranging from the aesthetic and moral judgements that can be made about 'bottle' blondes as opposed to natural blondes, to the highly charged racial politics that surrounds black people's hair against a background history of slavery and oppression. In this final chapter, we reflect on how hair and hair practices figure in the construction of human subjectivities.

THE NATURE OF HUMAN HAIR

Hair grows all over the human body, interestingly, at the same rate of about one to one-and-a-half centimetres a month, although hairs on different parts of the body have different life-spans before they drop out: 'Leg hairs, for example, last around two months, armpit hairs left to their own devices make it to six months, but head hairs grow non-stop for six years or more' (Barnett 2006: 39) (Figure 19.1). It is this capacity for our head hair, whatever its colour or curl, to carry on growing continuously, that makes it distinctive, and differentiates us from all other mammals who—with the exception of the musk ox—merely grow and shed with the seasons (Barnett 2006).

Our closest mammalian relatives, the monkeys and apes, possess beards, moustaches, coloured caps and even hairless rear ends that serve as a form of social identification; in our primeval condition it was the sheer volume of our head hair in relation to our relatively scant body hair that labelled us as human (Morris 1987: 21). Head hair that could grow to a considerable length provided a highly visible and unique species signal. Human technological advance provided the means to overcome the physical restrictions of long and weighty hair through cutting and shaving it with blades, knives and eventually scissors, or curtailing it with combs, pins and ties, hats and various head coverings (Morris 1987: 22) Function and form came together in the distinctively human capacity to modify, shape and reshape our hairy heads with endless stylistic innovation. This separated 'us' from 'them': the

Figure 19.1　Close-up of straight black hair growing out of the scalp (2003). Wellcome Library, London.

humans from the animals, and one human grouping from another. The musk ox might grow its hair long, but it has not yet evolved a salon culture.

Forms of hair management established hair as an early performative element in social enterprise and cultural organization, along with other forms of body adornment such as tattooing, ornaments and clothing (Turner 1991: 5–6; Wilson 1985: 3). Ancient tribal divisions were articulated through a system of distinctions between cut and uncut hair. Ancient Hittite men, for example, shaved off their beards, moustaches and even eyebrows, as well as a spot above the ear, but left their head hair and side whiskers to grow long; Moabite men shaved their foreheads back to the crown, combing the long remaining hair back to fall to the shoulders; ancient Egyptians shaved their heads, but large and intricate wigs were worn by high-class women and their servants (Corson 1965: 26–8). The relationship between growth and restraint offers a hairy equation that is constantly exploited and reworked in different formulations to signal shifting understandings of social status and identity across time and across cultures.

Marina Warner's (1995) classic exposition on hair in fairy tale and legend details how hair is a consistent theme in fairy stories, folk tales and traditional songs: enchanted or disguised, both sexes are metamorphosed into hairier and furrier, wilder and/or more domesticated versions of themselves. The meanings and values of such changes, she argues, shift according to gender, but are equally essentially grounded in sexuality. Wolves, bears, donkeys and goats offer a fantasy of bestial hairiness that operates to reveal men's baser animal instincts (and sometimes dumb stupidity); cats provide the female metamorphic alternative—the witch's familiar of choice—but other animal skins are also worn by the wronged woman or the fugitive as evidence, one way or another, of male contamination (Warner 1995: 354–60). Hair's presentation and representation reveals the nature of the fears and anxieties that disturb and define the human condition by being allied to a spectrum of animal-like qualities.

Warner's work offers an insight into how humans, though emphasizing their difference and distinction from animals, nevertheless continually build on this physiology of hair as something shared with all creatures of 'pelt, fur and hide' (1995: 354). Hair reminds us how close and how distant we are from the animal within. Occupying the middle ground,

COMBING HER LONG GOLDEN HAIR WITH A COMB OF RED GOLD

Figure 19.2   Lorelei, a siren, lures boatmen to their death. *Lorelei on the Rocks* by Helen Stratton (Edwin Wallace Collection).

Mary Evans/Edwin Wallace.

fauns, satyrs and mermaids offer an imaginative half-way house, and their head hair and hairy bodies function as a metaphorical device to explore and emphasize this liminal status. In tales of mermaids their hair becomes analogous with both sexual maturity and the very act of feminine expression. Long golden locks are spun and woven like the threads of narrative and the singing of songs, the movement of the brush and comb matching the backwards and forwards motion of the shuttle in the loom (Gitter 1984: 938, 941). But spinning and weaving have other connotations—of webs of deceit and of entrapment (Figure 19.2). Hair's magical powers are manifested in this generative capacity for symbolic uncertainty. Powell and Roach argue,

> hair is a performance, one that happens at the boundaries of self-expression and social identity, of creativity and conformity, and of production and consumption. Hair lends itself particularly well to self-fashioning performance because it is liminal, on the threshold, 'betwixt and between', not only of nature and culture, but also of life and death. (Powell and Roach 2004: 79)

Hairy and hairless, dressed and undressed, visible and hidden, human hair and its practices become part of a whole connotative moral universe of complex meanings attached to the human body, and the habitual modes of vision through which it is produced and consumed. All human bodies are created hairy and some bodies, regardless of gender, are created hairier than others. The discourses that surround hair's removal, trimming and shaping operate as ideological mechanisms, culturally regulating the display and management of the individual and collective social body. Hair's management and modification operate not just as an adjunct to the social body but rather, like dress and ornamentation, come to constitute the social body itself.

HAIR STEREOTYPES AND 'NATURAL' QUALITIES

As highly visible social markers, different hair colours and textures have particular physical and behavioural characteristics attached to them, creating stereotypes that are highly pervasive. In white people, dark hair and light hair tend to be diametrically opposed, the former being connected to seriousness, and the latter to fun (Synnott 1993: 103–27). Red hair is viewed as unusual, and pejoratively as 'weird', so that *ginger* can be a term of abuse.

Historically, red hair has had negative connotations of witchcraft, and of Judas's betrayal of Jesus (Roach 2005: 9–87). In contemporary Western society, more common associations are with a 'hot' temperament, clowns and Irish and Scottish identity. Studies show that redheads feel that they are treated differently from others, especially during their school years, and men are particularly affected by negative stereotyping. Ginger males are singled out for derision and classed as weak and sexually unattractive. Such discrimination on the grounds of hair colour appears to be quite socially acceptable, and women with light-red hair may prefer to describe themselves as 'strawberry blonde' to capitalize on the more positive feminine attributes of blondeness (Anderson 2001).

Figure 19.3   Unattributed photograph showing an ideal Aryan girl, used in Nazi propaganda, 1934.
Mary Evans/Weimar Archive.

Blondeness is also a particular type of whiteness, predominantly associated with the snowy north of the Scandinavian countries or northern Europe (Dyer 1997: 20–1; Young 1997). During the early-twentieth century, racial prejudice against people of Jewish, Celtic and non-white descent in Europe, America and the Soviet Union produced a new interest in blondeness. This reached its apotheosis in the Nazi project to engineer a racially 'pure' and 'perfect' German race by encouraging the breeding of Nordic-looking blonde-haired, blue-eyed children and exterminating the darker, 'undesirable' elements from the gene pool (Figure 19.3) (Pitman 2003: 167–201; Weitz 2004: 19–20). At its most reductive, the dichotomy of black/blonde identities is encapsulated by the central premise of the film *King Kong* (1930, with remakes), in which a savage black gorilla of enormous proportions is so entranced by a white blonde woman that he cannot harm her.

People of European descent have long exploited blonde hair's positive associations with light, goodness and beauty. Edwardian explorer Mrs French Sheldon claimed to have dazzled natives of East Africa in 1906 with a white gown and long blonde wig that apparently rendered her all-powerful and untouchable (Boisseau 2000: 33–35). Almost a century later, journalist Joanna Pitman (2003: 1–3) relates how in northern Kenya she was treated as possessing almost miraculous powers of healing because of her blonde hair, in a conflation of blondeness and Western medicine. Blondeness is also linked with certain stereotypes of femininity: infantilism, stupidity, glamour and sexual attraction (Figure 19.4) (Synnott 1993: 108–9; Cox 1999: 159–60). However, hair that has been obviously bleached and dyed has the negative overtones of artificiality, sometimes provoking a crisis of 'natural' identity. Bleached hair, as opposed to the healthy 'natural' goodness of sun-kissed blonde hair, has had a brassy, self-destructive, lower-class vulgarity (Cox 1999: 161). In contrast, more natural-looking dyes can be used by medium and dark-haired women who had been blonde as children to regain that former blondeness. This is conceptualized as a return to the 'real' genetically blonde self, so that a synthetic process is used to maintain the identity of 'natural' blonde (Ilyin 2000: 23).

There are two kinds of signification and identity formation at work here. On the one hand, hair colour is treated as just one manifestation of a particular genetic make-up that is imagined to affect the individual in a number of other ways. On the other hand, people can adopt a particular colour to change their persona as participants in a postmodern consumer culture that encourages body modification and maintenance as an essential part of self-expression (Featherstone 1991). Marion Roach's book, *The Roots of Desire* (2005), explores her own identity as a redhead through both the myths and stereotypes of red-headed femininity, but is framed around a personal journey to establish the exact genetic markers of her hair, creating a final sense of her own identity as a 'true', biologically determined redhead. Similarly, Pitman makes it very clear in the opening paragraph of her book that it was the natural action of the sun and not a packet of bleach that had produced her arresting head of blonde hair in Kenya, demanding that she too should be understood as a genetic blonde, free from artifice. Thus, hair is part of the more general question of where our sense of self resides in the body—in the brain, in the flesh, in the

Figure 19.4   The glamourous, seductive blonde. *Seduction,* 3 March 1934: front cover.
Mary Evans Picture Library.

senses, in our DNA or in the parts of the body that can consciously be used to signal to others (Merleau-Ponty 1962; Goffman 1971). The answer to this question is loaded with value judgements and negative assumptions about any claims to identity that are not 'natural'.

Here we encounter a nature/nurture paradox. In human identity, biological and cultural factors are blended, so that what is 'natural' must be questioned. Furthermore, the social articulation of race, class, gender and sexuality is intertwined, and each discourse has its own set of corporeal scientific proofs that tend to reify culturally constructed classifications. At the same time, the social conditions experienced by members of a particular race, class, gender or sexuality will affect the way in which the body is nourished, shaped, used and presented. Anthropologist Mary Douglas proposes that: 'The social body constrains the way the physical body is perceived' (Douglas 1970: 65). The values, customs and restrictions that society places upon the human body affect the way in which the body is experienced and understood. Thus, the lived experience of having a particular hair type (the 'natural'), and the daily dressing processes to which that hair is subjected (the 'unnatural'), affects and restricts a person's understanding of himself or herself. In the struggle for self-determination under racial discrimination and/or imperialism, the symbolic and biological connections between hair and notions of race and breeding have accorded a heavily loaded significance to 'natural' hair.

This is most powerfully the case with the Afro, a hairstyle that exploits the kinky texture of black people's hair in the creation of a soft, dense halo of long, tightly curling hair. African Americans have straightened their hair since the days of slavery, using chemicals, hot combs and grease, allowing women to achieve the 'femininity' of long, flowing locks, and men to feel well-groomed and sophisticated (Craig 1997; Kelley 1997). Thus, whilst straightened hairstyles might not qualify as an effective challenge to racial hierarchies (Weitz 2001), hair straightening should not be seen as a straightforward emulation of white hair textures, but as a styling strategy in a society dominated by white ideals of beauty (Craig 1997, 2002; Banks 2000). In the context of the American Black Power movement and of African nationalism, the Afro of the 1960s and 1970s was a style that demonstrated a self-asserted, anti-white-culture stance, which along with clothing such as the dashiki, looked to Africa for inspiration (Kelley 1997). As Kobena Mercer (1994: 100) writes, black hairstyling can be 'evaluated as a popular art form articulating a variety of aesthetic "solutions" to a range of "problems" created by ideologies of race and racism'.

It is highly significant that the Afro was also termed the *natural,* for notions of 'Africa' and 'nature' operated together as a counter to Western culture as artificial and oppressive (Mercer 1994: 105–13; Soper 1995: 71–81). In the Afro, a 'woolly' or 'nappy' head of hair was not stigmatized, but was teased out into eye-catching proportions and paraded as a revalorized component of self-asserted, liberated and truly 'authentic' black identity— a way for black Americans to 'be themselves'. It should also be noted that the Afro was a contested style within black communities. For many women, notably of an older generation, unstraightened hair signalled a lack of self-respect, so that hair that had been allowed to revert to its natural state would seem like a social nightmare (Cleage 1993; Byrd and Tharps 2001: 132–64). Very tightly curled hair is still 'bad' hair (Banks 2000: 107), and the existence of books such as *Nappyisms: Affirmations for Nappy-Headed People and Wannabes* (Jones 2003) attests to the continuing need for wearers of the 'natural' to defend their choice against a dominant culture which finds natural hair unattractive.

However, the Afro is a cultivated style—long hair combed and cut into a rounded shape. It is not a totally natural style, and neither is it quintessentially African (Mercer 1994: 111). Where slaves wore their hair long and bushy, this was the result of being denied access to hair care; styling the hair through a combination of shaving and bunching, cutting and growing, combing and braiding was an important part of collective and individual identification, and one of the few areas of free expression (White and White 1995: 56). The 'naturalness' of the Afro is thus very loaded as 'natural' hair was being used by black Americans to construct 'African-American' rather than 'negro' identity (Mercer 1994: 107). As a Nigerian living in New York puts it: 'In Africa the hair is purely to decorate. It's different here because of the race issue' (Ifoema Ibo cited in Byrd and Tharps 2001: 164).

Black hair's symbolic and physical antithesis—blonde hair—is no less totemic in terms of racial identity, yet has a very different relationship to concepts of nature. For Caucasian blonde hair, the high racial status of Nordic looks combines with the styling, make-up and body modifications of female beauty regimes that produce 'normal' femininity (Bordo 2003), to create blonde hair as a product of nature that is improved by culture, within certain limits. Cultural constructions of race and gender are thus naturalized in the body, and blondeness projected as a 'natural' asset worth striving for.

CONCLUSION: CONTESTING NATURAL IDENTITY

Clearly, it is hair's malleability and hair's relationship to the body that gives it great power and multivalence within the systems of representation and identity, whether the dominant social ideologies are challenged or confirmed. To be an Asian with naturally curly hair creates a disquieting lack of racial belonging and a concomitant loss of cultural identity. A recent Internet discussion hosted by the Chinese History Forum reveals that without the straight hair that is the badge of Asian genes, one Chinese woman had always felt 'talked about and treated like an outsider' (Spikeyli 2007). By contrast, Rose Weitz's study of women, hairstyling and social power gives the example of an Asian American who feels compelled to perm her naturally straight hair every few months to avoid looking 'too Asian' (Weitz 2001: 676). Such strategies undertaken to resist racial stereotyping whilst submitting to a dominant white-identified ideology of beauty can be related to debates around plastic surgery, such as the remodelling of Asian eye shape to create a more 'desirable', rounded eye (Kaw 1993; Gilman 1999: 98–111; Zane 2003). To perm Asian hair is also to transcend the flesh in a postmodern corporeality rooted in consumer culture (Figure 19.5). However, unlike plastic surgery, hair keeps growing, forcing us to deal with our biological roots on a regular basis, continually converting identity from an innate 'natural' genetic inheritance to a daily, performative act (Gilroy 1998).

Figure 19.5   A woman in Sichuan Province, China, having her hair curled
in a hair salon.
Photo by Robert Van de Hilst. Getty Images.

If the human body is an image of society, then hair's malleability makes it a doubly
valuable asset in social expression by exploiting an antithetical clash between the 'corporeal/
natural' and the 'cultural/unnatural'. The word *nature* is often used to mean the very
'essence' of human identity, but 'nature' also figures as something that is corrected by culture (straightening 'bad' hair) *and* something that offers an escape from culture (growing
'natural' hair to contest social norms such as racial oppression) (Soper 1995: 28–9, 33–5).
A crucial factor in hair's power as a social symbol is that, unlike clothing, hair is an intrinsic
part of the body. It is manufactured according to the dictates of our genes, springing forth
from our follicles to display physical characteristics that span the generations. Handed
down to us by our parents, and their parents before them, the colour and texture of our

hair is thus intimately connected to the notion of biologically inherited, essentially 'given' and therefore 'natural' qualities. Hair practices can communicate a desire to embrace, deny or contest the culturally constituted meanings of that lineage.

The key issue here is the near impossibility of natural human hair. In nearly all situations, head and body hair must be managed as an essential part of human social existence. As a result, hair in its totally natural state is rarely met with in society (Watson 1998), whilst concepts of natural hair become yet another representational tool to be used in the cultural construction of human identity. It is the centrality of the nature/culture opposition in Western thought that gives 'natural' hair its significant role in the symbolic definition of human identity, in addition to its role in biological designations. Whatever we do with our hair, we are constantly grappling with a 'natural' and a constructed self in our daily hair practices.

BIBLIOGRAPHY

Anderson, E. (2001), 'There Are Some Things in Life You Can't Choose ... An Investigation into Discrimination against People with Red Hair', *Manchester Sociology Working Papers*, 28.

Banks, I. (2000), *Hair Matters: Beauty, Power and Black Women's Consciousness.* New York: New York University Press.

Barnett, A. (2006), 'Tressed to Impress', *New Scientist*, 4 November: 39–41.

Boisseau, T. J. (2000), 'White Queens at the Chicago World's Fair: New Womanhood in the Service of Class, Race and Nation', *Gender and History*, 12 (1): 33–81.

Bordo, S. (2003), *Unbearable Weight: Feminism, Western Culture and the Body* (10th anniversary edn), Berkeley: University of California Press.

Byrd, A. D. and Tharps, L. L. (2001), *Hair Story: Untangling the Roots of Black Hair in America*, New York: St Martin's Griffin.

Cleage, P. (1993), 'Hairpeace', *African-American Review*, 27 (1) (Spring): 37–41.

Corson, R. (1965), *Fashions in Hair: The First 5000 Years*, London: Peter Owen.

Cox, C. (1999), *Good Hair Days: A History of British Hairstyling.* London: Quartet Books.

Craig, M. (1997), 'The Decline and Fall of the Conk; or, How to Read a Process,' *Fashion Theory*, 1 (4): 399–420.

Craig, M. (2002), *Ain't I a Beauty Queen: Black Women, Beauty and the Politics of Race*, Oxford: Oxford University Press.

Douglas, M. (1970), *Natural Symbols: Explorations in Cosmology*, London: Barrie and Rockliff: The Cresset Press.

Dyer, R. (1997), *White*, London: Routledge.

Featherstone, M. (1991), 'The Body in Consumer Culture', in M. Featherstone et al. (ed), *The Body: Social Process and Cultural Theory*, London: Sage Publications.

Foucault, M. (1977), *Discipline and Punish*, Harmondsworth: Penguin.

Gilman, S. (1999), *Making the Body Beautiful: A Cultural History of Aesthetic Surgery*, Princeton, NJ: Princeton University Press.

Gilroy, P. (1998), 'Race Ends Here', *Ethnic and Racial Studies*, 21 (5): 838–47.

Gitter, E. (1984), 'The Power of Women's Hair in the Victorian Imagination', *PMLA*, 99 (5): 936–54.

Goffman, E. (1971), *The Presentation of Self in Everyday Life*, Harmondsworth: Penguin.

Ilyin, N. (2000), *Blonde Like Me*, New York: Touchstone.

Jones, L. (2003), *Nappyisms: Affirmations for Nappy-Headed People and Wannabes*, Dallas: Manelock.

Kaw, E. (1993), 'Medicalization of Racial Features: Asian-American Women and Cosmetic Surgery', *Medical Anthropology Quarterly*, 7 (1) (March): 74–89.

Kelley, R.D.G. (1997), 'Nap Time: Historicizing the Afro', *Fashion Theory*, 1 (4) (December): 339–51.

Mercer, K. (1994), *Welcome to the Jungle*, New York: Routledge.

Merleau-Ponty, M. (1962), *The Phenomenology of Perception*, London: Routledge.

Morris, D. (1987), *Bodywatching: A Field Guide to the Human Species*, London: Grafton Books.

Pitman, J. (2003), *On Blondes*, London: Bloomsbury.

Powell, M. K. and Roach, J. (2004), 'Big Hair', *Eighteenth Century Studies*, 38 (1): 79–99.

Roach, M. (2005), *The Roots of Desire: The Myth, Meaning and Sexual Power of Red Hair*, New York: Bloomsbury.

Soper, K. (1995), *What Is Nature?* Oxford: Blackwell.

Spikeyli. (2007), 'Chinese People with Curly Hair', 14 September, http://www.chinahistoryforum.com/index.php?showtopic=19017, accessed 11 March 2008.

Synnott, A. (1993), *The Body Social: Symbolism, Self and Society*, London and New York: Routledge.

Turner, B. S. (1991), 'Recent Developments in the Theory of the Body', in M. Featherstone, M. Hepworth and B. S. Turner (eds.), *The Body: Social Process and Cultural Theory*, London: Sage Publications.

Warner, M. (1995), *From the Beast to the Blonde: On Fairy Tales and Their Tellers*, New York: Farrar, Straus & Giroux.

Watson, J. L. (1998), 'Living Ghosts: Long-haired Destitutes in Colonial Hong Kong', in A. Hiltebeitel and B. D. Miller (eds.), *Hair: Its Power and Meaning in Asian Cultures*, Albany: State University of New York Press.

Weitz, R. (2001), 'Women and Their Hair: Seeking Power through Resistance and Accommodation', *Gender and Society*, 15 (5): 667–86.

Weitz, R. (2004), *Rapunzel's Daughters: What Hair Tells Us about Women's Lives*, New York: Farrar, Straus & Giroux.

White, S. and White, G. (1995), 'Slave Hair and African-American Culture in the Eighteenth and Nineteenth Centuries', *The Journal of Southern History*, 61 (1): 45–76.

Wilson, E. (1985), *Adorned in Dreams: Fashion and Modernity*, London: Virago.

Young, R.J.C. (1997), 'Hybridism and the Ethnicity of the English', in K. Ansell Pearson, B. Parry and J. Squires (eds.), *Cultural Readings of Imperialism: Edward Said and the Gravity of History*, London: Lawrence and Wishart.

Zane, K. (2003), 'Reflections on a Yellow Eye: Asian i(\eye/)cons and Cosmetic Surgery', in A. Jones (ed), *The Feminist and Visual Culture Reader*, London: Routledge.

INDEX

shaving, 6–7, 67, 72, 73, 76, 77
sight of hair, 108
see also men
'masquerade', 24
Masson, Andre, 48
Mattera, Adam, 91
meaning, 8, 10, 184, 218
Mecca, pilgrimage to, 115, 117, 157
media
  eroticized male bodies, 103–4
  gay, 92–3
  inter-textuality, 218, 221
  surveillance by, 184
  see also magazines
Medusa, 101–2
Meindl, J. R., 113
melodrama, 196, 197, 224, 225
men
  artistic representations of the male body,
    101, 105
  eighteenth-century Britain, 20–2, 24–5
  ethnological differences in hair, 31
  hair removal, 90
  hair salons, 63, 64
  India, 149, 154
  Islamic, 7, 111–22
  long hair, 83
  male-on-male looking, 74, 102–3
  oppositional meanings of hair, 4
  performative display of hair, 99
  pubic hair, 43
  sexualized male body, 89–90, 103–4, 105, 107
  shaving of facial hair, 6–7, 67–78
  see also gay men; gender; masculinity
Mennonites, 113
menstruation, 149, 150
Mercer, Kobena, 133, 144–5, 220, 250
metrosexuals, 90, 91
Mexican Americans, 220
Michael, George, 86
middle class
  'Beats', 75
  eighteenth-century Britain, 22
  hairdressing, 56
  India, 160
Middlemarch (Eliot), 202
migration, 178–9
Miller, Janice, 9, 183–92
The Mill on the Floss (Eliot), 9, 194–6, 199, 201–2
minstrelization, 82, 83, 91
Mishima, Yukio, 43
Mngomezulu, Themba, 136
models, 231–3, 235–6, 237–9
Moderne, 58–9
Modernism, 58, 59
modernity, 9, 99, 202–3
  hair salons, 63

men's facial hair, 68
  shaving, 77
  The Woodlanders, 196, 198
monogenesis, 32
Monroe, Marilyn, 142–3
moral panics, 99
Morris, Chris, 120
Morris, Desmond, 97
Morrow, William Lee, 126–7, 130–1, 132
Mosaic law, 113
mourning jewellery, 176–7, 187–8
moustaches, 68, 84, 112–13
  India, 149
  Islam, 116, 117
  Turkey, 120
Murphy, Jill, 211
muscle men, 87–8, 89, 93
Muslims, 7, 111–22, 157
  fundamentalist opinions, 114, 118–19, 121
  secular opinions, 119–20
  shaving, 114–18, 119, 121
  women's hair, 178

Native Americans, 37–8
'natural' hair, 243, 248–50, 251, 253
nature, 252, 253
nature/nurture paradox, 250
'Nerds', 74, 75
'Nero cut', 85–6
New Testament, 113
Newton, Helmut, 237, 238
Nietzsche, Friedrich, 148
Nin, Anaïs, 43–5, 51
nonconformity, 74–5, 76, 77
Notting Hill (film), 99
Nova (magazine), 10, 229–39
  'A Little Knit', 235–7
  'Biba Doll', 231–3
  'Dressed to Kill', 233–5
  'Tight Is Right', 237–9
Now, Voyager (film), 208–9
nudes, 46–8, 51, 100–1, 203
nudist magazines, 49

October, Dene, 6, 67–78
Ofili, Chris, 144
Ojibwe, 37–8
Olympic Committee for Human Rights (OCHR), 135
Olympic Games, 133–5
Omar, Mullah Mohammad, 118, 121n4
Oppenheim, Meret, 174
ornaments, 16, 18
Osman Hill, William Charles, 29, 36

Padva, Gilad, 92, 93
painting, 176
Pakistan, 118

Salcedo, Doris, 169
Salomon, Nanette, 103
salons, 6, 55–65
    design of, 58–62
    historical origins of, 55–8
    science and technology, 62–3
    unisex, 64
salvage paradigm, 36
Sargeant, Jack, 6, 43–53
Sassoon, Vidal, 64
Satan, 113, 114, 116
Saunders, Jennifer, 205
Savva, Elena Louise, 206, 207
Schneider, Maria, 231
schoolmistresses, 9, 209–10, 211–12
science, 62
Scorsese, Martin, 67
selfhood, 7, 193
Sen, Sushmita, 160–1
sex, 43–4
sexuality
    art, 48, 105
    ballet dancers, 207, 212
    black women, 34
    cross-dressing, 235
    Desperate Housewives, 219, 223
    dominatrices, 212–13
    fairy tales, 244
    feminine, 9, 99, 106–7
    fetishism, 45–6
    India, 150
    metrosexuals, 90
    pornography, 49
    repressed, 208, 211, 212
    social articulation of, 250
    subjectivities, 243
    transgressive female, 107
    unconscious, 101
    women's magazines, 231, 235–6, 237
    see also homosexuality
sexual taboo, 3
shampoo, 160–1, 183
sharia, 114, 117
'shaves and shows', 104, 105
shaving, 6–7, 67–78
    culture and counterculture, 73–5
    domestication of, 68–71
    health and safety, 71–3
    India, 153
    Islamic perspectives, 114–18, 119, 121
    men's body hair, 90
    moral panics, 99
    religious traditions, 113
    women's pubic hair, 44–5, 49–51
    see also hairlessness; hair removal
Sheldon, French, 248
Sherwood, James, 105

Shirazi, Faegheh, 7, 111–22
Shiva, 150–1, 152
Shudras, 155
sideburns, 68
Signorile, Michelangelo, 86
signs, 218
Sikhs, 113, 157
Silvikrin, 160
Simpson, Mark, 90, 92
skinheads, 84–5
slavery, 28, 32, 126, 243, 251
Sleeman, M., 10
Smith, Kim, 6, 55–65
Smith, Tommie, 133–5, 137n13, 137n14
social class
    eighteenth-century Britain, 5, 22
    hairdressing, 56
    social articulation of, 250
    subjectivities, 243
    see also middle class
social cognition studies, 113
social control, 3–4, 6, 10
social status, 20, 22, 77, 244
'social theatre', 15, 23, 24, 25
Sodhi, Balbir Singh, 112
Sontag, Susan, 237
South Africa, 136
Spears, Britney, 104, 107
spinsters, 9, 208–9, 212–13
sport, 74, 103
    see also footballers
Sri Lanka, 29
stardom, 218, 221, 225
stereotypes
    Desperate Housewives, 218, 223
    disciplined femininity, 205, 208, 209,
        211, 212
    ganguro girls, 145
    gay men, 84, 85, 88, 92
    red hair, 246–8
    women's magazines, 235, 238
Stevenson, Karen, 57, 62, 64
Stewart, Rod, 143
Stewart, Susan, 136
Stone, Sharon, 104
Stowe, Harriet Beecher, 189
streamlining, 59–60
Streatfield, Noel, 208
structuralism, 218
'Struggle Chic', 136
Student Non-Violent Coordinating Committee
    (SNCC), 133, 137n2
style, 10, 75
suicide blondes, 142–3
Sunni Islam, 119
supernaturalism, 188–90
surrealism, 48

LaVergne, TN USA
29 December 2010

210543LV00007B/14/P